DARE TO OBEY

DARE
TO
OBEY

Dare to obey at your own risk.

JOHN WILSON

XULON PRESS ELITE

Xulon Press Elite
2301 Lucien Way #415
Maitland, FL 32751
407.339.4217
www.xulonpress.com

Unless otherwise indicated, Scripture quotations taken from the
Holy Bible, New International Version (NIV). Copyright © 1973,
1978, 1984, 2011 by Biblica, Inc.™. Used by permission. All rights
reserved.

Printed in the United States of America.

ISBN-13: 978-1-54564-596-3

TABLE OF CONTENTS

INTRODUCTION

When we dare to obey the commands of God to go into the world, teaching and making disciples, all we know at the time is that we are obeying Him. We know God blesses those who choose to obey Him. We know we want those blessings. Although God has blessed me tremendously with Rosalba, it doesn't change the fact that we are sinners. In this book, I hope you will enjoy seeing how God has really intervened in my life and the lives of my family. Many state they won't believe in a God who they cannot see or touch. Their future is dependent on their inability to believe in anything beyond what they can see and touch, even though many people have testified by their lives and stories to the awesome things that only God could perform. Sadly, this may include members of their own families, who have seen and experienced the wonderful things that God has done.

I encourage all readers who journey with me as they read this story to remember the consequences of death are a part of God's truth, just as they are a part of God's blessings. I was blessed because I dared to obey, but at the same time the consequences of death were very difficult for me to deal with in my wife dying from cancer. For a time, I was concerned, because the way the church's message has changed over time tells us that those who obey God will never suffer difficulties. I challenge readers to find anyone in the Word of God who did not suffer. If we dare to obey we will suffer. (1 Cor. 1:6)or will not suffer to maintain obedience.

Yes, God loves me, and He blessed me, but I too will die because of my sins. I chose to share the blessings and the consequences of sin with the readers of this book, so that we can all realize that even in the consequences of sin, God does bless us as well. Rosalba is in Heaven and has been blessed. I have been blessed by having confidence in God's Word and His promises. I'll continue to enjoy the memory of Rosalba, and how much she has motivated me both in life and in death to continue to obey and carry my cross to the end. One day, I, too, will be with Jesus and she will be there waiting for me. We will both be citizens of Heaven, where no paperwork, visas, or passports are requested.

Enjoy,
John Wilson

CHAPTER 1

STEPPING OUT IN FAITH

My name is John Wilson. I am a simple man who dared to obey God, and this has led me on an ever-exciting journey. This journey began when I was fifteen years old. I would come to the small town where my grandmother lived and I would help her on the farm. I use the word *help* carefully, because I was a teenager from the city and knew nothing about farming. My grandmother was a devout Christian and she would only watch television when Reverend Billy Graham was having a crusade. I had no interest in God or Christ in my younger years. My mother would always tell us that God would provide even though we had no money for food to eat. She never failed to pay her tithes, even though there was nothing to eat. I say *nothing* carefully, because there was food but it wasn't purchased in a store. The food we had at the time came from the trash cans located behind the store. Items such as over-ripened fruits, the contents of dented cans, or out-of-date bakery that had been disposed of. If this was the God my mother believed was providing, I didn't need Him. As I continued to rebel against God and Christians, my grandmother thought it would be a good idea to send me to a church camp with the youth group from her church. This was her idea, not mine.

I dreaded the thought of spending a whole week with a group of Christians/hypocrites. I hated God and had not ever seen a reason to have a hope in something I could not see, touch, hear, smell, or taste. *Where is God in a world so messed up and so disorderly?* With all these thoughts and doubts boiling up in me, we left for church camp. We arrived in the middle of the afternoon and it was around 100°F. Christians and heat were not a good combination for me. It was even worse, because now they wanted to run and hike, and only later to play games. Now, hot and stinky from all the activities they wanted to have a Bible study and prayer time. To me, this was a new definition to hell on earth.

When I had the chance, I would leave the group and find a secluded space under a shade tree to feel sorry for myself. One of these days under

1

a shade tree, a skinny girl came up to me and wanted to talk to me. All I remember is her name was Brenda from Corn, OK, and she had long brown hair and freckles. She asked me if she could talk to me and I told her it was a free world. She commenced to tell me about Jesus Christ. This was all I could bear. My mom taught me how to treat girls with respect, but I wasn't really attacking her, I was attacking her God. I began to use every foul word in my vocabulary, and after a few moments of my abuse she began crying. She looked at me with tears in her eyes and told me that no matter what I said or did to her, she loved me and God loved me. This caught me off guard and finally left me speechless.

Don't think that I fell to my knees and started crying for God to save me at that moment, but now I experienced a person who really believed in her God in a fearful moment. This experience has stayed in my mind and heart, even now. At the age of 16 I moved to Okeene, OK were my mom and dad grew up and I was born. My mom's mother Clara Federman and my dad's parents lived. Vernon and Georgia Wilson. My uncle Leland Fisher, married to my dads' sister, who allowed me to live with him if I promised to stay away from drugs. I can never thank him enough for his sacrifice. The instructions from my uncle Leland and my grandpa Vernon about dealing with life had always been firm but accurate as I was struggling with my past life of drug addiction and irresponsibility as a young man.

Five years later, I had just finished my second year in college and was working during the summer. It had been a difficult year and I really had no family or support system like normal families do. I was looking for answers to questions that had been percolating in my mind for the last five years. I knew about God and Christ, having grown up in church my whole life, but I didn't have a personal relationship with Him. I couldn't get the words Brenda had spoken to me out of my head, and my Christian/hypocrite analogy was falling apart. *Could this God thing be real? Do I have to sacrifice logic for faith?* I began re-thinking my previous stance about God. Nothing seemed to make sense anymore logically.

I was at work one morning and I just felt the need to ask Jesus to come into my heart and forgive me of my sins. This included my attack on Brenda five years earlier. Brenda from Corn, OK, if you have read this, I ask you to forgive me for all the mean things I said to you.

So now what? I asked Jesus to come into my life and forgive me of my sins and I didn't know what to do. I left work after my scheduled shift and went to my church and spoke to my pastor Robin Cowen . I told him about my prayer and confession and asked him the same question: *Now what?* He began by saying that he had always thought I was a Christian. I was no different from most people who attended churches today. I knew how to be "churchy." "We are plastic people going to plastic steeples." CASTING

CROWNS SONG "STAINED GLASS MASQUERADE" He must have seen something different in me because he began to disciple me. God must have really challenged my pastor when he got me as his assignment. He took me to the nursing homes to give a short message on what God had put on my heart. This helped take me to a deeper level of faith, because now I had to teach and preach about something I had spent so much time attacking my whole life.

I went back to college for my third year. I had a sweet and beautiful girlfriend in college who I had been dating for five years. She was my best friend and I couldn't wait to be with her. I was excited about the changes that God was making in my life. There always remained a question in our relationship though. If she was a Christian, why did she never tell me about Chris? If she loved Christ and me, why hadn't she shared her relationship with Christ with me? As I began to grow in Christ, she began to look for other things like drinking alcohol and going to parties, and I felt torn between God and her. It seemed easier to talk to God now rather than her. I didn't want to lose her because I loved her with what I thought was all my heart. Now someone else was getting most of my time and it wasn't her. She began to avoid me and I understood. Figure that?

One night as I was praying, something told me: *John you have to decide who your first love is. I need to know if it's your girlfriend or me. You have to decide.*

At the time, this was the most difficult thing I had ever had to do. She was my best friend, cute, athletic, and smart. We had spent the last five years of our lives together. I didn't know if I could do it. I fought off that voice for several weeks until it started hurting so much to see her walking away from God. Like a puppy, I was following her. One night we got together and I asked her why she never shared Christ with me during those years we had spent together before I made my confession. Before I knew it, I was telling her that I had to choose to follow Christ. What? Was I crazy?

I only saw her once since I made that choice. She went on to marry someone else, so it was clear that she was not what God wanted for me. So now I was in the same situation as before, asking God: *Now what?*

Since I began to follow God, many dreams and plans began to change. I no longer desired the field of chemistry or pharmacy that I had spent four years studying. Now what? I returned to my pastor and explained to him where I was in my life and my lack of interest in finishing the path I started in college. He told me the church was planning a mission trip to Monterrey, Mexico, and he would like me to go with them. One problem existed, though. The trip would cost me $600. That was all the money I had in the bank, and I needed it for the next semester of college. Now what? I prayed about it and decided to go on the mission trip.

Am I crazy or what? I have never been on a mission trip. I don't speak any Spanish except for what I had learned from Speedy Gonzalez on the Cartoon Network. "Andale, Arriba, Arriba."

I didn't have any spending money for food or anything else. I was scared, to say the least. *Is this what God wants me to do? Spend everything I have to tell my personal testimony to people who probably would never understand me?* I could envision all the negatives that were going to happen. The plane would crash. I would starve with no money for food, or I would have to beg to get something to eat.

The pastor Robin Cowan asked us to write a two-paragraph personal testimony so it could be translated to Spanish for the mission trip. All we were to do in Mexico was to go with the nationals door-to-door while they read our testimonies to the people who lived in the house. That seemed simple. I could do this. We arrived at the airport and took off for Houston, where we were to connect with another plane that would take us to Mexico. This was my first time on a plane, and my first time trying to connect with another one in a big airport. Thank God, I was traveling with a group that knew more than me. After making the connection in Houston, we were in the air to Mexico. *Are we flying over the ocean? Do the cushions float if the plane goes down?* Well, the plane did not go down as I feared. The plane landed safely in Monterrey, Mexico. We then were directed to fill out the travel visas so we could leave the airport. Thank God, this document was in English and Spanish. We filled out the visas, grabbed our luggage, and boarded the bus in route to our hotel.

So far so good, was going through my mind. We arrived at our hotel and paired up with our hotel partners. I was glad I was in the same room as my pastor. I didn't know he could play the guitar, much less *Hotel California*. This one caught me by surprise. Not a sin to play the song, but just to think pastor Robin knew one of my favorite songs and played it so well. We ate supper and went to our rooms for the evening to rest. I prayed and read my Bible, still nervous, thinking about the next day.

We woke up in the morning and took care of personal hygiene. We went down to the lobby for breakfast and our directions for the day. According to the instructions, several pastors from the mission churches were to take us to their mission areas where the work was to commence. There were three people in our group: Nancy, an older lady who could speak a little Spanish; Jerry, who was a little younger than me and didn't know Spanish; and me. They paired us up individually with the nationals and directed us to go in three different directions. Translators were supposed to be provided, but that didn't happen in our group.

We knocked on many doors, and as the doors were opened the nationals would read our testimonies to the families in the homes. The nationals were trained really well in the presentation of the gospel and did a really good job sharing the plan of salvation with all ages. I could have never done this without God's previous planning on how to use all of us. One problem arose: I was made the leader of the group. I couldn't speak with any of the nationals because none of them spoke or understood English. How could I direct a group of nationals and have Bible studies with the people in attendance when I had no translator?

My prayer began like this: *God, I know You didn't bring me here to fail. You must have someone available to use to help me lead this group.*

Soon after my prayer, a young man name Ruben showed up and offered his services as a translator. I knew nothing about Ruben, but his understanding of the English language was really good. Ruben worked teaching corporate employee's English. Now I could breathe. God had given me another sign that He was in charge, and all I had to do was speak of His love and His plan of salvation.

The second day began like the first. Hygiene, breakfast, planning, prayers, and then the pastors picked us up and took us to the areas where we were to work that day. The nationals were waiting for us when we arrived. We spent the morning knocking on doors as the nationals read our testimonies to the people who lived in those homes. Maybe this whole experience was a stronger message that a person from the USA needed God too. As I found out later, most Hispanics believed that we were rich if we lived in the USA. I guess they really didn't know me.

In the afternoon, we met at the church. Ruben hadn't arrived yet. The pastor Juan Antonio was talking and I didn't understand anything. I found out much later in life that he was asking for volunteers to take us to their homes to eat lunch. Due to the time frame, we didn't have time to return to the hotel for lunch. Nancy went with one of the elderly ladies from the mission. Jerry went with a couple of the younger guys from the youth group, and I was the last one left. The pastor was looking for volunteers to take me. No one volunteered. He finally asked one of the young ladies named Rosalba in the youth group if she could take me to her family's house for lunch. She seemed reluctant, but finally agreed. I wasn't comfortable at the time and I was sure she felt no different.

What can I say? If I figure out that part, how do I say it? Where are we going? We walked over hills on dirt trails that were well used. I was wearing a suit and a tie. No one accused me of being smart. A suit and tie in 90° weather. Ouch.

We arrived at a house that belonged to Rosalba's older sister Gloria. It appeared her husband Ramiro was a mechanic. Rosalba took me to this house because her brother-in-law spoke some broken English. Rosalba could dump me there and come back to take me to the church. It didn't work out that way for her. Her sister Gloria would not let her leave until she took me back to the church. I tried to have a conversation with the brother-in-law, Ramiro, but it seemed all my questions were about this beautiful young lady Rosalba who delivered me to their home. *What's her name? Is she married? How old is she?* For some reason, everything we had done that day was blocked out of my mind during that meal, and I desired to know more about her.

There were other girls present in the group of nationals Claudia, Lilliana, Ivet, and some were even more beautiful than her. Rosalba's beauty was different. I didn't know at the time how or why, but she was different. We finished lunch and walked back to the church. A short walk for them is two or three miles, but my feet in my dress shoes were starting to repent after all the walking. I had blisters on both heels and my feet hurt.

We continued to knock on doors, and Rosalba left as we began. Ruben showed up as we began. Although my mission hadn't changed, I seemed to be asking Ruben a lot of questions about Rosalba. He asked the nationals more about her for me. They said Rosalba attended their church, but they didn't know much about her.

I cleared my mind and focused on the job in front of me. We had a backyard Bible study to prepare for and I needed to plan the evening with Ruben, to make it easier for him to translate during the study. At 7pm the study started, and I began enthusiastically with the plan of salvation. I had almost finished with half of the study when Ruben stopped translating and told me he couldn't continue. I ask him why, and he told me that he didn't know Christ and couldn't translate with the same passion I was experiencing. I ask Ruben if he wanted to have a personal relationship with this Christ who loved me so, and he said yes. We excused ourselves for a few minutes as Ruben prayed for forgiveness and he asked Christ to come into his heart. We then returned to finish the study. Even with the excitement of leading others to Christ, I still had Rosalba on my mind. Why?

Even though I was experiencing doubts as to what direction I needed to take in college, I knew I was going to finish just so I could go to seminary afterwards. I had no desire for another girlfriend. I had no time or money for a girlfriend. So, the question remained: Why was my mind so focused on this girl Rosalba in Mexico who I might not ever see again?

The next day began like the others, but now I was more excited to go. Was Rosalba going to be there or not?

Rosalba was not there. I continued to think about her as we knocked on many more doors that day and had the privilege to lead more people to Christ. Wow, what a day.

That evening, before the Bible study, Rosalba showed up. All right! We had a short time before the study started, so I moved over to Rosalba with Ruben to find out more about her. I began asking Rosalba questions through Ruben. I don't know what he asked Rosalba or the way he asked her, but we were talking. I found out later that Rosalba had spent all this time trying to get rid of me. God intervened and used Ruben in his diplomatic way to soften her replies. This further emboldened me to press on. Little did I know how Rosalba really felt about me.

That night, the churches were planning a meal near the hotel at a nice restaurant. I asked Sergio if I could go with Rosalba whom I met at the mission church. Sergio Ortega is a Christian friend I met with the Hennessey, OK Hispanic church that traveled with us to this mission trip. He said it would be okay and he would advise the pastor to arrange two more seats for me and Rosalba. I asked Ruben to invite Rosalba to go with me to the dinner. Out of pity or embarrassment, Rosalba agreed. We were supposed to get together for the meal at 8pm and Rosalba arrived in time. She was so beautiful and radiant. We walked over to Sergio to get the details and he could translate for us. Little did I know what was going to happen next.

Sergio informed me that the restaurant had no more room for us and he couldn't cancel his meal to be with us because they would lose a lot of money for their reservations. So here we were, this beautiful girl Rosalba and me. I was alone with Rosalba and had no way to talk to her. Now what?

I didn't know what to do, and I couldn't say anything Rosalba would be able to understand. I knew Rosalba was hungry and I knew she had no money, nor did I. Now what? We began to walk together in the park located by the hotel in central Monterrey. I noticed a restaurant that accepted the only credit card I carried. I motioned to the restaurant and Rosalba followed. We entered the restaurant and were seated at a small table. I was hungry, but the menu was in Spanish and I didn't know what I could or couldn't eat. Rosalba ordered something called green enchiladas and I ordered one of the pictured products. Peach Melba is a dish with ice cream and peaches. You can't go wrong with ice cream, can you? The waiter brought the dishes we requested and set them in front of us. We began to eat, but I couldn't take my eyes off of Rosalba. She had the most beautiful brown eyes I had ever seen. I found myself doing nothing but staring into those eyes and losing myself. It must have been uncomfortable for Rosalba, because she wasn't eating very much. Rosalba later told me that these were the best enchiladas she had ever tasted, and she hadn't eaten all day. We finished at the restaurant and started walking in the park again, just looking at each other.

The next thing I knew, we were holding hands and it was 12am. I had no clue about the culture and traditions of Mexico, but Rosalba did. She was supposed to be home before 11pm and her father was very strict with that rule. How was Rosalba supposed to tell me? We went back to the hotel and I tried to say goodbye, but didn't really want to. I didn't know that the bus service quit operating at 11pm and Rosalba had no way home. Now what?

The taxi drivers did not speak English, but the desk manager did speak a little. I had no cash and no pesos. How was I going to get Rosalba home? I offered my credit card to the taxi driver and he waved his hand, indicating "no." How was I to know that the cabs didn't accept credit cards? Now it was about 1am and Rosalba asked to borrow the desk phone to call her parents. I could now tell that Rosalba was worried and I could hear someone yelling in the background on the phone. I didn't understand what was being said, but I knew that someone was mad.

I asked the desk clerk what options I had to Rosalba her home. Rosalba had mentioned to him that she would pay the cab the next day if he would take us to her house to drop her off and bring me back to the hotel. The fee for this service was forty-five pesos. This was how much money Rosalba would make after working all week. She later told me of this. The desk clerk then told me that I could get cash with my credit card from the hotel. I did this and sent Rosalba home, not knowing if I would ever see her again.

The next day, our team followed the same routine as the previous days, and Rosalba wasn't there in the morning. My heart felt heavy, even though I was very involved in the mission before us. Where was Rosalba? Would I ever see her again? That night Rosalba showed up at the Bible study. She had not attended the morning activities because she was working. Now she was there and my heart was racing as I tried to finish what God wanted me to do, so I could find out more about her. Ruben was there to translate for us.

Little did I know that she Rosalba was still trying to get rid of me. Ruben continued to field her comments with a softer presentation, which gave me hope that she was at least a little bit interested in me.

I knew that the last day was fast approaching and time was running out. We had been blessed by God and enjoyed a harvest only He could have prepared for us. Many questions ran through my mind. *What happens to these new believers when we leave? Who's going to help them grow in Christ and His word when we leave?* Dumb, I know. Like God had been waiting for us to arrive to complete something He had always been in charge of since the beginning. What about Rosalba ? I finally learned her name was Rosalba, but not much more. How in the world could I have a girl I was interested in who lived so far away from Oklahoma? How could I ever hope to grow a relationship with Rosalba when I couldn't even communicate with her? Now what?

Even though all these questions were real, I couldn't stop myself from asking Rosalba to attend the final gathering of the groups at the First

Baptist Church in Monterrey that night. We were to leave the following morning and I wouldn't see her again. Rosalba accepted my invitation to go together. Thank God. My heart was beating with sadness, but with excitement at the same time. Sad, first of all, because all was coming to an end and because I might not ever see Rosalba again. Excited, because I did experience something special in doing what God wanted me to do. In obedience, God had used me to harvest many lives for His kingdom. I was also excited because Rosalba came to see me and be with me. Why? I didn't know. Did she see something in me? Did I say something that might have gotten through to her?

The only thing I knew for sure, from the moment I laid my eyes on Rosalba, was the fact that I loved her. Don't ask how or why I reached this conclusion. I just knew without a doubt that this was the creation God had made for me.

With all these things in my mind, we sang some hymns and sat through the service holding hands. I gave her a picture of me that I happened to have in my wallet. No, I wasn't vain. This was a picture I was to give my mother, but I hadn't had the time to give it to her yet. The services ended and now it was time to say goodbye. Ruben happened to get Rosalba's address and phone number after the services, and he asked her if he could give them to me. Rosalba said it was okay with her, and that was all I needed to hear. I knew then that I could write her letters or call her by phone. Now what? How?

Then we were on the bus heading back to the airport. *What is she doing now? Where is she? Will she even remember me? Does she want to hear from me?* We held hands and kissed each other goodbye. Did this mean anything to Rosalba, or did she feel compromised to do so? This trip had now turned into a very long and very hard return. *Will I ever see her again? What about all those people who came to know Christ? What about them?* Many questions were in my mind, but no answers were coming yet.

CHAPTER 2

PRACTICING FAITH

The plane was running down the runway and all those questions were flooding my mind. I spoke to my pastor in hopes of finding definite answers. He told me that in God's world there is only one guarantee. If we asked for forgiveness of our sins and practiced our faith, we will be in heaven when our lives ended. That was the truth, but I was twenty-seven years old at the time and death seemed so far away. What about now? What about those we left in Mexico and Rosalba? Would I get to see any of them again? I needed answers to my questions now, not when I died.

Pastor Robin Cowan assured me that God had begun a good work, not only in me but in Mexico. He began this work long before I had been asked to join the mission to Mexico. He said that God also promised to see it through to the end. This gave me some peace, but my mind was still wandering. Remembering all the people we had left behind brought images to my mind. These were memories that I would never forget. How God had prepared the youth in Mexico so well with the plan of salvation for all age groups. How He provided Ruben to translate for me. How He was able to use me when I was totally useless. How He was going to use Rosalba in my life was a different question. I didn't want to get married and I couldn't even explain to myself how this relationship might start. *What do I do now on a plane back to Houston?*

We landed in Houston and boarded the next plane to Oklahoma. I hurt every mile that we traveled further away from Mexico. I knew that with no money, my chances of returning to Monterrey were not very good. I had Rosalba's address thanks to Ruben, and I also had her phone number. I had made some brothers and sisters in Christ Sergio and Leonor Ortega, who spoke Spanish, and this would be helpful in the future. I was excited for some reason and began to write letters every week to Rosalba. Little did I know that it would cost Rosalba two days' pay to translate each letter to Spanish. I poured my heart and soul into each letter with all the excitement of hopefully being with Rosalba and the mission church again. Some of the letters were six or more pages in English. I'm not a man of many words, but when I began to write the words just continued to pour out onto the paper. I wasn't even sure the letters were even arriving at her house. The postal service in Mexico is quite different from here in the USA. I later found out that her father occasionally gave money to insure the postal service man would deliver the mail. I had to wonder about her father Julian. Would he want his youngest daughter Rosalba receiving mail from some stranger in the USA? Would Rosalba even see them?

This made me decide to contact the florist to send some flowers to Rosalba in Mexico. How could I do this? Did FTD even deliver to other countries? I ask the florist if this was a possibility and she assured me that they did it all the time. I ordered two dozen roses to be delivered to Rosalba in Mexico and provided the address. I paid for the roses on a credit card at the time because I still hadn't received my first paycheck from my summer job. I had no cash on me. This seems to be a never-ending story, even to this day. The florist contacted another florist in Monterrey and ordered the roses for me.

How would I know if Rosalba received them? I couldn't resist anymore, and had to ask my friend Jacob to call Rosalba and translate for me. I found out later that when her mom Maria told her the roses had arrived, Rosalba believed they were sent by her old boyfriend. When she found out that they were from me, she asked her mother to throw them away. Her mom secretly kept one of the roses for her, for some reason. I called Rosalba a couple of days later, and it was such a pleasure to hear her voice. I enjoyed hearing her even though I couldn't understand a word she was saying. This is strange even to this day, because something was growing in my heart that I had nothing to do with. Rosalba acknowledged that the roses did arrive, but said nothing about ordering her mom to dispose of them. Rosalba had never dreamed of marrying anyone either, much less someone with a white complexion. Her dreams were to marry another Mexican man about her height, if she was to marry. She had planned to adopt a child and stay single. (I'm still trying to figure that one out.) We talked for about an hour as Jacob translated for us. I thank God that Jacob was a Christian and was willing to help me communicate with her. Meanwhile, all the letters I had been writing began arriving at Roalba's house. I told her everything about me, even the not so good things. I didn't want any secrets ever to be between us. I had no idea that many of the letters were never read until years later. She just could not pay to have them translated.

One day I came home and found that she had written me a letter as well. I was so excited to read it, but it was all in Spanish. I couldn't understand a single word. There wasn't a single "andele" or "arriba" anywhere in the letter. I went to Enid, OK, about an hour from my home, to buy a Spanish dictionary because I couldn't wait to read her letter. This helped me with some of the words, but the verbs were a big problem. They changed to suit the time or situation in which they were used. Once again, I had to look for someone to help me translate. Jacob wasn't available, so I drove another hour to Hennessey, OK, to get Sergio to help me. I guess this had to be hilarious to him, that I cared for Rosalba so much that I would go to such lengths to read her letter. He was more than willing to help me, and I was so glad.

My ears hung on every word as he translated. Rosalba told me of her dreams of finishing college and that she worked as a seamstress six days a week, and really didn't have the money to pay for translating all the letters I sent her. She was trying to support her elderly parents, now in their sixties and retired. She didn't have money to pay for college either. As Sergio read Rosalba's letter, my heart began to ache because I could relate to wanting something and having no money to pay for it. I worked all summer and during college and hardly ever had money to eat. She sometimes would go all day without food at work and college at night, and never had money for even a soda. How could she be so positive when everything was so hard to achieve? I didn't remember a single moment with Rosalba that she wasn't smiling while I was there.

One call and one letter down, and I began to breathe again. When would the next letter come or when would she call again? I found myself unable to wait, so I continued to write more letters and anxiously await her reply. I would drive to Hennessey frequently to call her. Pastor Ramon Alemon went on the mission trip with us. Pastor Ramon is the pastor of the Hispanic church in Hennessey, OK. He would often help me translate as I talked to her. Pastor Ramon, Sergio, and Jacob were probably tired of me bothering them constantly for help.

The next semester started in college and I added Spanish classes to my schedule. My professor was a strict professor from Venezuela. After the second day in class, she would not speak English to us. The only time she spoke in English was when she was irritated with our inability to learn. I made the mistake of telling her that I had met someone in Mexico and this was why I was taking Spanish. I say *mistake*, but I wouldn't trade anything for her higher demand on me learning. I had to learn Spanish because I met so many wonderful people in Mexico and I wanted to be able to communicate with them more. My professor would often correct me on the proper way to speak to a woman in Mexico or any other Spanish speaking country. "Don't dare say it this way" and "Be careful to use these words that way." These were things the textbooks didn't talk about. I would constantly annoy my Spanish-speaking friends in person or by phone so I could practice my Spanish. They were patient with me and spent a lot of time laughing at my misuse of the language. It didn't matter, I was going to learn. Nothing was going to stop me.

One night, about 11pm, my phone rang. I answered the phone and it was Rosalba. I panicked because I still could not understand her. I looked in my books and found the correct way to say "wait a minute." In this minute, I ran to Jacob's house a block away and knocked on his door. He answered the door in his robe and slippers. I excitedly explained to him the Rosalba called me and I desperately needed his help. He agreed to help me, and together in robes and slippers, we walked to my house to communicate with Rosalba. Fighting off the yawns and the tiredness, we ventured into the world of this girl who lived in Mexico. What was Rosalba going to say? What was I going to say? It couldn't be too mushy, because of embarrassment. That didn't last very long, because she said that she missed me. Wow! She missed me! Now what? I told her that I had never stopped missing her since I left Mexico. I told her that I remembered every detail about our time together.

And then it happened. I ask Rosalba if she wanted to get married.

I can still remember the look on Jacob's face as he translated this proposal to Rosalba. I was not on my knee with a ring in my hand, or anything traditional like we did things here in the USA. I was following my heart and it was going crazy, it seemed. This was far from common sense and even bordered on the crazy side. I couldn't help myself. It just seemed to jump from my heart and out of my mouth. I had never even contemplated the thought before. Now I was just waiting, unable to breathe, to hear her reply. Would she say yes or would she think I was crazy? *I must be crazy.*

Rosalba said yes, and Jacob and I were surprised. *What did I do? How in the world am I going to marry a girl in Mexico?*

As it turned out, I was crazy. I asked Rosalba if I could visit her soon. She agreed and I used my credit card once again to purchase a plane ticket to Monterrey, Mexico. I hadn't even paid for the roses yet. So there went my return as I spent $400 to see Rosalba I had spent about ten to twelve hours with Rosalba during the mission trip. I was excited because now I could count down the days until I would be with her again. She assured me that her brothers were going to pick me up at the airport in Monterrey. Who were her brothers? I had only met one of her sisters and her husband during the mission trip. Was Ruben available to spend time with us?

I was traveling back to Mexico and I knew enough Spanish to get myself in trouble. This time I had brought enough cash with me to pay for a taxi. I got the money on the credit card, of course. What was I going to say? Rosalba said I could stay with her at her mom and dad's house. I was glad for this because I didn't have money for a hotel during the week. The plans were made and my anxiety was on a very high level. My life was changing and it seemed that I had no control over what was happening. That was scary in itself.

I didn't know anything about marriage. I didn't even have an example to compare to. My mom and dad got divorced when I was five years old. He left and only came back but once a year to make sure we were still alive. I prayed many days for God to help me learn in His Word about marriage and its importance. I didn't want to even get close to repeating the same thing my mom and dad failed at doing. I feared this thought and spent many days studying and talking to my pastor Robin Cowan about my decision to marry. Many questions remained that had to be dealt with. My lack of knowledge, lack of money, and I had no idea about the expenses a woman had to deal with in life. How could I marry a girl in another country and bring her home?

This was going to be another impossible challenge to overcome. Now the nerves were really out of control. I asked a Rosalba to marry me and I didn't even know how we could be together. She couldn't live here legally and I couldn't live in Mexico legally either. Was I stupid or what? How could I ask Rosalba to marry me without dealing with this issue first? Now what?

I asked for a day off from work and drove to Oklahoma City to the Immigration office. I arrived and took my number and waited in anticipation for a quick, easy answer to the problem I created for myself. What would they tell me? Was it even possible? How would I tell Rosalba I couldn't marry her because both of us would be illegal here or there? A marriage wasn't legal in Mexico if both were not citizens of that country. I could marry her here in the church, but it wouldn't be recognized because she was illegal. What if they discovered that she was Illegal after we got married and shipped her back to Mexico? This was not going to suffice. I was going to do it right the first time. I didn't want to live in fear, and I definitely didn't want Rosalba to live with this fear.

The officer called out my number and I walked to his window nervously. I began to explain the situation I made for myself and he laughed at me. He said, "You must really love this girl so much that you would propose to her without any answers." I agreed and desperately asked for his council on how to make this problem go away.

"I love her and I want to be with her but I want to do it legally."

He directed me to the proper forms that I must fill out to start the process. I wasn't yet aware of the time process it took for Immigration to do their work. I asked him about the process and the time frame I must wait before I heard something. He told me that it would take six months to process the paperwork once they received it. He gave me the forms and directed me on how to fill out all the documents so that I wouldn't have to repeat it.

The time finally arrived and I was sitting in the airport in Oklahoma City, waiting for my flight to Houston. I was nervous, because now I was flying into Mexico alone. Someone was with us before to help us fill out the travel visas in Mexico. Now I was alone and wondering if I could do it myself. *Will I know Rosalba's brothers or are they waiting for a white guy who matched the picture I left her?* I shaved off my beard. Would they recognize me? How would I know them? Would Rosalba be with them? Every question left me more nervous than before, and I was sure my blood pressure was soaring. I found myself praying more and more.

Are You sure this is what You want me to do, God? Messing up my own life is bad enough, but now I'm getting involved with this wonderful girl. Are You sure?

I somehow felt a sense of peace in the midst of my fears. The plane landed in Houston, and somehow I needed to find my connection in thirty minutes. The anxiety increased because I had to travel to the furthest gate for my connection to Monterrey. I barely made it and took my seat near the window. I had to see for myself that I was traveling back to Mexico. I hoped the cloud cover wasn't that bad. I was nervous because I was closer to seeing Rosalba and I had no clue what was going to happen.

I finally felt the plane descending after the three-hour flight. My ears were popping and my heart was pounding as I tried to think of what I could say when we arrived. My Spanish was the basics: *Hello. How are you doing? Where is the bathroom?* God, help me, please. We taxied into the airport in Monterrey and waited for the doors to open. As we exited the plane into the airport, I saw all the soldiers with their M-16s and prayed that I wouldn't do something stupid. I filled out the travel visa and paid my airport taxes and handed the officer my documents. He waved me on and I walked down to the baggage claim area. Thank God, the directions were in English. I got my luggage and exited to the area to be picked up.

There she is! God, she's even more beautiful than I remember.

I refrained from hurrying over to Rosalba, but I wanted to run. She was with her brother, Samuel, and his wife, Edi. I said hello in Spanish and shook her brother's hand. We exited the airport where he had parked his pickup. I placed my luggage in the back and sat in the back seat of the pickup with Rosalba. I tried to speak in Spanish, but she spent more time smiling at me than talking. I couldn't imagine all the stupid stuff I had to be saying in Spanish without even knowing it. *Maybe I'll get points for trying in the end.*

The trip from the airport to her parents' house lasted about forty-five minutes. I didn't even know if Rosalba understood a single word I had spoken. Now I was nervous again. She hadn't said a word yet and I wasn't sure if I was sinking or swimming. Now what? *Is Ruben going to be there to help me? How am I going to communicate with her and her family without making a fool of myself?* "God please help me again," I pray. I seemed to be praying this prayer a lot lately.

We arrived at Rosalba's house and I unloaded my luggage and followed the pointing gestures made towards where I was to sleep. After taking my luggage to the room, we ate supper. We sat at the table and everyone was talking, but I hardly understand a single word that was spoken. I wanted to say, "Slow down, I can't understand because you're speaking too fast." I understood a few words only, and I wondered about all that was being said.

When the meal was finished, Rosalba must have had compassion on me. She grabbed my hand and led me out the door. We walked around the neighborhood, holding hands and making faces. I tried my best to talk to her, but I was very unsure of my progress. She continued to smile and occasionally laughed. This concerned me, because I wasn't telling jokes or anything humorous. *Where's Ruben?* I asked Rosalba if we could go to Ruben's house to visit for a while. Ruben had become my good friend during the mission trip and I missed talking to him. I now had double motives to see him again. We took a bus to his house and found him there. Thank God! Now we could go over everything I had kept bottled up inside me.

We had to go over all the immigration papers and fill them out correctly. I needed Ruben to instruct her on how to do it and what we needed to provide to Immigration. This was a fiancé visa and it had to be done correctly or they would return it and we would lose the application fee of $300 and the six months of waiting would be wasted. Most likely it would involve another trip to Mexico to do it right the next time. I wanted to make sure every "T" was crossed and every dot in its place. I hated doing this first because there was so much more I wanted to do. I couldn't get that first kiss off my mind, and I was waiting to see if the second one was going to be just as good or better. Paper work and documentation were a priority, due to the lack of time I had to complete it. Birth certificates, letters, doctor visits, and immunization shots kept us busy during this week.

Once the immigration papers were complete and notarized, then we could spend some free time having fun. I was glad Ruben was with us, and he brought his sister with him. This was fun but also helpful. I'm sure Rosalba was nervous being alone with two guys. Having Ruben's sister with us helped relieve her fears. We went to movies. We went to the mission church on Wednesday night to visit with the pastor and the youth who helped us during the mission trip. We walked in the park where we had walked together during the mission trip.

God, Rosalba was beautiful. The more time I spent with her, finally able to communicate with her, my heart became totally convinced that this was what God wanted me to do. After this week with her, I never had another doubt about her being my wife. I knew God was opening this door, and everything was way over my head. God had told me that if I did His will and obeyed His commands, He would give me the desires of my heart. The only problem I had was that I did not know the desires of my heart were different from the desires of my mind. Now what?

God always says, "Trust Me." I'm slowly learning how to do this. It's like the saying: "You can't teach old dogs' new tricks."

Father, help me please! I found myself asking this more often as the trip went on. When Ruben and his sister left, we had some time to spend alone. It seemed the only thing I could do was hold Rosalba. I saw the moonlight reflecting off her black hair. I had never seen eyes that shined so bright in the light of the moon. As I held her hand, I couldn't stop thinking about how soft her skin was, and how beautifully pigmented. A girl made for me with a natural tan. *God, You are so good.*

I can still remember the clothes Rosalba wore every day we spent together that week. I was not going to take a single second for granted. She smelled so good and I would await the next breeze to blow her fragrance my way. She had such a beautiful smile and laughter. It was so contagious, and comforting as well in a really difficult situation. My heart had fallen and I still didn't know if Immigration would permit our marriage to happen. What would I do if they said no? Every second I was there, the problem grew substantially. It wasn't just my heart involved now, because I had dragged her into this without properly planning beforehand. Now what, God?

Every day we spent together, my mind was counting down the seconds left that we had to spend together before I had to leave. *How or what do I do to convince Rosalba that I really love her and want to be with her?* I had to trust in God to show her that I loved her, and it was impossible to do it on my own. There was no way I could make this happen by myself. Did I even want to get further involved in this? It would hurt her and me so much if the immigration papers didn't go through. Was I wasting both our time?

What about college? What about seminary? Would I ever be able to do either of these with a wife? Having a wife usually meant having children. How would this interfere with getting to seminary? How much did a wife cost? Would she like fishing? What about golf? What church would we attend? She didn't understand English and I didn't understand Spanish yet. Should I leave my church to attend a Hispanic church? It was my responsibility to help her grow in Christ. How would I do this if I couldn't speak the language?

I decided then that we would attend the Hispanic church in Hennessey, OK, with Pastor Ramon. I might not immediately understand the studies or sermons, but at least she would grow in Christ. I would increase my personal studies so that I would not lose my love for Christ. I would miss my church and the brothers and sisters in Christ who had influenced my life. Could I handle this? I wasn't really that mature in Christ, to be able to sacrifice this time of fellowship with other Christians in English.

I realized that my mind was wandering with all those questions while I was with the most beautiful girl I had ever been interested in. *Focus, John. Your time here with Rosalba is almost over.* So, with her hand in mine, I gently smiled and looked deep into her eyes. Hopefully she could see into my soul and know that I was truly in love with her. Do eyes speak in different languages as well? I hoped not, because now that was the only thing I had in my kit to use. I hoped she liked blue eyes.

We continued to enjoy the rest of the week being together. *God, she is so beautiful. Help me, please.*

CHAPTER 3

LIVING IN FAITH'S REALITY

I t was now Friday morning and I had to return to the real world. My brother-in-law Samuel drove me back to the airport with Rosalba by my side. I was back to staring into her eyes and holding her hand. I hoped with every second that she was looking deep into my soul and able to see how much I had fallen for her. It was really hard for me to leave and the trip to the airport seemed like it happened much too quickly. I had to say goodbye and go through security, and she stood and watched me leave. *Does her heart hurt like mine now does? Whoever says love is easy must not have ever really experienced the real thing.*

There wasn't a single part of my mind or emotions not affected as I left Rosalba there. The reality remained. I had to return to Oklahoma and work. Monday would arrive before I was ready. I made the usual flights to Houston, and then on to Oklahoma City. I didn't notice the time because my mind was entertained by all the memories of Rosalba and her family. I had the privilege to experience more of their customs and culture. I met her family members who lived in Monterrey and they seemed to be good people. I still did not have the opportunity to talk to them due to my inability to speak Spanish.

I arrived in Oklahoma City and now had to drive two hours to my little trailer house in the country. I liked living in the country after living in the city for most of my young life. It was quiet, and if I wanted to go outside to enjoy God's creation, it was there. God now had opened my eyes to another beautiful creation of His, but Rosalba was in a city of 7 million people. As I drove home I wondered if she could live in the country. I lived in a small trailer park with five other families. If I walked out the door the cows were about fifty feet away and mooing all the time. Most of the noises were from God's creations that lived in the country. To me, this was heaven, but to her ... I didn't know. Reality told me I was home, but I believed I left a big part of me in Monterrey with Rosalba.

21

I went to church the next Sunday and shared with my brothers and sister in Christ all of my experiences during the trip. I shared with them my visit with the mission church and the thanks they sent with me for all the work we did while we were there. I was still amazed by the youth group and their excitement for Christ. Their pastor Juan Antonio was very diligent in teaching them discipleship and they were growing in Christ every day.

I talked to my pastor Robin about my time with Rosalba and all the things we did while I was with her. I told him that even though most of this didn't make sense to me, I loved her. He reminded me that God always worked the best when we didn't understand what was happening. He said God's will on earth is as it is in heaven. I told him I agreed, because Rosalba must have come from heaven. He prayed with me and said if this was God's will, then it would happen. I hoped and prayed he was right. I missed her already, and I went home and wrote her more letters.

I explained to Rosalba where I lived. What I did at work. I told her about the classes that I planned on taking the next semester. I just wanted to talk to her so much. When I finished my letter, it must have been eight pages long on front and back. My mind wandered as I remembered the moon reflecting off her black hair and her eyes. I remembered the full, soft lips that gave me the kiss goodbye when I left. I cherished the times we spent walking together in the park and in her neighborhood. What about those legs? Her smile would just warm my heart in an inexplicable way.

Monday morning arrived and reality returned. I had to go to college and then to work. I would wake up shower and drive to Weatherford, OK, and go to work 3:30pm until 1am. My job wasn't that difficult. I sat on a machine and filled bags with cement nine hours a day. I got dirty, but it wasn't that hard. I needed the money and it paid pretty well for this area. It also helped to keep my mind from straying while all these questions about getting married and immigration were testing my faith. I wasn't comfortable yet with the thought of possibly sacrificing college for marriage. The thought of this, with the complications with immigration, made it more difficult. *Am I doing the right thing? Is this what God wants me to do?* I remembered Paul in the Bible. He wanted to go east and God changed his plans and sent him west instead. Was this a Paul moment for me?

I woke up the next morning and went to mail my letter to Rosalba, wondering if she was as anxious to receive it as I was to write and send it. I wrote another one every time I would think of her. I would explain how I was feeling and what I was thinking. I was always open with her in everything. I wanted her to know who I was, not what she hoped I was. I didn't like surprises and I don't think Rosalba liked them either.

Rosalba also had doubts. She spoke to me later about some of her thoughts during this time. People in her life wondered if this was real or was it a scam. They had heard many stories about how guys would marry girls in Mexico and turn them into prostitutes in the US. They had also heard that many women from Mexico later found that their husbands had another wife or lover in the US.

I sent her pictures of my family as well with the letters. Once, I sent a picture of my brothers' wife and her two girls. The next thing I knew, she was calling me and asking about this woman and these two girls. She thought that they were mine. She was angry and determined to believe that I planned on using her. I explained to her that this was indeed my brother's wife and children, and Rosalba relaxed with a deep sigh.

Reality was often very hard and sometimes seemed more than we could handle. Case in point: I was in Oklahoma and she was 900 miles away in Mexico. I had no time for marriage. I had no money. I still didn't know anything about what marriage included. *How much does it cost to take care of a wife? What do I need to buy to provide what she needs? Can I even communicate with her? What about church and my responsibilities? How do I study the Bible with her in English or in Spanish?* The biggest question remained: *I have never had a physical relationship with anyone else. How do I do this correctly with all her current fears?* Many questions remained as I waited on God to work. *God, am I listening to you? Is this what God wants or what I want?*

Life continued and never waited for us to find the answers we sought. I still had to work and go to my classes. My Spanish professor was really pushing me harder once I told her that we were going to marry. We had not set a date, but I knew we were going to marry.

The following Saturday, I remember playing golf with my grandfather Vernon on my dad's side. He was a great guy but didn't say much. Later, as we sat in his living room with my grandmother Georgia, I brought up the subject of getting married. They asked the normal questions: *Why are you are doing this? Who is she? What's her name? How do you know she's the right one? How are you going to support a wife and continue school?* These were all great questions and I had been asking them of myself all the time. My grandfather looked at me and asked if I was crazy.

He said, "You have only seen her two times and you can't even talk to her. How are you going to marry a girl you can't even talk to?"

These were all questions that check our reality world and shake us up when we cannot find the answers. *What am I going to do?*

My grandfather looked into my eyes and I was sure he could see me trembling with the fear of making this decision. He told me that I had never spoken more passionately about anything in all my life. He encouraged me to continue praying for God's direction. He also told me that I had never made brash decisions in my life. He told me, "Son, whatever you decide you're going to do, do it the best you can."

I took a deep breath and realized that this was much bigger than me and I needed God to help calm my fears and continue to open the doors here in Oklahoma and in Mexico.

I had many examples of what I didn't want my marriage to be like, but I had very few that would serve as good examples. My grandfather and grandmother were an exception. They seemed to connect and they enjoyed being together. They had similar interests and likes. Could I be so fortunate that God would provide me someone I would enjoy being with?

My nerves were sensitive to all these questions and I began to exercise and fast to present myself to God in a way that He could mold me into what I needed to be. I never doubted that Rosalba was going to be my wife. I continually doubted if I had what was needed to treat her as the bride of Christ. *God, help me? What does a man of God need to be to represent Christ to Rosalba? I am nothing like Christ. I am a sinner saved only by YOUR grace. Am I ready for this?*

The words echoed in my mind: *I can do all things through Christ who strengthens me.* (Phil. 4:13) My problem was that I didn't know what "ALL" included. I was now seven years old in Christ, so what did I know? Having no knowledge is not a place I liked to find myself in. *Now what? God, would You please still my soul?*

I got home and found a letter from Rosalba, but it was time to go to work. I got to work looked for my Spanish-speaking friends to help me translate. My friend Jacob was on the floor above me, but I couldn't just stop working to have him translate the letter for me. What if she wrote something that would embarrass me? Don't misunderstand me: I wanted to hear what she said. I didn't want others to make fun of me, and I knew they would if they knew too much. My desire to hear what she wrote was greater than my fears of embarrassment.

This is what we did: I would call Jacob on the intercom and read a sentence. He would listen and then tell me, one sentence at a time. I would write it out in English above her Spanish words. We did this all night without stopping the work we had to do. Thank God for putting people in my life to open all these doors. It was a great night. *Rosalba loves me! All right!*

Somehow, I knew everything was going to be all right once I learned that she loved me. This was great. Sometimes I wondered if I even loved myself, and often wondered if anyone other than my mother could love me. I knew now that God loved me, and now a beautiful lady in Mexico loved me. *So, what do I do now?*

I wrote another letter. I poured out the contents of my heart. I told Rosalba how relieved I was to know now that she loved me. She might have wanted to say this in Mexico, but would have been embarrassed by Ruben, who was translating for us. That was okay. I was glad she said it in her letter. I tried to remember every detail of her beauty as I wrote my letter to her, I used the creation of God to make my comparisons to her beauty. I knew the same God who created the bright beautiful moon created her. The light from the sun also came from God. Her beautiful smile existed because God had been a big part of her life.

I also asked Rosalba if she had ever asked Christ to come into her heart and forgive her sins. Catholicism dominated religious life in Mexico, and I wanted to make sure she had a real relationship with Christ. She later explained to me how and when she accepted Christ into her life. She spoke of her baptism later.

I mailed my letter and checked my mailbox twice to make sure she hadn't sent me another one. I went to school and remembered the mistake of telling my Spanish professor the plans we had to get married. Big mistake! Every day she would call on me to respond to her questions. My new name was Juan not John. She would speak a sentence in Spanish and awaited my reply in Spanish and then in English. I remember once she paired me up with a female classmate. We drew character titles out of an envelope and then we had to role play. She was a sales lady and I was the customer. I was buying shirts and socks. I had to ask her about colors and sizes. I then had to check out at the end.

I asked her, "Cuanto cuestas?" My professor went crazy. She said, "You don't ever say that to a female. You are asking her how much she costs. You are speaking to her as if she's a prostitute."

My face turned several shades of red that day. I learned a lot during that time in college, but nothing compared to what Rosalba would teach me later.

I received more letters in the mail and I tried to translate them myself at first. Now I had an understanding about how the verb changed by time and person, it seemed easier. This was exciting. I was in love and still learning. Sometimes love can block our minds and we fail to learn. Many times, we make poor decisions when we think we are in love. I don't think examples are necessary.

Back to work I went, and still waiting on some type of reply from Immigration. I couldn't plan anything until I heard from them. I became well known at the Immigration office in Oklahoma City. Every day I had off work and school I would drive the two hours to check on the status of her papers. I wouldn't leave until they updated me on the status of her papers. I didn't want this to get tangled up in the normal government bureaucracy. They were patient with me and told me that there was a process and they were going to push mine because of the love story I shared with them.

They knew I loved her by my actions and dedication towards doing everything correctly. I left the office the same way every time. I asked God if HE was moving the right people the right way to make this happen. God must have been tired of listening to me sometimes. I often wondered if my love for Rosalba was becoming more important to me than my love for God. I hoped not, because without HIM this would never happen. I not only needed HIM, I wanted HIM in charge of this relationship.

Waiting sometimes can be so difficult. I opened the mailbox and nothing was there. No letter from Rosalba and nothing from Immigration. I woke up and went through the same motions all the time. Go to school, work, and church. Something seemed to be missing all the time. Something was wrong. The picture was not complete because she was supposed to be here with me. That hadn't happened yet. *God, are you there? What's Rosalba doing now? Does she still want to be with me? What's the delay?*

I had to realize God was still working with both of us to prepare us for HIS future. Rosalba was still dealing with a former relationship with an old boyfriend. She still loved him, as I later learned from her. God had to close that door for her to have the freedom to say yes to me. I was a basket case. I didn't know anything about marriage, and what I did know was not HIS definition of it. "What are You trying to tell me?" seemed to be my favorite question as I fasted. "What else do I have to learn?" I was twenty-seven and I thought I knew everything. Little did I know, everything I thought I knew was incorrect.

How do you love someone like God loves them? Am I looking at Rosalba through God's eyes or mine? Am I looking at how to make her happier, or myself? I was looking for a queen in my life, and never stopped to wonder if I was the king I was supposed to be. *God, what do I need to learn to love her the way You love me or the church? Work in me, please, and make sure that I'm right in YOU so I can love her without limitation.*

I never liked living in a world of "what if?" How could I avoid this? I read the Bible all the time looking for the road map HE had provided me. Many times, I didn't find the answers I was looking for. I asked my pastor Robin and he did his best to guide me, but sometime the answers were elusive and not to be known.

I decided to go to the Hispanic church in Hennessey, OK, the next Sunday. I had to learn more about their customs and culture. I didn't like surprises in my life. If I was to use my time waiting, then this was one way to learn more about Rosalba. The relationships I developed with the brothers and sisters in Christ there were awesome. They were patient with me as I asked multiple questions about customs and culture. They shared with me about the importance of family. This is something that the USA has lost sight of in the last fifty years. I have worked in nursing homes and seen patients waiting for two or more years, and never receiving one visitor. That was sad. I didn't want my life to be like this.

I was learning to cherish every moment with the Hispanic congregation. They taught me so much and I began to enjoy being with them, even if I couldn't understand half of what they were saying. I could see in their lives and actions and how much they cared for their families. The elderly parents or grandparents always stayed with their children. They were not abandoned in a nursing home or something like it.

This meant so much to me, because although I had a family, we hardly spent time together. In Rosalba's family, they looked for each other constantly. This proved to me that I was not ready to be with her yet. I needed to find out what family meant. Now what?

I dug out my Bible and continued to study and read the stories of Ruth and Esther. I also read the story of King David and the poor choices he made. What about Job? He basically lost his whole family. *What do YOU want me to learn, God?* Being in the back seat during this time of learning was difficult. I couldn't see what was ahead and remained moving all the time, while not knowing the destination. *Where is this going, God?* The problem that bothered me the most was to know that my own family was so separated. The truth was that my family only got together for weddings and funerals. Was this normal, God? I chose to believe that it was not supposed to be this way. Families ought to look for each other.

I continued to wait on God's plan. I received another letter and wrote about eight more during the same time frame. Rosalba had to know my love for her was still alive. *Is she thinking about me now? What is she thinking about now? What dress or clothing is she wearing now? Does she have money to get to school? What about the bus or her meal?* I sat at work and I was picturing her walking home several miles because she had no money left to pay for the bus or her meal. Waiting to get home and finally eating her supper at the end of a difficult day. How her feet must have hurt after walking all the way home.

Her father was older and had retired. They had no income coming into their home. Rosalba had to pay all their bills and she made about $45 a week. This was not very much money, but she pushed herself harder every day to help them and finish college. This must have really bothered her, knowing that her parents would suffer if she got married. The whole time I had known her, she had always focused on others rather than herself. Who was going to take care of them when she left? This must have been a very difficult time for her parents as well. Their youngest child was getting ready to marry some guy from the mission trip. *Who is he? What are his motives? Can we trust him?*

I left my mind to wonder as I got on my knees to pray. There were just so many unknown questions that needed to be answered. In my fasting and prayer time, I was growing in my relationship with Christ. I no longer felt the same desperation for all the answers in the world. I needed to simply lay my concerns at the foot of the cross and HE would take care of them when HE wanted. I prayed, asking God to remove everything that was not Christ-like in my life. HE was constantly working on me.

I planned on another trip to Mexico to spend time with Rosalba, but this time I would drive. I had a two-seat Toyota SR5 pickup. It was a standard and a simple vehicle to drive. I had never driven through Dallas before. Now I would have to drive to Monterrey through many big cities. I couldn't wait to see her again, but I had to get there in one piece. The plan was to drive to Laredo, TX and Rosalba's brother Samuel would meet me there. We would spend the night with an uncle of Rosalba. The next day, we would drive to Monterrey. It was hard to imagine, because the thought of fifteen hours of driving usually made me tired and exhausted before I even left.

I cranked up the volume on the radio and cruised to Dallas. Once I made it through Dallas, my next big hurdle was getting through San Antonio. After San Antonio, it was a pretty easy drive to Laredo. It was amazing how the fauna and flora changed as I drove south.

My heart was once again pounding because now I was driving my pickup into Monterrey. People at work had filled my head with bad stories about things that happened to their vehicles when they were in Mexico. Sometimes their vehicle was wrecked, stolen, or both. I sought God's peace as I drove. I chose to drive because I didn't have the money to fly. In a way, I was glad I was driving. We could take my pickup to the movies, church, or just to go shopping.

One thing I had to do was buy vehicle insurance in Laredo. Jacob directed me to a reputable business that sold the plans I needed for Mexico. I didn't know anything about it. I stopped at the business he suggested and paid the money for a one-week visit. I then had to drive across the border into Mexico. I was nervous from all the things I had been told before. As I went through the border check station, an officer directed me to go to a designated building to fill out the visitation visa. I did so and paid the fee for it. The officers then directed me to go to another building to get permission for the pickup. I arrived at this business and they directed me to another office that focused on this only. The officer came and examined my pickup and put a sticker in the windshield. I paid the fee and asked for the best way to get on the right roads for Monterrey.

Four or five more hours, and I would be with Rosalba, I hoped. I now had to stop and get gas. Jacob advised me to get the green gas, not the red. Thank God, I remembered to change my dollars to pesos. I pulled into the gas station, and in Spanish requested they fill my tank. Fifteen minutes later, I was on the road again. Rosalba was closer every minute. *God, help me find my way to her.* Little did I know that one of my greatest challenges was about to happen. I now had to drive through Monterrey at night. I'm glad Samuel is with me.

I finally made it to Rosalba's parents' house and unloaded my suitcase. I knocked on the door and there she was. *My God, You really created a fine piece of work in Rosalba.* That same smile met me at the door, and once again I somehow knew everything was going to be okay.

CHAPTER 4

A FAITHFUL REUNION

I was there with the most beautiful creature I had ever seen. I thanked God for helping me make it from Oklahoma to Monterrey. It was a long trip, but it seemed shorter than it really was. Once I held Rosalba in my arms, I knew everything was going to be okay. Somehow, I felt more secure and hopeful that life was going to be okay.

It's a wonderful feeling when the doors open in ways that bless your life. I still to this day consider her coming into my life a blessing. The only blessing greater than this was when Christ came into my heart and forgave all of my sins.

I held Rosalba in my arms for the longest time that night. I never wanted to let her go. Her hair smelled so good and the light still reflected brilliantly from her dark brown eyes. It was a little cold, so we enjoyed the embrace even more. I could feel her heart beating against my chest and Rosalba felt like she was already a part of my life. I had never felt this way for anybody in my whole life. I felt at peace with God and my own conscience.

It was late, but that didn't seem to matter. Neither one of us could sleep, so we sat in her living room and I got to practice my Spanish more. She continued to smile and laugh as I spoke. It didn't seem to matter now, because I wanted to talk to her so much. I would talk to her about my life in Oklahoma and my family. I explained how my days went at school and at work. I told her about my Spanish professor at college, and how she was pressing me to be the best. My Spanish was still faulty, but I could keep a simple conversation with her. I had a harder time understanding people when they spoke to me. My professor taught us Spanish from Venezuela, and it was different enough to get lost in a conversation. I would have to ask Rosalba to speak slower so I could process what she was saying.

Rosalba finally said that she was tired and needed to go to bed. It was about one in the morning, and we were both exhausted. She showed me where I was to sleep and it took no time at all for me to fall asleep. I actually fell asleep thanking God for everything He was doing in my life.

In the morning, we woke up about eight in the morning and ate breakfast. I offered to help, but Rosalba told me to remain seated and she would serve me. This was rare to me because I had spent the last ten years serving myself. This was part of her culture and I had to respect it. She explained to me that there was no greater joy than to serve the one you loved. Wow! How was I going to serve her? The Bible told me that I must serve Christ and serve my wife as Christ served the church. How would I do this? I found myself in prayer again, asking God how I could keep Him number one in my life and love Rosalba the way He wanted me to. She was so beautiful in the mornings and at night. How often did this happen on a normal day? She was beautiful when she woke up and before she went to bed. No makeup was used, and she didn't need it. Her complexion and pigmentation were perfect.

Rosalba asked me if I would like to go for a walk, and I was more than willing. We walked to the corner of her street and found an ice cream shop. She introduced me to the owner, who was friends with her dad. He was a great guy and made great ice cream. I believe mango and strawberry were my favorites. Rosalba enjoyed the one made with nuts. That afternoon I was invited to go with the family to the river nearby to have a picnic. It was fun, as her brothers would sing some of their favorite songs as we sat around visiting. I didn't have Ruben with me at this time, so I had to pay very close attention to everything that was said. Rosalba's family would ask me questions. Some I could understand, and some I couldn't. It was time to eat, and Rosalba brought me two tacos that her sister made just for me. I felt wanted, until I started eating the tacos. Inside were jalapeños. My mouth was on fire and nothing seemed to stop the burning. Someone told me that this was my initiation into the family. Even though my mouth was on fire, I felt comfortable with her family. I continually watched Rosalba and hoped that every detail about her would burn into my memory, because I knew that this week would end quickly. I wanted to remember every smile, laugh, movement, and touch. I really enjoyed being with her. We went swimming in the little water that was in the river. It was fun with all her family there. I remember seeing her with her wet hair and the water beading down her face. What was wrong with me? Every little detail about her meant something very special to me. *What are You doing to me, God?*

I knew I was hooked after this trip. I couldn't quit watching Rosalba's every movement. Every smile burned deep into my heart and left a lasting memory. We left the river and returned to her house. We called Ruben to see if he and his sister would go to the movies with us. He agreed and we picked them up and went to see the movie. I was glad it was in English and the subtitles were in Spanish. I noticed how intensely Ruben paid attention to the movie. He later explained that his desire to learn English motivated him to really pay attention. There were some phrases and sayings in movies not found in the dictionary.

After the movie, we went to eat pizza. I enjoyed Ruben and his sister. He helped me have more detailed conversations with Rosalba. Some of the words I used confused Ruben, and I would have to explain to him another way, to say the same thing in another way. This seemed to help him understand the language better.

It was time to say goodnight to Ruben and his sister. We dropped them off at his house and returned to Rosalba's. The rest of the night, I just held Rosalba and said nothing at all. I just wanted to feel her in my arms. I wanted to feel her heart beating against me. I wanted to hear her breathing and found myself breathing in sequence with her. We were becoming one and I did nothing to take credit for. This was all God from the beginning. Nobody would ever be able to convince me otherwise. In His infinite wisdom, He had provided for me a dream that I never knew I dreamed about. Deep within my soul, He could see that I needed her. I never doubted God and His wisdom, but I continually doubted mine. Now I felt that my will was coming into alignment with His. The things I thought were important before now seemed like they were less important. God had put me and Rosalba together again, and every moment seemed so special.

I asked her if she was receiving the letters I sent her and she assured me that she had received many, but didn't have the money to get them translated yet. I couldn't write very well in Spanish, even though I tried in one of the letters. I spent an hour trying to explain what I was trying to say. I would repeat what I said in the letter and she would correct my Spanish with love and laughter. I remember as we were walking that night, we saw a dog walking across a field. I told her in Spanish that the dog was lost. She laughed, because I could not roll my tongue with the double "r" sound. I learned it that night. The dog just sat in the field, looking at us. After several tries and no response from the dog, I told her it must be an English-speaking dog. I said "dog" and he started coming to us. We spent most of the night laughing at each other and our situation.

I could still see in Rosalba's eyes that doubt still remained about making everything happen. I remained nervous as well because I still hadn't received any news from Immigration yet. I had to continue to trust in God to finish what He had started in us. This was a problem way out of my control. I had no choice but to wait on God. Until He did His thing, I was going to enjoy being with His creation. Rosalba was so beautiful and her skin was so soft. It was amazing that the hair on her head was so thick, but the hairs on her arms were so fine and delicate. I was continually amazed by

God's creation. How could one person be so beautiful inside and outside? I had seen many beautiful girls, but their beauty came at a cost and was expensive to maintain. She was able to be beautiful just as God created her.

The next day, we went to visit the museums with Ruben and his sister. It was incredible. We got to see the Mayan and Aztec Indian artifacts. I was interested in history, but I still could not keep my eyes off Rosalba's beauty. We would walk back and forth, looking at the pottery and tools they used during this time. It seemed we couldn't stop looking at each other in the eyes. Something was there that connected us together in a way I will never be able to explain. I don't want to explain it. I just wanted to dive deep into the dark brown eyes before me.

After the museum, we went to the mall and walked around. Rosalba would look at the clothes and hold them up to her body and ask me if I liked them. I knew she had no money to purchase any of the items, but she enjoyed doing it. She was a seamstress and she focused on every stitch and color. She would be able tell if the clothes were made properly or not. I just enjoyed seeing her holding the clothes up to her body. She really cared what I thought about her. She wouldn't have asked if it were not true.

We continued to talk and walk through the mall, and it was great. I enjoyed Ruben and his sister. They were so fun to be with and talk to. Ruben was very interested in everything about the USA. He would constantly ask me about certain phrases used in movies or songs that he didn't understand. We would visit for a while and then continue on our way to see more. I found that Rosalba really appreciated the little things. The little statues or items seemed to tell more about her life. She always looked for these little things in life. Some would consider them insignificant, but not her. She was so creative that something small to you or me was an open door for her creativity. She could make a rock beautiful. Some people like me have no imagination or creative ability. Her mind never said "no," or "it's not possible." She didn't suffer for lack of creativity. She didn't have many clothes in her closet and this forced her to be creative with what she had. She never had a problem coordinating her clothes in different ways. Not me. I always had a difficult time making colors match. She looked so beautiful in everything she wore.

We left the mall and returned to Rosalba's home after dropping off Ruben and his sister. At her house, we sat on the couch and she just laid her head on my chest. I wondered if she was listening to my heart to see if it would divulge some of my secrets. No need, because I had no secrets. I just sat there and imagined what it would be like to hold onto her forever.

Is this possible? God, could You let me see into the future YOU are creating in our lives? Is it possible that tomorrow is going to be as good as today, or worse?

Enjoy the day, John. Don't worry about tomorrow.

We went to our beds and rested for the night. I laid there pondering being with her always. Many wonderful thoughts passed through my mind as I tried to still my soul. I eventually fell asleep before all these thoughts and questions finished passing through my mind. I thanked God for this day, and fell asleep during my prayer. Isn't it amazing how well we can sleep when things are good in our lives?

I could handle this relationship so far. Many more things had to fall into place for this to come true. Could this love story really come to pass, my God? I continued to pray that He would intervene with Immigration to finish the paperwork. I had already made several trips to the Immigration office, and I had made many phone calls. Now what?

We woke up to prepare for another day, and it was a good one. Not too hot or cold. Rosalba greeted me with a wonderful kiss as I went down the stairs to the bathroom. She looked so good and I just wanted to embrace her, but I needed a shower. The showers and bathrooms were very different from what I was used to. Everything was concrete: floors, walls, and ceiling. No problem. The shower felt great, and there was hot water. I dressed myself and exited the bathroom. There she was, waiting to do stuff with me.

Her mom Maria wanted us to go the open-air market. If you don't know what this is, let me explain. This place had all types of vegetables and fruits. It had tortillas and bread products. My favorite part was that they sold food also. I always liked the tacos de barbacoa. They came with the pico-de-gallo and salsa. This was my favorite meal so far, and Rosalba didn't mind if I ate three or four tacos. They were small tacos. Three bites and you finished one. There were all types of crafts and decorations from various parts of Mexico. She would always look for the trinkets. These fascinated her the most and she would spend hours looking at everything. I didn't mind as long as I was with her and holding her hand. I enjoyed seeing her eyes react when she found things that interested her.

Rosalba would turn around and say to me, "Don't you think this is awesome?" I loved the way she expressed everything.

We returned to her house to eat breakfast. One thing I wasn't aware of was that they hardly ate like this. I didn't know that most of the time they ate only rice and beans with corn tortillas, because the money just wasn't available to do so. This really bothered me, because they were such a wonderful family.

After breakfast, I helped Rosalba do some things for her dad. He was elderly and dealing with bronchitis and had a hard time doing manual labor. This was when I noticed that she was going to be a great helper. She worked so hard. Things I thought she couldn't move or lift she was doing so. I knew we would make a great pair. I never had trouble working hard, and continue to do so.

We finished doing the different jobs that needed to be done and we went for a walk. I felt more comfortable with Rosalba now because she kept her words simple and spoke a little slower as I requested. I was glad, because now I could really hear and understand what she said. Not just hearing but listening. There is a big difference. She showed me the schools that she attended and we went to see one of her old bosses. He and his wife were really nice people. They entertained us and I enjoyed hearing the effect she had on them as an employee. They really appreciated her because she was always a good worker and her personality made it easier to work with her. We finished our meal and visited some more. We discussed how his clothing business was going and some of her coworkers that she had left when she started going to college. They really had a great relationship with each other as they shared memories of things that happened. We excused ourselves and left as it was getting dark. It was a good visit and I was glad to share in Rosalba's world, but I wanted more alone time with her.

There was such a short time to spend with each other and I wanted those times to be ours, but I knew she was only trying to let me into her world. Rosalba enjoyed her time working for these people, and they made her feel important and needed. Most businesses lack that desire to have a close relationship with their employees.

We returned to Rosalba's house and went walking in the cool of the evening. I couldn't see the stars because there were so many lights in such a large city. I felt kind of strange not being able to enjoy the night skies. She had always been fascinated by the moon. As it glowed upon her beauty, she returned praise to the moon for its glory. It was like they were connected together. When the moon was not visible, she missed it. As we stared at the beauty of the moon, I ran my hands through her dark black hair and focused on how the moonlight reflected off of it. Her hair was so thick and wavy and felt so soft and silky in my hands. As I ran my hands down the side of her face, I enjoyed the soft, subtle texture of her skin. Her skin was so soft and so smooth. I believed God was preparing me to love her as Christ loved the church. Jesus Himself was looking upon the beauty of His true church. All of those who were really in love with Him and wanted to be with Him. All of those who waited for Him to appear and kept themselves pure until that time came.

I already admired her mother Maria. Every day, morning and night, I saw her praying and reading her Bible. I knew who did the encouraging and motivating of the children to go to church every Sunday. She was really in love with Christ. I thanked God for a parent like her. I wasn't sure about her dad yet. I didn't see Christ in him or hear him talking about Him either. I met some more of her family and they were good people. They offered to do many things with me, but mostly wanted me to travel with them to other places in Mexico. I couldn't do this because my travel visa was only for the areas around and in Monterrey. I had to state on my tourist application where I would be staying and couldn't leave that state without telling them first. Another reason I said no was due to the fact that I knew they didn't have the money to pay for it and didn't want to take my money. I also wanted to be alone with Rosalba, to spend more time discussing our future.

We really had spent no time discussing what kind of wedding Rosalba wanted. I knew this would take a lot of time to plan the details. I had no plans other than to be with her forever and ever. But as we all know, women and men are quite different in this aspect. I couldn't stop listening to the details as they rolled out. Don't get me wrong, she didn't want a big fancy wedding. She wanted a simple but nice wedding, and I was going to do all that I could to make it happen. She wanted a beautiful dress and she deserved it for her purity. She wanted to be married in the church where we worked during the mission trip. Of course, she wanted her family to be there with her. I listened, but my mind traveled back to Immigration. I had still not heard anything from them, and if they said no, what was I going to do? How would I break the news to her if this happened? I prayed continually: *Father, please intervene in this matter for me. This is YOUR plan, not mine.*

I had no idea how I could face this myself, much less tell her. How would I deal with it? I loved her with all my mind, heart, and soul now. I breathed when she breathed. I was awake when she was awake, and I slept when she slept. I could almost feel her presence even when she wasn't near me. I had invested all that I was in this adventure and I was not about to quit yet. This was my Jordan River, and I wouldn't wait to get to the other side.

Get your mind to the present time, I told myself. *You have a beautiful woman in front of you and very little time to let your mind wander off into the unknown.*

Maybe it was one of God's angels prompting me to turn back to reality. What is faith if you never have to practice using it? Everything so far showed God's hand was making it happen. He would deal with Immigration and everything would be all right.

I looked at Rosalba again, and it was like she was telling me, *welcome back*. She was amazing as she looked deep into my eyes and knew I was concerned about something, and yet she really didn't know me. This was the third time we had been together, and she knew something about my soul already. It was like she placed her hand deep into my soul and lifted me out of despair. I believed God knew she was what I had been lacking in my life. He was going to provide me with a real helper and friend in a time that I really needed her.

I never had time to really spend with a girlfriend in the past. Since the age of thirteen, I would go to school and immediately go to work in the evenings. No time for girls and no time to really enjoy being a teenager. It was all right because it taught me to work hard for what I wanted. Rosalba was someone I wanted, and I was going to fight for her, and Immigration was not going to defeat me. She was a gift given to me by God and I wouldn't let her go. *God, please help me with my faith. Let me know somehow everything is going to be okay. I can't bear the pain in her face if Immigration says no. Would she even believe with all the doubts that have been placed in her head about Americans and how they use Mexican women as prostitutes? I can't compete with all of her fears and doubts. I don't even know of a case where this has happened, but I live in Oklahoma.*

Friday arrived, and I had to leave on Saturday morning because I was driving. What else can I do to assure Rosalba that I was serious about her and I wanted her to be part of my life? It frustrated me intensely that I couldn't tell her in a way that I loved her with all my heart. Ruben was doing his best to translate everything that I had tried to tell her, but maybe embarrassment might have inhibited him so he didn't say it the way I said it. Nevertheless, I had to do it myself in whatever way possible to let her know that I loved her. I wondered if time was my enemy or my friend, but then I realized time belonged to God and I knew God was not my enemy.

I held Rosalba's hand and constantly gazed deep into her eyes, looking for a way to let her see how much leaving again was the last thing I wanted to do at this moment. How could I do this? It seemed I was running out of time, and I knew less than before.

God, does she love me? Have I done enough to show her my heart? Most of all, can she see YOU in me? How long must we wait to receive the answers that we long to hear? Will she be okay when it's time for me to leave?

My mind was filled with more questions than ever before as I waited on the hand of God to move people and time to make this happen. *Is this YOUR will, God, or am I looking or trying to make this happen myself?*

Saturday came much too fast, and now I had to say goodbye again. *How long this time, God, must I wait to be with Rosalba again?* My heart was hurting with every tick of the clock. I found myself paying attention to the clock more than giving her my undivided attention as time ran out. Could she see how much leaving her caused my heart to hurt in ways I couldn't describe? I had never spent time with a person who affected my life so much. So little said, but so much distress involved when it was time to say goodbye. If I knew when I was to return, it might have helped me to hurt less, but I didn't know what was happening that day, much less the next. Wow! How could a relationship like this grow to be a life-changing event?

We arrived at the moment when I had to leave and her brothers give me the needed directions to get out of Monterrey the easiest way possible. *Thank you* was the last thing I could say to them before I left. I looked deep in Rosalba's eyes and said, *Yo Te Amo,* (I love you) and that I would write and call every moment I got. I knew she believed me now, because she had many letters left to translate and more coming soon. I told her I would call her as soon as I heard from Immigration. I held her close, never wanting to let go, but I knew that I had to no matter how much it hurt. *Does she know how much I love her? Did I do everything I could to show her so?*

I thought of when it was time for Christ to leave the disciples and how difficult it must have been for Him. How difficult was it for the disciples (church) when HE left? How much was it hurting Rosalba as I drove away toward Oklahoma?

CHAPTER 5

FAITH BUILDING

I drove home in my little Toyota pick-up, trying to focus on the road as my mind wandered through the memories of the last five days. Monterrey to Laredo came before I realized it and I had to stop and turn in my traveling visa and the permission to drive my pick-up in Mexico. If I forgot to do this, they would charge the value of my vehicle to my credit card, and when I returned I would have a very difficult time entering again. Mexico had laws also, and so I did my best to follow them because someone I loved still lived there and I wanted to see her again soon.

Laredo to Oklahoma was longer that I remembered, compared to my trip down there. Nobody in Oklahoma even knew I went to Mexico. If something had happened, I would have been on my own. I had to trust in God alone because nobody else was there to help me. I didn't have any friends who lived anywhere close to Mexico. God knew this and He continued to guide and protect me going to Mexico and returning to Oklahoma.

I got home at about five in the morning. I was so tired from the trip and needed to call Rosalba to tell her I arrived safely. She cared when my own family didn't even know I was in love with a girl in Mexico. I needed to talk to her more than I felt the need to talk to my own family. *Why do I feel this way? Do I love Rosalba more than my own family or is there something else that I'm missing? Why do I feel the need to talk to her more than my own family?* I felt my life was changing in ways that I couldn't explain, much less understand.

I asked Jacob to help me call Rosalba before we went to work at six in the morning and he was more than willing. Jacob had nothing invested in me or Rosalba but was always willing to help me. I wondered why all the time, because I had never gone out of my way to help anybody. Until then, I had always focused on what I wanted and nobody else was important to me. Selfish, I know, but this was who I really was and I didn't know what was happening to me. Why were so many people willing to help me in this situation with Rosalba when they had nothing to gain from if? I didn't understand this at the time because I was so focused on what I wanted, and nobody else really mattered to me.

Now, I realize how selfish I had been, and this was what God had been trying to change in my heart. I knew I could find a girl in the USA to be in love with and it would have been much easier than going through Immigration and traveling to Mexico and back. Why did God put Rosalba and all these people in my path? They didn't owe me anything, yet they were always willing to help me even though I had never done anything to help them.

I opened my mailbox at the Post Office and it was full, mostly with junk mail. I sorted out the trash and found a letter from Immigration, and I opened it carefully. I didn't want to damage the document or potentially see something I was not prepared to see. I opened it slowly and began to read.

The letter stated that they had received and processed my application. All RIGHT! My heart must have leapt from my chest and bounced around on the floor for a while and I had to take time to breathe again. The wind left my body and I found it difficult to breathe, because now we could set a date to be married, once we completed the requirements in the reply from Immigration. They had set up an appointment in Oklahoma City at the Immigration office on April the 24th, 1989. Wow! I had six months to make this happen and I didn't have a clue how I would do it. I knew the first thing I had to do was call Rosalba.

Wait! The first thing I had to do was get on my knees and thank God for answering my prayers. Then I would call Rosalba. I prayed with so much excitement and I wasn't sure what I said. I don't know if I spent more time thanking God for making this happen or thanking Him for Rosalba. I couldn't forget that He sent me there and He opened the doors to find this wonderful and beautiful lady. I needed to slow down and take a deep breath and realize that there was much more to be completed. Just because there was an open door didn't mean God opened it. I needed to focus on God even more now than before. I was closer to having a wife and I still didn't know how to treat a wife. There was still so much selfishness in me that God had to deal with before anything fruitful was to happen. Now what, God?

After praying and thanking God for this answer, I called Jacob to see if he could call Rosalba and translate for me. I didn't want to take the risk of any misunderstanding at this moment in time, because I had to ask her to marry me. Did Rosalba understand me when I asked her to marry me? If by some miracle, she did say yes, then what would I do? Worse yet, what if she said no? My heart seemed to stand still as Jacob dialed her phone number.

I still had one of those old dial phones and each number seemed to pass so slowly. Finally, Jacob finished dialing the twelve numbers to reach her.
Is Rosalba home? Will she answer the phone?
I was glad she didn't have caller I.D., because if she did, she might not have answered the phone. How would she react when she heard the news about Immigration? Did she have in her mind doubts about Immigration saying no, and in that way, she had an out to this situation? Or would her heart leap from her chest as mine did as I read the letter? The next thing I knew, Jacob is talking to someone on the other line, but I didn't know at the moment if Rosalba was on the other end. He asked if he could speak to Rosalba and said that the call was from the USA. There was a moment of silence as she came to the phone. These pauses seemed like an eternity to me because I admit I was so anxious at the time. Every moment was so important to me and I had to know what she would say. How would I ask her to marry me again if she didn't understand me the first time by phone and the second time by letter? It seemed so bland and cold to ask her on the phone, but what else could I do or say. I had just come home from Mexico and I didn't have the money yet to return and ask her personally to marry me. I had to use what was available to me at the time, and time had become very short to reach the date set by Immigration.

I heard Jacob talking to Rosalba on the other line, and everything in me froze up with fear and emotions. Jacob made the normal salutations, and then said he was there to help me communicate with her on the phone.
What do I say and how do I say it? I must have practiced it a thousand times in English and Spanish and now my mind was blank. Jacob must have been laughing about my nervousness and knew this phone call was an answer to my prayers. He carried on a conversation with Rosalba while I found my words. He prompted me to state what I wanted to say to her. He told her I had good news to share with her and I couldn't wait to share it with her. He then paused and asked me to state what I wanted to share with her. I must have mumbled to tell her that I loved her and missed her. This was true, but it wasn't the first thing on my mind at the time. I wanted to say: *Immigration sent their response and we have very little time to respond. Will you marry me now?*

Jacob helped me find my breath and helped me relax. He said, "Slow down and tell her what she needs to know." I told Jacob what I wanted to say: *Rosalba, Immigration has given us permission to marry. I love you and we have very little time to go forward with the plans. I need to know now if you will marry me.* Jacob's face turned red as he translated my words to Rosalba. Then I heard him laugh. Oh no, not a good sound to hear after asking someone to marry me. It turns out that she was saying *yes, yes,*

yes, over and over again and this made Jacob giggle because of her excitement. Now what?

I had been waiting for about a year to hear the word "yes," and now that I had not mis-understood her before. I didn't have a clue what to do next. Jacob was waiting for me to continue the conversation, but I had no idea what to say next. I stammered the next question: *When do you want to get married?* Once again, Jacob laughed and my heart skipped another beat. What did she say now that had him laughing again? This time he was laughing because Rosalba said: *Now, as soon as possible.* Then I stopped and realized something very important that hadn't caught my attention before.

I had applied to Immigration for a visa for a "fiancée," not a wife. How would I explain this to her? Let me try it here: *I want to marry you but I can't do it legally in Mexico because it would make void all the papers I have filed with immigration. I will marry you legally in the USA when we get to Oklahoma.*

How do you think Rosalba would process this in her mind, after all her doubts concerning how Americans treat women from Mexico? Was I going to turn her into a prostitute? This conversation was now in peril because I didn't know what to say. Fortunately, Jacob knew what I was going through and he could answer her questions. He knew I was in love with Christ and my life had been dedicated to serving Him at work and at home. He had seen the change that God made in my life and assured her that my heart was pure and nothing would ever put me in the same category as those who used women in such a way.

Once we cleared this hurdle of flustered questions, I hear him say *when.* When do we want to get married? Now my mind went many directions and it seemed harder to breathe. *When do I set the date?* I had no idea how to plan for a wedding, much less two weddings. *What am I going to do now?* I stammered the reply that there was no way I could plan a wedding there and here, and I asked Rosalba if she could plan the wedding there on April the 19th, 1989.

Jacob said she would be more than willing to take care of the planning for the wedding in Mexico. I took a deep breath and started thinking that I had six months to plan a trip to Mexico for my wedding. I was excited but nervous at the same time because I was getting married on April the 19th and I had no money to get a tuxedo, much less make another trip to Mexico. Now what?

I figured out that if I didn't go back to college that semester and if I only ate one meal a day, I could save enough money for the wedding. Okay, that took care of the wedding in Mexico, but what about the wedding here in the USA? How was I going to pay for two weddings? All this time I was speaking to Rosalba through Jacob and all these questions were passing through my mind. I kept remembering the saying: *Be careful what you ask for because you might get it.* I now had it, and I had no idea how I would do it.

We ended the phone call with a great big "I love you." Jacob must have been thinking I was going to hug and kiss him, because he kept his distance. We say goodbye and Jacob left after I thanked him for all his help.

I spoke to my pastor Robin Cowan about my situation and he told me he would take care of the details for the wedding here in the USA. I didn't know how he would do it, but he told me he would take care of all the details. I had never thought about marriage, much less ever been involved in the planning of one. I thank God for my pastor and his willingness to take on this responsibility for me. He knew I was indeed in love with Rosalba because he had been there since God opened up the door for this to happen. I remember one of the ladies at church prophesying that I was going to meet a beautiful señorita in Mexico and fall madly in love. How true were her words, whether she knew it or not.

I returned to work the following Monday and did my job, but my mind was far from my job. My mind was on the wedding with Rosalba and how I would do it. It couldn't be too hard because all I had to do was drive to Mexico and rent a tuxedo and drive home, right? Oops. A couple weeks later I got a phone call, and Jacob was there to translate for us again. Rosalba was talking to him and he looked at me and said she was requesting $500 for her wedding dress. My first response to Jacob was, "Tell her father, because it's his daughter that is getting married." Jacob spent the next ten minutes explaining to me that the customs in Mexico were that the groom paid for all of the wedding. Ouch! Where was I going to get $500? I told Jacob to tell her that I would send her a check for the dress as soon as I could possibly do so. He repeated what I said to Rosalba and she said she would be waiting on the check because she had already ordered the dress. I didn't know now who was more excited: Rosalba or me?

I had so much to learn and I didn't ever realize it, because I sent Rosalba a money order for the $500 for the dress. She called me again a couple weeks later and told me she couldn't cash the check I sent her and wanted to know what to do now. I asked her if any of the banks in Mexico could cash the check for her. She said that was not possible if she didn't have an account in the bank. Now what? Rosalba's oldest brother Armando said he could cash the check at the business where he was employed. This lifted a weight off my shoulders, because I had no idea how I was going to get $500 in cash to her in Monterrey. The business where she ordered the dress was waiting for the money and had given her a short time frame to show them the money before they would make her dress. She was concerned and worried about how or when I was going to make this happen. She didn't really know me at this point, and I didn't think she had a different opinion about all Americans being rich, as so many other Hispanics thought.

Boy, was Rosalba in for a big surprise once we were married. I had never focused on the future because I was too focused on the day I was living in. There wasn't room in my life to plan for a future, much less planning for a wife. Her brother, Armando, cashed the check at the company where he worked and she ordered the dress. Thank God for another open door and another hurdle crossed.

I finished my call with Rosalba and Jacob spent more time with me, assuring me this indeed was the custom in Mexico. The groom did pay for all the wedding in Mexico. Over time, I found this to be true from all of my friends in Hennessey, OK, who went on the mission trip with me. Sergio explained the custom and culture to me in a way I could understand as well.

Jacob went home and I found myself on my knees once again because it was still hard to breathe and I didn't have a clue what I was to do next. I would continue to work until that day came, and it finally did. I wrote many letters in this six-month period, continually explaining to Rosalba my good points and my poor decisions in the past. I wanted to make sure there were no secrets between us. I had seen so many people make these mistakes, trusting that the spouse or would never find out the past.

I drove to Mexico and I had nothing with me other than my papers and the papers Immigration provided for Rosalba. I had my suitcase and my personal hygiene bag, and that was it. I didn't rent a tuxedo here, because that meant paying for it daily, and I was going to be there for a week. All I knew was the time and date for the wedding, which was April 15, 1989 at 7:00pm at the mission church where we had worked during the mission trip. I was super nervous and I had fifteen hours of road time to prepare and think about this moment. I knew Rosalba had the dress, but did everything fit the way she wanted it to? What was left to do when I got there? I knew I had to get my tuxedo, and of course I forgot my dress shoes. What else was waiting for me when I got there? At this point, all I wanted to do was to hold Rosalba and tell her that I loved her. I could imagine what she looked like in her dress. I was limited to my imagination because I had yet to see her dress, but I knew she was going to be so beautiful. She was already beautiful and I couldn't really imagine her to be more so.

I reached Dallas and was really trying to pay attention to the road, but it was not easy with all these thoughts going through my mind. I thanked God that it was later in the day and there was not that much traffic in the Dallas area when I got there. I made it through Dallas, Austin, San Antonio, and then Laredo. Laredo was always the hold up on this trip because I had to stop and get my travel visa and permission to operate my pickup in

Mexico. I had to get automobile insurance for Mexico for the week because my insurance did not cover my pickup outside the USA. This usually cost $100 for one week, and I came prepared for it this time. I had learned this from my last trip and had to use my credit card to cover the cost. I didn't bring enough cash for this insurance and also to pay for my expenses during the last week I was here.

Two hours at the border in Laredo and now I had all my stickers and permissions to continue in Mexico. Onward to Monterrey, to be with my soon-to-be queen Rosalba. I tried to visualize standing there next to her in the church and wondered if I would have to say anything in Spanish. My understanding of the language was better than before, but still wanting. Could I repeat after the pastor Juan Antonio if he asked me to? How would I be able to understand him if he asked me to repeat after him during the ceremony?

Three hours later I arrived, about five in the morning, and I was tired. My eyes felt like they had weights hanging off my eyelids. I knocked on the door and there Rosalba was in her pajamas, and now I remembered why I just drove fifteen to seventeen hours straight to be with her. She even looked good at five in the morning in her pajamas. I held her in my arms for the longest time. I couldn't even remember how long or how tight, but I wondered what she was thinking as I embraced her. At five o'clock in the morning, most people wouldn't want you hanging on to them for a short time, much less for many minutes. She was patient with me and looked into my eyes and told me she loved me, and for some reason this time it meant so much more than before. I don't know why it was different, but it was like it burned deep into my mind and my soul.

Every time I arrived at Rosalba's house, her neighbors would let me park my pickup in their lot across the street. Accidents and vandalism had begun to get worse in the area and they wanted to protect my pickup. So even though I was tired, I ended my embrace with Rosalba to park my pickup in their lot. I grabbed my luggage and returned to her house, and she directed me to the same room as before. It seemed it was always hot when I went to Mexico and it was difficult to sleep because of the heat, but now I came more prepared because now I had my fan. Even when it was cold outside, I needed a fan blowing on me to help me fall asleep. I kissed Rosalba good morning and went to my room and prayed to give God thanks for getting me there safely, set up my fan, changed my clothes, and went to bed. I slept really well for several hours because I was in the same house with Rosalba and I knew that everything was going to be okay.

I woke up about eleven o'clock, and after praying we ate lunch together before we began to take care of all the items we still needed for the wedding. After lunch, I excused myself to shower and prepare myself for another day. The shower felt good and helped rejuvenate me for all the shopping we had to do that day. Rosalba had to buy some shoes, I had to get my tuxedo and shoes, and then we had to plan for our wedding pictures. You know what? I actually enjoyed doing all this with her, even though I was driving through one of the craziest cities in the world. The traffic in a city with 7 million people was intense, to say the least. I knew God was protecting me as I was driving, and I could actually understand the road signs in Spanish. I did have one big problem with directions because Rosalba didn't have any idea concerning street names or addresses. She just hopped on a bus and it took her wherever she wanted to go, but without the bus she just knew the area of the stores where she was interested in going. In Mexico, there is not much parking available and had to be paid for. Many times, you had to pay someone to look after your car and put money into the meter, in case you returned later than you anticipated. This was okay to me because they were working and trying to make money by doing a job, and I didn't have to worry about getting a parking ticket. I did get pulled over one time by a traffic officer once, because I didn't have a tag on the front of my pickup and spent the next thirty minutes explaining to the officer that I didn't need one in Oklahoma and the permission Mexico had provided me was all I needed to drive in all of Mexico. He finally agreed and let us continue on our mission -- reluctantly -- without a ticket, but it was a little scary because I wasn't in America and I wasn't Mexican. Thank You, God, once again, for protecting me in a potentially dangerous situation.

We drove on to the next store to buy our shoes and I was surprised. It was really easy to find shoes for her because she had tiny Mexican feet, but not for me, because I wore size twelve in the USA, and this was like thirty-four to thirty-five centimeters in Mexico. It was very rare for anybody to buy shoes this size in Mexico. We must have gone to twenty to thirty stores trying to find my size. I finally give up and settled for an eleven-and-a-half shoe size. I could make them fit, but they were very uncomfortable. I bought them, at the same time wondering if I could get married in my black socks only, because I didn't like wearing shoes that didn't fit properly. I was not going to say anything to ruin Rosalba's day, because up to now everything had been perfect. How long would I have to suffer with these shoes, anyway? So, with our shoes in hand we walked back to the pickup and paid the attendant for watching our vehicle and continued on to the next store and the next project.

This was where we were going to get our pictures taken after the wedding. In Mexico, the photographer doesn't come to you, you have to go to them for the pictures. It was awesome here, because they had very large pictures for about $80, and this included the frame. We reserved a time and paid for the picture, but we would have to wait two weeks for the picture to be finished. This wasn't a problem because Rosalba's family said they would pick up the photos for us and bring them to Dallas where some of her family lived. We would be able to pick them up when we went to Dallas to visit them.

We finally finished shopping for shoes, pictures, and flowers, and returned to Rosalba's house to rest for a while. After lunch and resting, we went to the church to see what else we needed to finish before the wedding. I really enjoyed seeing the entire youth group from the mission trip. I had really missed them during this period of absence and I took advantage of the moment to play a guitar with Mario and Demetrio. These were brothers who helped with the music during the backyard Bible studies we had during the mission trip. They played so well that it seemed as if only one guitar was playing. To this day I remain impressed by their ability to worship God with the best they had. After playing the guitar and learning a different strumming style, my beauty Rosalba and I returned to her home for supper and a visit with her family.

Rosalba had asked Ruben to meet us at her house at a certain time. I wasn't aware of why at this time. When we returned to her house, all of her family who could be there were present. I didn't know at this time why they were there, other than to meet me and to get to know this white boy who was going to take Rosalba to the USA. Ruben invited me to sit down in their living room and then the questions began. Mom and Dad, brothers and sisters, aunts and uncles, and the nieces and nephews all were there to ask me the questions of their choosing. Ruben translated as her father asked me if I would promise to keep their customs and cultures in the USA when we returned. He then translated for an aunt, asking me to promise I wasn't taking her to the USA to abuse her or use her. Other questions Ruben had to translate were: *What will she be doing in the USA? Do you have enough money to take care of her? Where do you intend on living?* Many questions, but I still had to explain to all of them that I wouldn't be able to marry her legally until we returned to Oklahoma. I had to explain to them that the papers from Immigration prohibited me from doing so because my papers were for a fiancée, not a wife. So, I looked at Ruben and begin to explain to him this issue with Immigration and the papers. He gives me a doubletake, as if saying, "I can't tell them that because they might kill me." I explained to him that this was the option Immigration provided me, and all the arrangements had been made for the wedding in Oklahoma the next week on April the 22nd, 1989 at 2:00pm, with the same pastor Robin Cowan who was with us during the mission trip. So, Ruben wiped his forehead and began to translate all this information for her family. I was watching to see the reaction from everybody while he explained this new situation they were not aware of. The questions only intensified.

I finally had to tell Ruben that I had always been accountable to God for all my decisions, and this one was more serious than all of my previous decisions in my life, other than asking Christ to come into my heart and forgive me of my sins. I believe they saw the commitment I had to Christ, and the evidence was there because of the mission trip and my commitment to be with Rosalba, when I had traveled several times over a great distance to be with her. Her family gave me their blessing and I took a deep breath. I invited Ruben and his sister out to a movie and a meal to say thanks for fielding all the questions and translating for me in a difficult and uncomfortable situation. They said yes. I was really excited because I wanted all Rosalba's family blessing before committing to this marriage and I didn't want Rosalba to suffer with the thoughts of one or two of them disagreeing with the wedding.

After the movie and meal with Ruben and his sister, we went for a walk in the park by the hotel where I had stayed during the mission trip. We went back to the restaurant called VIPS, where we had tried to eat our first meal together during the mission trip, where neither one of us could communicate with each other. We were seated and ordered something to drink and continued staring into each other's eyes and looking into one another's souls to learn about each other. Now I could talk to her in Spanish, but I didn't have to say anything in these moments because much could be seen in silence and gazing deep into one another's eyes. We must have spent two hours with our drinks and looking after each other. I was now looking at these full, luscious lips that God had given her, and slowly and gently leaned toward her to enjoy those lips in a way God created them to be used. What a great kisser she was, with those moist, full lips so soft and subtle. It was like the Lay's potato chip commercial, "Nobody can eat just one," because I couldn't have just one kiss.

Eventually we decided to leave before someone asked us to leave because of our displays of emotion and passion for each other. Yes, I said passion, because I was a male and I had waited patiently to be with my beautiful bride Rosalba for a year-and-a-half. Enjoying those wonderful lips was a prelude to something that would be much greater when that time came, but now we had to return home due to the late hour. We drove home and sat with each other until early in the morning. It was fun asking her what she wanted to do in the USA and talking about things I said in my letters to her before. We finally said goodnight to each other about four in the morning and went to bed. As always, I took the time to thank God for every second of the time He gave us to spend together.

The next morning, we woke up to another day and we took care of our prayers and hygiene before we got together for breakfast. Rosalba spent time helping her mother prepare breakfast as I tried to visit with her father,

Julian. He told me of his life and how he had served as a judge and finished his working days delivering items for the stores. I enjoyed the visit because it taught me more about how hard he worked to raise and support eleven children. I couldn't imagine more than two, much less eleven children. How in the world did he and his wife do this? We visited for several minutes until we were told that breakfast was ready, and he thanked God for the meal that was set before us.

After breakfast, Rosalba wanted to visit with some of her school friends and invite them to the wedding if possible, and if not, then say goodbye, because after the wedding we were driving back to Oklahoma because I had to work the following Monday. We also had another wedding to prepare for, and she would have to meet my family at the wedding. Most of them had never seen her or heard me talk of her, and probably never even thought about it, but they would attend if only to say that they were there.

We finalized the visits with her friends and went out to eat some pizza. I was asked to leave because I wore dress shorts to a pizza joint and they did not permit short pants. *What? It's a pizza, guys.* I could understand a nice restaurant with steaks and seafood, but not a pizza joint with food and trash on the floor when we entered. We left, and I hoped I didn't embarrass Rosalba. How could I know that a pizza joint would have a dress code? She told me that it was okay and they didn't have that policy before, and she didn't understand why they had one now. Thank God, because I was embarrassed and a little angry at the same time. I believe she noticed this and tried to calm me down as we went to another restaurant to eat.

I couldn't believe it. This place had maybe six cold pizzas and a couple flavors of ice cream, and a dress code. What, again? We went to another pizza place in downtown Monterrey. It was a popular place for the youth and really crowded, but had no dress code, and the pizza was hot and there was a much better variety. We enjoyed our meal as we discussed the details for our wedding the next day. I couldn't imagine all the things going through Rosalba's mind at the time.

Rosalba was getting ready to give herself to a man from a different country who she still couldn't talk to. She was about to leave her family to go to Oklahoma with me after the wedding. She was going to a new country and a new family with different cultures and customs. This was not a vacation where she would be back in a week or two. She was leaving her mother and father, who had come to depend on her to pay some of the bills and run errands to the store for them. She was saying goodbye to her lifelong friends and classmates who had been with her for twenty-two years. She was leaving her coworkers and college classmates and college in general, because now she couldn't finish in the same school. She was leaving her room at home and her neighbors, both of which she was really fond of.

Rosalba was really making a total life-changing decision that would be that way forever. I couldn't even fathom all the doubts that were going through her mind as we sat and enjoyed pizza together. I didn't even know if I could eat if I had to make the same decisions that she was making at this moment in her life. This made and motivated me to love and care for Rosalba even more, so that she would not come to regret this week and the coming day. For me it was much easier because I just had to learn to live with a wife, but nothing in my live was really changing. I could go to my church, be with my friends, visit my family, go to my job, and enjoy my home. But what would I do about her happiness and losses? How or what could I do to help Rosalba say to herself that this was the right decision? Her whole life was about to change, and for what?

This question has haunted me and motivated me to love her with no conditions and no limitations. She was giving up her world for me. Could my love for her be enough to fill all those voids once filled by so many different people?

We finished our pizza and drove home. I was very quiet and Rosalba was concerned that I was still angry about the dress code, or maybe something she did or said. She wanted to know what happened and why I was now so silent. How could I tell her all the questions had been passing through my mind and how this was going to impact her life? The questions only continued because she was going to the USA and she couldn't even speak English. How was she going to find friends she could visit with? How many Hispanics were available to her in Oklahoma where I lived in the country? I was putting her in a very difficult situation, and I said that I loved her? I was bringing her to the country, where about six families lived, after she had spent her life with about 7 million people, where they all spoke Spanish.

I was very happy that Rosalba decided to marry me, but I was so concerned that I was also getting ready to introduce her into probably the most difficult situation she had ever faced in her life. How do you say you love somebody and put them in such a difficult situation? No one to talk to and she didn't know how to drive -- what was she to do? Even though I asked myself all these questions, I had no answers other than that I loved her more now than life itself and I couldn't live without her. She was in my mind day and night, and I found it difficult to focus on the things I had to do myself. I constantly asked myself if my selfishness motivated me to take her away from her life and introduce her to very difficult situations like this.

I looked into Rosalba's eyes and I didn't know what to say, so I held her closer while hoping that my embrace would make her understand the challenges that she was about to face. I felt her heart beating against mine, but now I thought mine was beating much harder after all these questions were running through my mind. If anything could be called unfair, this would easily qualify due to all the obstacles she was going to face in Oklahoma. We hadn't even discussed how it got cold in Oklahoma and it snowed, and these were things that Rosalba had never had to deal with before. Her house was made of all concrete and mine was made of wood and glass. She had never been alone, but now she would spend at least half a day alone while I was at work. Even though I could go home during my lunch break, she would be alone the rest of the time. All these things, she would have to learn while trying to learn how to be a good wife, friend, lover, and sister in Christ. I was overwhelmed, and I wasn't the one trying to adjust to a total change in my life.

We said goodnight again and I spent the next hour asking God to show me how to love Rosalba the best way possible, so she could endure this change that was about to happen after tomorrow. Now what? *God, please help me and help us.*

CHAPTER 6

A BLESSING FULFILLED

I awoke to a new day and another opportunity to talk to my Father in heaven. I had become very close to Him in the last year, and many times I could feel His Spirit guiding me in the path He wanted me to go. Don't get me wrong, because I'm not saying that He speaks to me or I can see His face. I'm simply saying that in times when I really needed His guidance, a small, quiet voice echoed in my head and I tried to focus on what He was saying, and every time I listened I was blessed. I needed this today more than ever because I was getting ready to promise to take care of anther creation of God. I was not only promising my God, I was promising Rosalba and her whole family. I remember that her father, Julian, asked me if I would help her keep the customs and cultures of Mexico and her family. I would do that as soon as I learned what they were. This was but another question I had swirling around in my head, and the day was just beginning.

I showered and shaved to get ready for this wonderful and blessed day. It was blessed because two creations of human form had come to realize a wonderful time in life that God Himself had ordained. Rosalba was going to promise herself to me and I was going to promise my God that I would love her and take care of her until death separated us. This by itself made me very nervous, due to all the questions I mentioned before, but I was aware that my God was using His Spirit to guide and direct me throughout all of this marriage planning. He sent me to Mexico and used me to reach the lives of many people He was working on before I ever arrived. He also was working on my life and the life of Rosalba in ways that made life seem to stand still until we knew that we loved each other. He had opened many doors before I ever knocked on them, like the door to communication, the door to loving someone when it seemed impossible. He opened the path through the rules, regulations, restrictions, and delays that we encountered working with Immigration.

I heard Rosalba's sweet voice calling for me as I finished praying, and I couldn't wait to see her another day. I came down the stairs in her family's home and there she was with a gorgeous smile and a twinkle in her eyes. I believed that she was just as nervous as me, if not more, but it sure didn't show. She said she was excited and I was too, but still in a trance due to all the questions going through my mind. It was hard to find my positive side as I thought of all those questions, while still waiting on that still, small voice to tell me that it would be okay. I felt led to do this with her, but the human side of me still questioned her future with me in Oklahoma, away from her whole world.

I kissed Rosalba and gave her a big hug, and even then, she could tell that something was bothering me. I didn't have a very good poker face and everybody could read me like a predictable ending in a book. She asked me if I was all right, and I tell her the truth: I was concerned about her future in a different country, a different language, and different customs. I was concerned about taking her a long way from her mother, friends, and family. I asked her again if she was sure she loved me enough to sacrifice all these things for me. She confirmed that she loved me with all of her heart, and that would be enough to help her overcome all the differences that she might encounter. Somehow this made me feel a little more at ease as the time arrived for the promises to begin. In a way, I was a little anxious, even though I had to drive home after the wedding.

I gave Rosalba a kiss and a big hug once again. I wanted her to know that my commitment to God and to her was final. She was going to be my wife in a few hours, and I was committed to love her without excuse, exception, or lack of time management. She was going to become my charge today and I knew God was going to hold me accountable the moment I said, "I do." I had no idea what I was doing because I'd never seen a good marriage up close and personal to compare to or imitate. It wasn't because they didn't exist, but because I didn't take time to focus on them.

At the moment, I was dressed in short pants and a dress shirt because it was hot in Monterrey. I wanted to be comfortable until it was time to dress for the wedding. We finished breakfast and spent some time talking with each other before it was time to prepare for the wedding. I asked Rosalba once again if she was sure this was what she wanted to do and she confirmed to me that it was. She said she loved me and wanted to marry me.

After about two hours of visiting with each other in broken Spanish, I hoped that Rosalba understood everything I tried to say to her. Now it was time to prepare for the wedding, and to tell the truth, I was very nervous. I hoped Ruben was there to translate for me on this very special day because I wanted to be able to understand every word Pastor Juan Antonio said in this commitment we were about to make to each other. I put on my tuxedo and it fit fine, but I was wondering, after a week of delicious

Mexican food. I put on my new shoes and I hoped that they would stretch a little as I wore them.

I descended the stairs and saw Rosalba in her wedding dress, but I was not big into the superstitions that this world had to offer. I only knew she was beautiful in this dress and I could compare her to the bride that Christ gave His life for. I was willing to care and love her until it was time for me to carry my own cross into the Father's hands. I hoped that He could see my love for Rosalba was pure and righteous. This would be the only way I could love her the way God expected of me, and nothing else concerned me more than the thought of pleasing Him. I was going to stand before Him someday and give an account to Him based on the truth that He was recording starting today. I was more concerned about this fact than I about the shoes, language, nerves, or the drive home.

Rosalba's dress was so big that I wondered if I could find her inside of it, because the only things showing were her face and her hands. We had to take our pictures before the wedding, so we had to drive to the studio before the wedding in downtown Monterrey and I didn't know if I could fit her into my pickup with her dress on. So, she decided to remove her dress and dress casual until we arrived at the studio to take the pictures. God, she was so beautiful, with the dress or without it. We arrived at Angel Studios in Monterrey and got out of the pickup and went into the studio to get dressed for the pictures. I was a little nervous as we waited for the pictures to be taken, because it was hot and here I was dressed in a tuxedo and beginning to perspire. Rosalba came out of the dressing room and I held her hand as we moved toward the photographer for the pictures. She stood at my right side as the photographer prepared us for the pictures. He directed us in how he wanted us to stand and which way he wanted us to face as he prepared his cameras and lights. We did our best to follow his directions, as he spoke Spanish very quickly and I couldn't understand what he was saying. She gently grabbed my hand and pulled me in the direction he requested. I really needed to work on my Spanish more than before, because I understood very little of what he said to me and I felt a little embarrassed as she was aware that I had much to learn. I had studied intensely during college and with the Hispanic friends and brothers and sister in Christ that I had come to know during the mission trip, and during the time that I needed someone to translate her letters to English for me. I was remembering one time in the past when I went to a Sergio's house about an hour drive from my house with a newly arrived letter from Rosalba. When I got there, they were desperately trying to find out where in the world a mouse had died in their house, because the smell was so intense it was hard to focus on anything else. Sergio stopped what he was doing and dedicated his time to help me with the letter. To tell the truth, I couldn't even detect the smell during those intense moments as I waited to hear every word Rosalba had written in her letter.

I was brought back to the present time and moment. The photographer was giving me directions and I wasn't paying attention. Gently, Rosalba grabbed my hand and told me to smile as he took another picture. Isn't it amazing that during the most intense moments in your life, your mind can still wander in different directions? I looked at her and smiled, not because the photographer was directing me, but because she was gently guiding me with love and doing her best not to embarrass me. What a wonderful start for us, that in this time of such a change in her life, she was more present than I was. I gently squeezed her hand and smiled to tell her that I was once again back in reality, yet remembering everything God had shown me as this moment unfolded. I could not believe how many people God used to make this day possible. I have no clue to this day how many people were used to make this day happen, but it was a privilege for me to meet the people God led me to during this time.

The photographer stated that he had finished and asked us more questions about how many copies we wanted of each stance and what sizes we would like to have. I didn't know exactly what she wanted, but I wanted the biggest one they offered to hang up in the living room. This picture was huge and measured two feet by four feet high. With the frame it only cost $80 for everything. Wow. You would never get a picture this size in the United States for that price.

As the photographer finished with the paperwork, we excused ourselves so Rosalba could remove her dress and once again fit into my little Toyota pickup. I waited for her outside the dressing room. I knew this couldn't be easy for her to change so many times in one day, and in about another hour later she would have to once again change back into her dress for the wedding. As Rosalba came out of the dressing room, she looked at me with those amazing eyes and my heart continued to melt. I knew now that she could see into my heart and know I loved her with everything that I was and with everything that God had given me. I offered her my hands so that I could carry her dress, which we had to continually put into a large box and continually remove. It was so large that we had to put it into the back of the pickup because it wouldn't fit inside the pickup. I opened the door for her after placing her boxed dress into the back of the pickup, and she smiled as I showed her that I was a gentleman.

I drove slowly so the dress wouldn't be messed up in the bed of the pickup, and because of the crazy traffic in Monterrey. We arrived at the church about an hour before the wedding. Almost everything had been prepared, but there was no punch. I knew we didn't need it, but I had never attended a wedding without some type of punch being served. I asked

Rosalba if she would go with me to the ice cream store near her house and help me buy a five-gallon carton of strawberry ice cream. She agreed, and off we went to buy the ingredients for the punch. It was really an easy form of punch to make. We bought the five gallons of strawberry ice cream and several bottles of Seven Up, and returned to the church to prepare it. I poured all the Seven Up into a large container, and then I placed all the ice cream in the container. We had enough time before the wedding that the ice cream would melt into the Seven Up, giving it an intense flavor. Rosalba found a room in the church where she could once again prepare herself for the wedding, and for the fourth time she put her dress on for the ceremony. I wondered if she was tired by now, with all the times she had to change, but she seemed excited every time she had to do so.

With thirty minutes left before the wedding, Ruben had not arrived yet. I spent my time visiting with the youth group that helped me during the mission trip. Some of the girls were sad because I did not choose them. I didn't know this until after Rosalba and I were married for two years. One of the girls, Lilliana, was so upset that she spent a year in depression. This made me so sad, because Lilliana and another girl, Claudia, were also beautiful, but God had opened my eyes to Rosalba, not them.

Remember that I had no plans to marry anyone, but God changed my heart when I found Rosalba. I wasn't looking for anyone, but if I did I would have looked for someone with a beautiful presentation and someone with a beautiful spirit, mind, and body. She most definitely would have to have a relationship with Christ and be able to show me her fruit. I could see the fruit in Rosalba compared to the other girls. They were beautiful, but they were not the one God wanted me to commit to for the rest of my life, and this was all that I was concerned with. I did nothing to mislead them, because when I first laid eyes on Rosalba I knew this was the woman God wanted me to spend the rest of my life with. I focused on finishing the mission God had put me there to do, and all my free time was used to get to know her more, and only her.

The ceremony began, and I had to once again bring myself to this moment and leave the past behind, because I was about to promise to give my life to be with Rosalba. "For better or worse, till death do you part" is a very powerful and unforgiving promise to make to someone. I had spent a considerable amount of time fasting, praying, and studying to prepare myself for this moment, if that was possible. The music started in this small mission church, packed with all of Rosalba's family and our friends. Ruben arrived and he stood beside me, not only as my translator but as my best friend. I thank God that he became part of this story God was showing to the world through both of us. Pastor Juan Antonio of the mission church stood beside us as Rosalba's father Julian escorted her to the front of the church to give her away. I realized that this had to be very difficult for both of her parents, because Rosalba was the last and the youngest of all their children to marry and leave home. She was not only leaving, but traveling a long way from their home, and the chances to visit her when they wanted were very slim due to the distance. They didn't have a car or the money to travel to the United States.

As I watched Julian leave Rosalba by my side, I knew I had to do everything in my ability to help them become legal residents in the USA, so that if they wanted to visit it would be much easier. I wanted them to be part of our lives, as God put us together, and I wanted my children to be with them as much as possible. Most of all, I wanted Rosalba to have her mother Maria with her to advise her in the married life. I had no problem with her parents because I respected them both.

Pastor Juan Antonio brought me back to the present by stating my name in Spanish. Quickly I focused my attention to what he was saying at the beginning of the ceremony. He spoke slowly, as I requested him to do, and I understood almost everything he said, but I let Ruben translate just in case I misunderstood something. Ruben smiled at me because he knew I was nervous, and he knew I really loved Rosalba. He had asked me many of the same questions that I had been asking myself about my marrying a woman from Mexico when I couldn't even speak her language. He knew I had been trying my best to learn Spanish, and he was amazed that I had learned as much as I had in such a short time. About halfway through the ceremony, I heard a strange noise and I noticed that the shoes had split down the middle. What could I do at this time? There was nothing to find in a world of small feet. I was just glad my pants were long enough to cover the ripped shoes and nobody would notice.

Then came the moment I had to repeat the vows in Spanish. I was very nervous because if I said something wrong I would be embarrassed, and maybe all in attendance would start laughing as I mumbled something wrong. Thank God for His help and for placing Ruben in my life to help me during this time of promising myself to God and to Rosalba. I finished my part, and now came the time for her to repeat her vows. I hoped she knew I loved her so much. She did so without hesitation, and once again looked deep into my eyes. Now I felt I was part of her life. I could look into her eyes and experience things that didn't need words. I had grown used to this because of our inability to communicate during this last year.

The pastor brought my wandering thoughts back with, "You may now kiss the bride," which he said in Spanish. I held Rosalba softly but firmly in my arms and kissed her now as her husband. From this moment I know I would be held responsible to God for everything I did or didn't do to lead her in His path. A rush went through my body as I finished kissing her.

After the kiss, we walked from the front of the mission to the foyer for the celebration. I had no idea what they were going to do. They put chairs in a circle and lifted us up in two different circles as they sang some choruses in Spanish. After the celebration, we were seated to eat a meal with everyone there, which was their custom and culture, and I was good with that. Why not? They were all part of this marriage and had spent their money and time to prepare for the event. I thanked God for their time and sacrifice. We were seated at the head of the table and did the normal married things like cutting the cake and feeding each other. I hoped she wouldn't stuff the cake in my face. She gently placed the cake into my mouth, and I did the same as we began our life together.

We sat together as the ladies of the church served us our plates of food. Boy, it was good. They served us red enchiladas with cheese from Chihuahua, Mexico, with rice and ranchero beans followed by punch and the wedding cake. Rosalba was so precious as she carefully placed each bite carefully into her mouth, so as not to make a mess. I knew she was so hungry because she had not really eaten much throughout the day, due to lack of time, and nerves. I knew if she could, she would have grabbed the enchiladas with her hands and eaten with more freedom and pleasure. The food was very delicious and I thanked the ladies of the mission for everything they did for this special moment for both of us, and the youth group who were more than willing to help set up the tables and chairs for this special moment.

Eventually, most of the people left the mission church, and Rosalba and I returned to her parent's house for the trip home. I wasn't ready for this time, but it would take us at least two days to return to Oklahoma because we would be delayed on the American side of the border to process Rosalba's papers as my fiancée. I didn't know how long it would take to process the papers, but we had to say our goodbyes to the people left at the mission church and to her family as well. This was going to be a most difficult time for Rosalba, as the separation began and the tears started flowing, including mine. I didn't know if I could have done what she did as the wedding ended, as well as her time in Mexico with her family. My heart hurt for her and I felt a little bit guilty for causing her this pain. How could I avoid doing this to her? I had passed this thought through my mind many times, and pain was the only response that came to my mind. There was no way for her to say goodbye to her life, family, friends, and everything in Mexico that she had come to love during her twenty-two years of life.

I was twenty-eight and really never had a close relationship with my family. I had no time to create friendships, because going to school and work gave me no extra time to commit to the relationships and friendships.

Rosalba didn't have this problem, and she would stop long enough to show others how much she was concerned for them.

We returned to her parent's house and changed clothes before we began packing up our things for the trip to Oklahoma. It was a slow process as Rosalba tried to decide what she wanted to take or leave behind for her parents. Little by little, she placed her clothes and items into the boxes so I could load them into the pickup. I carried box after box as she said goodbye to her family. I prepared a tarp to cover the bed of the pickup, just in case it began to rain.

I said goodbye to Ruben and thanked him for everything that he had done for us and for being my friend. I stood outside by the pickup as Rosalba continued to say goodbye to her family. I had no desire to hurry her through this moment, even though I knew the trip home was going to be difficult. We still had to drive through downtown Monterrey on our way home, to drop off the tuxedo that I had rented for the wedding.

Rosalba finally came out of her parent's home and brought the last things to the pickup, so I could finish loading them, and then covered everything with the tarp. She continued to say goodbye to her family as her mother Maria cried. This hurt me as well, because I knew I was taking her baby a long distance from her, and tomorrow seemed a long way away. Rosalba now cried, and my heart really hurt because I had to witness one of the most painful moments in her life. This was the start of a painful time in her life, and I had to help her do something I had never had to deal with in all of my life.

We got into the pickup and rolled down the windows. With Rosalba's tears still flowing down her cheeks, I started my pickup and slowly pulled away from her parent's house onto the road home. What could I say to her in this moment to help her? Was there someone out there who could help me find the words to stop the pain and anguish that she now experienced as I drove away? Her tears turned into sobs of sadness and my heart was really hurting as I drove further away. What could I do now? Could I turn back and leave her with her family after marrying her? How would I comfort her as we got further away from her home? I didn't think stopping the pickup to hug her would help us during this moment.

Now what?

CHAPTER 7

A BLESSING FOR WHOM

We drove through Monterrey and stopped to drop off the rented tuxedo. I was really concerned for Rosalba, because the sadness seemed to have gripped her heart and was squeezing the life out of her. I returned to the pickup and tried to have a broken Spanish conversation with her, and got nothing in return. She was lost in her own thoughts of what was going to happen to her life. I couldn't even imagine what was going through her mind at the moment, but I knew that it reached her heart because her sadness was genuine and reached over to my seat and affected me as well.

I had no experience in how to council someone on how to deal with an unknown, like leaving everything you knew and loved behind you. How do you tell someone something you have no knowledge about, such as leaving all your family, friends, jobs, life in general, customs, and culture to venture into the unknown with a guy you just married?

I'm sure Rosalba was asking herself right then, "What in the world did I just do?" I knew she was asking herself many questions, because she didn't speak as I drove though Monterrey, except to give me directions on an easier way to get out of Monterrey. The tears were still flowing and I was sure she questioned God at this moment about the decision she had made to marry me. I couldn't blame her for a moment. My part in this relationship was not easy, but it had very little comparison to the weighted cross she had decided to carry just to be with me.

I drove in silence, mostly because everything I seemed to say caused Rosalba to cry more, and I feared to say anything else. We were now out of Monterrey and driving to Laredo. This had to be the longest trip of my life as I took one of Mexico's treasures out of their country. I kind of felt like I had just stolen one of Mexico's most beautiful artifacts away from them. I don't know why, because I told myself Rosalba's life had to be better in the USA. There had to be many more opportunities for her with me rather than in Mexico, but all my thoughts were still focused on how I tried to

63

convince myself I was doing her a favor by bring her to the USA. *I have to be right,* I continued to tell myself, as her sorrow continued and the silent tears rolled down those beautiful cheeks.

Rosalba's eyes were now red due to the extreme grief that she was experiencing. The three hours to Laredo seemed more like five or six hours as the silence captivated us both with the reality we found ourselves in. I had taken a bride for myself, but I left half of her in Mexico. She had agreed to marry a man she really didn't know and go to a country that was new to her, and speak a language that was alien to her. The grief that held her heart hostage from Monterrey to Laredo was compounded by the fear of the unknown she was about to face in the USA.

What is going to happen to me in the USA? Is this guy really going to love me, or use me, as I have heard from so many of my friends? Does he really love me or does he have other plans in store for me? Where is this Oklahoma, in case I have to come back home? Will he let me come home to see my family? Will he let me call them, or will he let them come and visit me? How could I have let myself come to this decision without knowing more about him or where he lives? I know these questions were going through Rosalba's mind, because at a later date she shared them with me.

We arrived in Nuevo Laredo, Mexico, and I had to stop and turn in my tourism pass and the permission sticker in the windshield of my pickup. I stopped at the office that provided me the vehicle permission and asked Rosalba to come and help me communicate with them, and also to use the bathroom if she needed to. She reluctantly exited the pickup and wiped the tears from her eyes, and I wondered if she could really help me. She might have been thinking that she still had time to change her mind now, because she was still in her country. Until she crossed the border, she was still a citizen and they would help her escape from me. She still had a chance to escape the unknown reality that was staring at her more intensely the further from home she went.

I held Rosalba's hand as we walked to the office and stood in line for the next available officer to wait on us. Her hand was so soft, and I thought I could never let go of it. I softly called her name and looked deep in her eyes, and told her in Spanish that I loved her, all the time hoping she understood me. I think in some small way it touched her heart, because it was the first time she smiled since we left Monterrey. I held her in my arms as we waited our turn, and I felt her trembling. I knew she was not cold, because it was about ninety degrees outside. I know her fear was real and I had no clue how to make her feel more at ease as we waited.

The officer called us to the window and we walked the short distance to be helped. He asked for the permit for the pickup in Spanish, and I really did not understand exactly what he was asking for. I had all the papers in my hands. Rosalba gently grabbed my hands and helped me choose the papers he was requesting. She grabbed the permission documents for the pickup and handed them to the officer. The officer accepted the documents and began to stamp them one by one until he handed them back to us and dismissed us to another officer. This officer's job was to remove the permission sticker from our pickup and inspect the items we had in the bed of the pickup. I removed the tarp so he could verify I had nothing illegal, and when he finished I took a deep breath and once again tied down the tarp.

He dismissed us and we exited the parking area and began traveling to the bridge to cross into the Laredo, TX in the USA. The line of vehicles going into Mexico was very long and we waited about two hours to cross into the USA, where we still had to go into the office on the USA side to verify the documents Immigration had provided me for a fiancée. I was nervous as well at this moment, but comfortable at the same time because I could now speak English and I also followed the law and I didn't leave any room in this situation for the "WHAT IFS," as I called them. I didn't like surprises when it came to something like this, not something as important as it was to me to make Rosalba's life here as stress-free as possible. This first process was so important for her to see that I was real and that I had completed all that was necessary to make her life better. "In what way?" I was sure both of us were asking, all the way from Monterrey to here. I knew if I didn't take care of making everything legal and as smooth as possible, she would be unsure about us and our decision to be married.

We finally arrived at the point where the officer requested our documents on the USA side of the border in Laredo. I handed him my birth certificate and the papers that Immigration had provided me for Rosalba. He ushered us through the checkpoint and guided us to a place to park, and asked us to remain in the vehicle until he could verify the documents. After about thirty minutes, he returned and asked me to get out of the vehicle and tell him what we had in the vehicle. I got out and explained to him that we were going to Oklahoma to get married the next Saturday, and the items in the bed of the pickup were mostly clothing and small treasured items that had sentimental value that Rosalba had brought from Mexico. He asked me to remove the tarp so that he could verify what I said was true. As I removed the tarp, another officer brought the drug sniffing dog to check my pickup for anything illegal. I was nervous. Not for me, but for Rosalba and what she must be thinking as all this process went on. The officer asked me to unload the items in the bed of the pickup onto a table beside the pickup, so he could further investigate and verify we were not bringing in contraband prohibited by US law. As he sorted through our possessions, he directed us to go into the office for the paperwork to be processed. We went through the door he directed us to. A line of people were also waiting for their papers. We waited patiently as Rosalba sat in silence once again. She seemed to be in a state of panic, as she continued to tremble. I tried to encourage her that everything was going to be all right, but I didn't know if I was helping her or not. She might not have even understood a word I said.

I knew God was helping us during this time, but how did I relate this to Rosalba in one of the most panic-filled times of her life? I did see many little things that might have gone unnoticed by those who didn't pay close attention to the things going on around them. One example was the wonderful character of all the officers involved in passing us through the process. I'm sure they saw and heard us trying to communicate, and they must have wondered how in the world the two of us could have gotten together. I saw them smile at me as I talked to Rosalba in Spanish, and they must have been thinking, "What in the world is he saying to her?" I could feel their gazes on me. Not in a threatening way, but more of a compassionate way, because they could see how I was trying to comfort her in my broken Spanish.

They could see s Rosalba was indeed a panicked bride entering into a new and unknown world, and they also could see her trembling. They asked me many questions about our relationship, how we met, how long we had spent with each other, and how in the world could I marry a girl I couldn't even communicate with. I think they were worried more about her than about me. If I were them, I probably would have questioned me the same way. At this moment, they didn't see an excited bride-to-be, but rather a beautiful young Hispanic woman trembling in fear. They asked her many questions about me in Spanish that I could not understand, but it was nice to see her smiling. Maybe they were laughing at me and how broken my Spanish was, or maybe they could see how I was acting like a fish out of the water. Maybe God let them see an example of true love that could overcome all the fears and obstacles and remain strongly embedded in Him and in the grace that He provided. Even though they encountered two young people in love, they also saw the hand of God working to overcome incredible odds and bring these two people of total differences together.

Even to this day, I have to give God the glory for helping us through these moments, because we were grasping at whatever we could to keep ourselves steady in the strong winds buffeting us.

We haven't even made it one mile past Mexico yet, and we had a long way to go, but it was vital to complete this process the correct way. I wasn't going to let impatience jeopardize what God had done for us. Rosalba would look to me, grasping for anything she could hold onto in the moments of her fear, and I was constantly in a state of prayer, in my mind pleading with God to continue to open these doors one at a time.

Please, God, give me the confidence to take one step at a time and continue to trust in YOUR infinite wisdom, power, and might as You allow me to feel Your Spirit's presence in my life and Your angels surrounding me.

It was true that I was nervous, especially when the officers were asking Rosalba questions in Spanish, but every time she addressed the officers, she would look into my eyes and I knew it was going to be okay. The officers would laugh with her and then look at me and laugh some more, but she was now smiling and that was okay with me because it beat the silence that I had to endure from Monterrey to here. She was beautiful as she laughed, and there was no falseness with her laughter because it came from deep within her. She didn't wear a smirk or a quirky smile, but genuine smiles with a wide-open laughter that touched my heart and made me love her even more. Maybe God allowed me to see this to calm my own heart and my own doubts as I struggled with her continual tears as we left her world to travel into the great unknown.

The officer came to me and told me that all was in order and I could replace our items into the pickup and tarp it as before. He told me not to forget to present our marriage license to Immigration as soon as possible, to continue to obtain her residency paperwork. The officers congratulated us and encouraged us with their best wishes for our wedding the next weekend, and we drove away. I could still see them smiling, laughing, and waving as we pulled out of the parking spot.

Now it was just us two again, leaving Laredo, TX for Oklahoma, a mere fifteen hours away. I planned on stopping in Dallas for the night to rest and give her time to spend with her two sisters and one brother who already lived there. I believed this would help her find some confidence that someone she could see and touch was closer to her, in case I was a bad person who wanted to use or abuse her. She lacked confidence in God, me, and what she had decided to do when she married me. I could sense her fear and doubts as she glanced at me from time to time. I couldn't do anything because I had to focus on the highway so I didn't kill us before we ever become an "us."

Rosalba talked to me and pointed to places in front of us, but I didn't understand what she was saying because she spoke quickly and excitedly. I thought she was concerned over how I was driving, or she thought I was driving too fast, so I drove a little slower. I had a full tank of gas in the pickup and I could most likely reach Dallas, TX with one tank and still have some left over. She continued talking to me, and I tried to remember how to say in Spanish, "Slow down because I don't understand what you are saying." It didn't come to me, and I slowed down a little bit more to calm her nerves.

So many insects hit our windshield, from Laredo to San Antonio, so I stopped to wash it. As I stopped, Rosalba opened the door and ran into the gas station. After washing the windshield I followed her to see if something was wrong. I entered the store and couldn't see her anywhere, and my heart started beating intensely. Where did she go? I continued to look as the need for the restroom hit me. I took care of business, and as I exited the bathroom I saw her standing nearby, waiting for me. She smiled at me and pointed to the coolers where the drinks were stored. I went with her. She took a Coke from the coolers and I took a Dr. Pepper. We walked through the store and she grabbed some stuff to eat.

I thought, *John, what a moron you have been. Dedicated on reaching Dallas at a certain time, you never stopped to think Rosalba might need a bathroom break or maybe a meal.* I realized even more so that I was not alone anymore. I knew she was there, but I was caught up so much in my own thoughts and deadlines that I didn't even address the basic needs of life. So, I take a deep breath and I told her I was sorry for not realizing her needs from Laredo, TX to San Antonio, TX. She smiled, and I think she told me that it was okay.

I opened the door for Rosalba and we resumed our journey from San Antonio to Dallas. From now on when she began pointing, I promised myself that I would stop and make sure she was okay. What else could I do to make her feel more at ease as I drove to Dallas? I turned on the radio in hopes that I might find a station in Spanish, to make her feel more at home. Music was supposed to calm us, right? There were several stations to choose from. I tried to follow her eyes as the music played, and if she smiled or nodded, I left it where I thought she liked the song. I programed the Spanish stations so it would be easier while driving to change the stations during commercials or when songs played that she didn't like. After I did this several times, Rosalba learned how to change the stations by herself by watching me. This made it so much easier for me because I didn't have to try to read Rosalba's expressions as I focused on the highway. Thank God for the radio, because even though I didn't understand a word of any song in Spanish, I could tell she was finally starting to relax and breath normally again. We stopped two more times before we arrived in Dallas, and took care of bathroom issues and stretching our legs, then continued on. It was now dark outside and we needed to drive about two more hours before we reached Dallas. I could tell she was tired because she fell asleep a couple of times. In the quiet of the night. During the drive, I would continually glance at her and thank God over and over again for making this possible, while asking continually for His guidance during everything that happened to us from now on.

I would need Him many times, because besides being responsible for my relationship with God, now I was also responsible for helping Rosalba learn more about God. It really sank into my mind and my heart that I would someday stand in front of God and give an account for everything I did or didn't do to love her like Jesus loved the church. In a moment of fear, I asked God to help me maintain my relationship with Him because I couldn't love her the way I needed to unless I loved and desired to be with Him even more than before.

As Rosalba slept and I drove, many questions came to my mind: How exactly did Christ love the church? How or why did He give Himself for the church? I tried to think of times in the Bible when specific answers were provided concerning these questions, but not much came to my mind as I drove. I remained in a moment of panic as I thought about what I had done, because I don't know how I would answer to God for my own life, much less now my marriage to Rosalba. *God, how am I going to do this when I can't even talk to her yet? How am I going to read the Bible to her when I cannot read or even understand Spanish well enough to know myself, much less teach her in a language she cannot comprehend?* The more I thought of these things, the more uneasy I felt in my heart, and the more I asked God to lead and guide me in this day and all that remained.

I felt the long day and events wear on me and I fought off the sleepiness that wanted to overtake me. Rosalba must have known and woke up to play with the radio again. Just to know that she was awake gave me the confidence to continue, because if I started to fall asleep, then at least she could say something or touch me to wake me up. We had another sixty miles or sixty minutes before we had to find her sister's house in Dallas. We didn't have GPS systems at this time, and we had to use ordinary maps to guide us. I was glad it was evening when we arrived in Dallas, because there was a lot less traffic compared to the mornings and afternoons. While Rosalba played with the radio to find the music she wanted to hear and made sure I stayed awake, we finally arrived in Dallas. I had to find a house in a large city that I had never been to before. This was the first time I had left I-35 in such a large city, and I was looking for a house out of millions of houses, doing this at night and in a sleepy state.

Rosalba had a book with the telephone numbers to her family in Dallas and I stopped to look at the map for some kind of direction to this unknown address. To somebody who lived there, it was probably easy, but it wasn't that way for me. I knew about Dallas and about Ft. Worth, but her family lived in some of the smaller cities in between them, and I had to find them on a map about eleven o'clock at night. We didn't have cell phones at this time and I had to stop several times to review the map and try to continue in the right direction. I would have asked Rosalba to help me to read the map, but she knew less about Dallas-Ft. Worth, or maps than I did. She had never been to the USA, and she couldn't read or understand any of the road signs. I needed to be really careful not to get lost in the middle of the night. Sometimes I had to stop at a gas station to get directions. Most of them didn't know anything about the place I was looking for either.

Finally, I arrived on I-820 east into Bedford, and found the apartments where Rosalba's two sisters lived. Rosalba looked at her book and found the numbers to their apartments as I parked the pickup in a designated area for visitors. Now we had to determine what to do with all the items in the pickup. Should we leave it all there under the tarp, or unload everything for the evening? How much did we have to unload and where could we put it all until we were ready to leave the next day? We finally decided to unload everything into her brother's apartment and try to rest, but this wasn't to happen, as they offered us coffee at midnight. I had no problem with coffee, because I could drink several cups and still be sleepy, but my new bride could drink one cup and stay awake all night visiting with her brother and sisters, and you know that this made me happy.

This was a cross-carrying experience, because now Rosalba would be a new face in the world according to John, and she needed this family time when the world according to John became a little crazy for her and she needed some kind of normality in her life. She could find this in her family, and I was more than willing to accommodate her to help her overcome the difficulty of this cross-carrying moment.

We finished the coffee and I could no longer keep my eyes open, because most of the conversation had lost me from the beginning. I didn't have a clue where the story had started or where it was going. This caused the desire to escape to "slumber land" to climax into a good night's sleep.

Day one in John's world, and what did Rosalba think of it so far? Did she have any hope to help her into tomorrow or was she clinging to desperation in a world that was alien to her?

God, what else can I do to help her be the best daughter You have in a new and different world that is alien to her? How do I help encourage her and strengthen her to face this new and difficult cross-carrying experience? I never asked You for a wife, but YOU saw into the depths of my soul a desire for a friend, lover, and helper, and You provided me Rosalba. I now have her with me because YOU chose her, but I lack the ability to communicate with her. Plus, I lack all the knowledge that is necessary to care for a wife, friend, lover, and a sister in Christ. I thank YOU for Your guidance and Your instruction, but I will continue to seek YOUR face for the wisdom that I lack to carry the cross You have given me.

We were now in the USA, and for the moment with her family. What would happen when we arrived in Oklahoma and she was not surrounded by her family, but alone with me in the middle of nowhere? *Now what, God? What's next?*

CHAPTER 8

A BLESSING THROUGH STRANGERS

In the morning we had to leave for my home and Rosalba's new life with me in Oklahoma. We ate breakfast with her family and reloaded all the things we unpacked the night before when we arrived. I had never met her family here in the United States, and many of the questions I had to answer in Mexico were repeated, but now I have no translator. I did my best to answer every question in a very broken Spanish language. We finished loading and putting the tarp on the bed of the pickup and now it was time to leave Dallas for our home in Oklahoma.

I didn't live near my family and never had. Not because I didn't want to be with them, but because God placed me there for some reason. We said our goodbye and got into the pickup to leave. Like before, Rosalba began to cry. It didn't get easier, whether she cried leaving Mexico or leaving Dallas, because I knew she was leaving everything she knew to marry a virtual stranger.

We finally got back on the road bound for Fairview, OK, and the tears and silence again filled the cab of the pickup. I said whatever I could, in the way only I could say it, not knowing if she could understand me at all. I knew now how to say "I need to go to the bathroom," which was very important for both of us as we traveled for six more hours. I was careful to pay attention to her desires for food, drink, or rest stops on the way home, and we stopped a couple of times to get something to eat, drink, and to use the bathroom. As we crossed the Oklahoma and Texas state line, it was more difficult to get a Spanish radio station to tune in on the radio, and now I was asking myself how I could entertain her. The music in Spanish seemed to keep Rosalba connected to her world now so far away, with every mile taking us further north. She kept silent most of the remainder of the trip as she stared out of her window at the hills and trees in the Turner Falls area. I wondered if she had ever seen anything as beautiful where she

71

lived in Mexico. Her wandering eyes led me to believe the answer would be no, because she was so fixated on every tree, pond, or lake that we have passed on our journey.

We stopped at a BRAUM'S which to me is the best hamburger and ice cream business in the world. I knew Rosalba would enjoy this because the ice cream was heavenly. In BRAUM'S we used the restroom and ordered from the menu, which I had to try to explain to her. She could order from the pictures but not by the words on the menu, and I ended up reading off the menu to her in Spanish. She finally chose what she wanted and I ordered for the both of us. While we waited for our food, I held her in my arms, hoping to make her feel safer and loved in this most difficult time starting out in her new life. She has now faced her inability to speak to the man who will be her husband, her inability to read the menu, and her fears increasing by the moment.

The people at the counter called our number and we went to get our food and drinks and find a table to eat. I could still feel Rosalba's nervousness while I watched her. I did my best not to stare so she could eat and enjoy her meal, but it was not easy because I needed to know if she liked the food. The only way I could tell was by her expressions. We said grace for the food in front of us and thanked God for keeping our way safe. She ate so slowly, and it looked like she was enjoying the whole meal.

When we finished our meal and disposed of our trash, we loaded up again in the pickup. We left this city, and I was sure Rosalba was asking herself just how far we had to travel to get to her new home. I told her we had about three more hours left to get there. I tried to imagine what she was thinking and what to say next. I couldn't read her mind, but I could see the preoccupation in her face. I would say something to her and she would respond with a smile and look away, leaving me to wonder if she even knew what I was saying. This trip was suspenseful for both of us as I pondered how I would communicate and she pondered what she could have been thinking. Every second was like walking a tight wire over the circus and wondering if I could make the next step without falling. I'm sure it was worse for her because she didn't like heights.

As I write of this moment in time, I am coming to fully understand what an incredible woman Rosalba was during this time. There was no way I would have done this if I were her, because I really don't like that much change. There was a lot of change coming in her life.

I hoped my family could help her find an identity in this new world, but wasn't sure how. None of them spoke Spanish and the barrier to communication still existed, even though I knew they would love her with all their hearts, as I had. The questions remained as I drove through Oklahoma City towards our home, and the silence provided a thought-provoking backdrop.

I would rather have been talking to her about anything versus the silence. She had nothing to do other than look out the window and try to keep her mind from spinning out of control from every thought going through her mind. I try to communicate with her using the words that I knew, like when we would pass cows. I knew how to say cows, trees, clouds, and the sky, but I didn't know how to talk to her about anything she wanted to hear. Things like: *How are we going to make this work when we can't even talk to each other? Why did you ask me to marry you when you knew there were so many differences between Mexico and the USA? Why would you bring me here without me knowing the language first? How am I going to exist here without my family?* I'm sure there were a thousand questions that I didn't even know about and probably should have known about before we agreed to marry.

What now? I continued to drive and my mind filled with thoughts as the miles passed one at a time. I didn't have a clue what would happen next. Rosalba brought one suitcase with her clothes, and I wondered what else she would need when we got home. What did women need to maintain their lives? Here I was, married, and I couldn't even answer a basic question about women. I should have known this before I married. My house was full of guy things and guy furniture. I had nothing in my home that a woman needed or might even want. I had two Mustang cars and a bass boat that I had just purchased the previous year, but nothing for her other than a roof over her head and the basic necessities. I just remembered that the refrigerator was close to empty, and whatever was in it had probably expired due to my being in Mexico for a week. I didn't even have anything for her to eat that she would want, unless she liked packaged frozen meals or cereal. I knew I didn't have any Mexican food like tortillas, enchiladas, tacos, rice, or refried beans, which were the staple foods in Mexico. I was now more nervous than ever before as I realized I was not prepared at all mentally or physically to take care of a wife, much less a wife from Mexico.

I looked at Rosalba in the passenger seat as all these thoughts went through my mind. I now felt sorry for her, and I began to see exactly how much of a sacrifice she had made to be with me. *How would I make this work, my God?* I prayed. *I know I didn't misunderstand You, God, because I have never been this close to You or been more assured of Your guidance than in this moment.* I prayed that God would still my soul, because I felt the pressure building up inside me the closer to home we got. *I need You more now than ever before because now I'm not only responsible for my life with You, but now I have to maintain my relationship with You and help Rosalba be all she can be in You as well. I'm sure I cannot do it without You, God.*

If I was feeling like this now, I couldn't imagine how Rosalba was feeling at the same time. I prayed for God to give her the strength and patience that I knew we were both going to need.

"Help Rosalba, God," I prayed out loud. It seemed like she looked at me wondering what I was saying.

It's amazing how many thoughts can go through your mind after you think you have all the answers and God gives you what you asked for. He knows what we need and He provides it for us, but we are limited to our own thoughts and abilities, many times not even knowing how God is working in our lives.

This was where we were now, because God knew what He was doing, but He hadn't sent us the memo. We were both lost in this situation, and the only thing we knew was that we loved each other enough to get married. The same thought went through both of our minds many times during this drive home. *What in the world am I doing getting married, much less to someone from another country? How could I marry someone I can't even talk to?* These were real cross-carrying experiences where only God could guide us both, because where could we find a book talking about the problems that we were going to have to overcome? Was there a book out there that addressed how to marry someone from another country who cannot speak our language or even communicate with us? A book titled: **Marriage for Dummies in English and Spanish**, perhaps?

I am embarrassed to say that during this time, I never even asked Rosalba what was going through her mind as we made this trip. There were so many things we had to address, and I never really sat down with her and asked her what was in her mind.

I often wondered: *What is Your plan with us, God? Why did You put us together? Why did You put her through a cross-carrying moment like this? How can I love her enough during her most difficult moment in time?* The many questions keep me on my knees even to this day, asking for God's guidance and direction. *What am I going to do now, God? When I get her home, what do I do? What do I say and how do I say it?* At the time, I couldn't imagine a more difficult time in my life, but as usual I would be wrong, because even though this would prove to be difficult, we were together to overcome the odds.

We were now close to where I lived and I pointed to where the trailer home was parked. I told Rosalba that I lived on top of that hill up there. She looked as me in desperation and asked, "Where is the city?" Oops! I had written her many times in the past about all the details concerning where I lived and about my job, friends, and family, and I had assumed that she had read all the letters. I found out later that she had not read this letter talking about me living next to where I worked, and about the fact that there were only four or five other trailers near me. I could only imagine the level of panic now going through her mind now and it was only controlled by her body and mind being stressed to the point of exhaustion. I had removed her from her country, culture, family, friends, and now I was removing her from the city.

As I write this book, many years later, I am asking myself over and over again the question: *What were you thinking, man?*

It was about six o'clock in the evening. I pulled into the trailer park and helped Rosalba out of the pickup. Her eyes were wide, looking for some type of hope, I'm sure. I opened the door to the trailer house and helped her in, and awaited some kind of response when a woman enters a guy's house and how big her job would be just becoming apparent to her. I tried to keep my home clean, but I was sure it didn't seem like that to her, because it must have had all kinds of guy smells that she couldn't handle at the time. The house had been closed up for a week, and was probably stuffy and uncomfortable to her, coming from her home in Monterrey. A house of wood versus a house of concrete was sure to have many differences, and if I could distinguish them, Rosalba could distinguish them better. I was sure that if she ever had a question about all Americans being rich, she had now found out the truth. None of her family in the USA had houses and they all lived in apartments at the time we were married. This had to be better. At least we had a place to live that belonged to us. I hope that was what she was thinking. In all reality, the only thing going through her mind was: *When can I go back home?*

I went back outside to start unloading the pickup and Rosalba continued to view the task at hand: *How am I going to make this our home and not just his? Does he have anything here that I can use? What does he have here that I need? Where is the city? How do I tell him what I need? How do I get the personal items that I don't feel comfortable discussing with him?* This was a very difficult time for both of us, and we were going to need a big God to help us overcome the obstacles in our path before we could move on.

Right now, we were both really tired and I had to get ready to work in the morning. This led us to another big and uncomfortable moment for both of us. What about the sleeping arrangements? I only had one bed in the house, and addressing this issue became a very embarrassing moment. How would I do this? I tried to overcome my embarrassment by thumbing through my English/Spanish dictionary as I prepared to address this issue. We were still not married legally, and that wouldn't happen until a week later in my home church. *Now what am I supposed to do?* I asked God in this very moment. *How do I tell Rosalba and expect her to understand not just the language barrier but the legal marriage barrier?* I decided to give her the bed to sleep in and I would sleep on the couch until we were legally married. It seemed she felt comfortable with this decision. I took my pillow and blanket to the living room with my work clothes for the next day. I showed her how to operate the controls in the shower and where I kept the towels and other things that she might need. I walked her through the kitchen and showed her what we had and hoped she would be able to find something that she would feel comfortable eating the next day until I returned from work. I had food in the cabinets, but I wasn't sure it was food that she would eat or even like, and there was no time or stores open at the time to go and buy things she might desire or need.

I ask Rosalba if she would want to pray with me before we said goodnight to each other. Thankfully she agreed. So, we got on our knees in the living room and I prayed to God for HELP as we started our lives together and a new responsibility for me and a new world and responsibility for her. I heard her praying in Spanish at the same time, and this encouraged me, because I now knew that I was not in this alone. She was trusting in the same God for HELP as well.

I kissed Rosalba goodnight and left her in her room to sleep while I went to the couch in the living room and prepared to start a new day the following morning. I felt the need to pray again by myself before I could go to sleep, because I still felt this overwhelming pressure about the whole situation and some anxiety. Before I finished praying, she appeared behind me, crying from her fears as well. Before the night was over, she asked me to sleep with her. We decided to put pillows in the middle to prevent you-know-what from happening until the proper time. So, with pillows in place, I put my arm over them to embrace her until both of us fell asleep, exhausted from the very long day. I finished my prayer to God as I fell asleep, and somehow, I got the feeling that everything was going to be okay before I surrendered to the night.

The alarm clock sounding off at 5am came way too soon, but not because of the hour of the day. It concerned me more that I had to leave Rosalba by herself in a strange and new world, and indeed everything was strange and new to her. I got dressed for work and she woke up with me to see me go, and with fear of the unknown in her eyes. I encouraged her that I was only five minutes away, and if she needed me she could call my work phone and ask for me by name, and someone would contact me to come to the phone. I gave her a kiss and told her that I would be home at eleven-thirty to spend twenty-five minutes with her until I had to return to work. I didn't think either one of us could patiently await this time.

I went to work, never really able to keep Rosalba from my mind as I performed my tasks. My mind was far from my job, wondering what she was doing by herself in this alien world. Eleven-thirty seemed like it would never arrive, and I was out of the door as soon as I could so I wouldn't waste one minute getting to her. I knew Rosalba was scared and she knew nobody here whom she could call or visit. When I got home and opened the locked door, she ran to embrace me. Not an embrace of love, but more of fear and relief that I did come when I told her I would. How hard it must have been for her every second, minute, and hour that she waited for that time to come. The twenty-five minutes passed in what seemed like a couple of minutes before I had to return to work. I kissed her goodbye and reminded her of the phone, and the fact that I was only five minutes away, and I would be home at three-thirty in the afternoon.

God must have known about the level of fear she was dealing with, because while I was working a missionary couple came to visit with her and they both spoke Spanish. I came to understand at a later date that these wonderful people were Jacob's parents, Luis and Mariana, and he had asked them to come and visit with her because he remembered how hard it was for him and his wife when they both came to the United States to live here. Jacob's parents spent most of the time with Rosalba as she waited for me to come home, and I thank God for their visit and all they did to calm her nerves. I never asked her what they talked about because I was able to see that she was a little less fearful after their visit, and that was good enough for me. I knew they were both godly people and had also experienced living in other countries that were alien to them.

The Bible tells us to be careful with the people we entertain because they could be angels from God, and I believe this couple were angels from God. Not because of the fact that they spent time with Rosalba, but rather by the substance of what they shared with her to relieve her fears and help her be more at peace in this new alien world.

I returned home at three thirty-five in the afternoon and Rosalba was there waiting for me. She ran to me with a big kiss and a hug. At this time, I was not aware of the visit by Jacob's parents while I was at work. Many of the things I am writing in this book, I found out the details two or three years later, after we had learned to communicate better. Many things, I found out even twenty years later, because she had forgotten about them until we revisited just how much she had to overcome to become an American.

I thank God for these visitors and the time they sacrificed to make Rosalba feel at home in a time when fear almost won. God wouldn't allow it. After this day, I could always sense a new hope in Rosalba, even though everything was new and strange to her. Don't misunderstand me, she still had deer-in-the-headlights moments, but now she seemed to be assured that God was going to take care of her.

After I got off of work, I asked her to walk with me and I took her to meet Jacob and his wife Merthala, who lived a couple hundred feet from our home. Now she could put a face with the name and voice of one of the people who had talked to her on the phone while she was in Mexico. Now I felt like the stranger, because due to her excitement to converse in her native language, the conversation moved quickly and nobody remembered that I didn't speak much Spanish. I now felt like the alien, and I could only understand a few words of the conversation, but it was okay because Rosalba was happy and she deserved every moment she could get. She was as beautiful as before while she spoke to Jacob and his wife, and I quickly remembered why I fell so in love with her. She gleamed in a beauty of hope that everything was going to be all right and she could exist in this new world. It helped that they lived so close. After visiting with them for a couple of hours, we left because I still had to shower and take her to the store to purchase the items she needed for herself and for the kitchen.

I took Rosalba to Enid, OK to a Walmart, so she could find everything she would need at one store. I was glad she was with me, because I never would have guessed all the items she selected. I would have been embarrassed by many of them, because I never knew women needed so many things to exist. I decided not to elaborate on the items because even writing them down embarrasses me, even though I'm sure everybody reading this already knows what those items were. We paid for everything with the credit card again, which should not be a surprise by now because I was no way prepared for the married life. I was glad that she was able to get what she needed and that she could purchase the food she liked to eat. This was food that was part of her world, her life, and food she knew how to prepare.

I took Rosalba to eat at El Chico's Mexican restaurant for supper before we returned home. I think she was happy because she ate everything on her plate. Maybe this was due to the fact that she didn't eat anything all day from fear or the lack of food she recognized. After eating and paying for the meal by credit card once again, we left for home in the country. I hoped she would have a better second day.

Thank You, God, for helping us have a better day and for the hope You provided for both of us in a situation that seemed so overwhelming.

CHAPTER 9

LEARNING TO WALK TOGETHER

That evening, we followed the same sleeping arrangements from the night before, and we prayed together before going to sleep. Praying together was something I would never compromise on during our marriage. Looking at our circumstances, I think that it was obvious why. There was not a moment in our relationship where God was not much needed to make this marriage work and to make it work the way He wanted it to work. We needed direction from Him on everything we did, how we said it, and how we responded to every situation we were to face together. I didn't have the opportunity to fail in this relationship because I would be held accountable to God Himself for everything I said and did individually, as well as for everything I did or didn't do to guide Rosalba as Christ guided the disciples and the church to be. He is the Son of God and I am only a creation that lives because He wants me to live. I needed to always remember that Rosalba had been given to me from my Father above and His rules would always be more important than any thought or rule I could ever make or desire to make. I needed to revere His words concerning how to serve and guide her and how to be there when she needed me. I knew that I didn't have the answers for my own life, much less for hers, and now I was responsible for the direction of our lives together. In all reality, I should never have left my knees in prayer, due to the responsibility I was now accountable for. Could I do this? I asked myself these things many times and continued to do so every day, because only God knew about tomorrow and I didn't know about today or the next second.

We prayed and went to bed with the pillows between us, my arms over the pillows, and my hand resting on her shoulder. This seemed to help us both, but the full-size bed was definitely going to be an issue in the future, because there just wasn't room to role over and not fall out of bed.

Once again, the alarm awoke us to a new day and we spent a moment in prayer to ask God for strength, protection, and guidance for the new day He created. I prepared for work as Rosalba tried to open her eyes. These early mornings were new to her because she didn't have to wake up until seven in the morning to go to school and afterwards off to work. She was always awake with me as I prepared for work and I really liked the fact that she was with me, because now I had a reason to come home other than to eat. I kissed her goodbye as I left for work and assured her again that I would be home at eleven-thirty. I wished, just like most people getting married, that all we had to do was walk with each other in God's presence like Adam and Eve. I didn't have to be reminded that I too was a sinner and I had to work to pay off the consequences of my sins as well. It did bother me to have to leave her, and after one day together it didn't bother me any less.

Work was just that, work, and I was waiting for eleven-thirty to come so I could go and be with Rosalba as long as I could. It came and I went home quickly. When I arrived, there was a great smell of food coming from the house. I had never really experienced this in the past, coming home for lunch, because ham or bologna sandwiches really had no pleasant aroma to give off. This was great. I came into the house to my beauty smiling at me. She gave me the biggest kiss. I wished there was a way to measure it on a scale or something for future use or comparison. She had the table set and the food served, because she knew my time was short and too quickly for both of us, I would have to return to work. The meal was so good. Even today, I remember the first meal that she served us that day: red enchiladas with rice and re-fried beans. I have never tasted anything like this in any restaurants that I have been to. We thanked God together for the meal He had provided and helped her to prepare, and we finished everything, which was perfect, because there were no leftovers to put in the refrigerator. I went back to work and hoped as always that three-thirty would come quickly, because I wanted to be with her again as soon as possible. Finally, off work and at home with my girl again.

What were we going to do today? Now I had all night to spend at home with Rosalba, and we still had a big communication problem to overcome. I asked her if she would like to go for a walk before it got dark, because this was a way God could at least entertain her with His creation, and I didn't have to come up with a lot of broken conversation in Spanish. We walked for about an hour before we went back home. I had hoped Jacob was home so he could help me converse with her. I had never been one to be able to sit with someone for fifteen minutes and have a conversation, much less several hours. The words just never came to me and I had tried to limit my conversations so I wouldn't become annoying to the others involved. How much was there to talk about, even if I could converse with her? I could tell her about my day and everything I did, but there were limited ways to tell someone I filled bags with gypsum-cement products. It bored me, and I could imagine how boring it would be for her as well, but what else could I say?

I knew she was anxious to communicate with her family in Mexico, especially with her mother Maria. Rosalba was the youngest child in her family and the last to leave their home, and I knew this would be very difficult for her and her mother. She needed to call her family and I couldn't say no because it just wasn't possible. So, I handed her the phone and I asked her to call her mother and father and give them an update on her situation in Oklahoma. Her face lit up like children when they receive what they really want for birthdays or Christmas, and her reaction made me feel great as well. We did have to learn how to dial Mexico from Oklahoma, because I had never done it myself before. My friends Jacob, Sergio, or my pastor Ramon in the mission church in Hennessey had made all the calls on my behalf. I stumbled through the phone book to find the right codes to dial from Oklahoma to Mexico and to Monterrey. Rosalba dialed the numbers as directed, and within a few seconds her mother Maria answered the phone. It was like she was in Mexico again, talking with her mother in their living room. She held the phone to her ear with excitement and gratitude that she could still communicate with her family. Statistics say women can speak 165 words a minute, versus men who only speak 100 or less. I now agree with whoever came up with those numbers. I found it amazing that she could continue to talk for more than an hour with her mother. I didn't understand anything she was saying because she was speaking so fast and I could only understand a few words in most of her sentences.

Rosalba's face radiated with glee as she spoke to her mother, and I was even more aware of why I married her. She had a beauty much deeper than her physical beauty and something inside her had appealed to me since I first saw her in Mexico. I couldn't really explain it accurately because I had never experienced it in the past. I could compare it to a cool breeze that blows over you on a hot day. You don't know from where it came or where it's going, but you thank God for the cool breeze.

Finally, I heard her Rosalba say goodbye. This I could understand because I had to say it many times when I had to leave her in Mexico. I was now content, because one hour had passed and she found somebody that she could talk to and she was happy and sad at the same time. I'm sure it hurt her to say goodbye to her mother, not knowing when they would talk again, much less see each other in person. She was also very happy as she ran to me and gave me a big hug of happiness, gratefulness, and sadness as she cried on my shoulder. I was happy for myself and for her as well, but I knew she was not going to be able to call long distance every day to

Mexico. I could see the costs of being married were going to be more than I had planned for, and I had to make some decisions for the future to help her maintain some type of peace in her life.

I had the bass boat, and I really had not had one single good experience with it. Every time I used it, something mechanical would happen and end the trip or create more concern every time I wanted to use it. I constantly had to ask myself what was going to fail next, and I no longer enjoyed having it. I placed it in the paper for sale, and within two weeks I had sold it and gained more financial liberty, so I could better provide for her and allow her more time to phone her family. Many times, the phone bill was $300 or $400 a month, and this was about what I was paying for a new boat that never functioned properly. It was a good decision to make, because Rosalba was much more important than a good boat or this mechanical nightmare that I was making payments on. How could I use it with her, anyway? She feared the water and she didn't know how to swim. There were no lakes, ponds, or public swimming pools in Monterrey, so where would she learn to swim?

The evening and the following day proceeded like the other days, but now I was off work. I had planned to go to the mission church in Hennessey, with our brothers and sisters in Christ who had worked with us during the mission trip to Monterrey. I was excited because now I could visit with them and remember the details of the mission trip and how Rosalba and I met each other. She was excited to go to church and visit with Sergio, his wife, Leanor, and Pastor Ramon. They had made an impact on her life, and I was sure she held them responsible for the fact that she was here with me. If we didn't have a God helping us by using them to help me communicate with her, then she wouldn't be in this situation that was uncomfortable for her.

We prepared ourselves to go to church, and we were both excited because we both missed them and Rosalba really desired someone to talk with. She looked beautiful as always, and focused on every hair being in place and that her teeth were clean. She took very good care of herself always, and she always had great pride in the way she looked. This was something I needed to learn in my life, because although I took care of myself, I really didn't care what people thought of me. I remember once my pastor Robin Cowan asked me to prepare a service for the nursing home and I showed up at church wearing sweats to present the gospel to those in the nursing home. He asked me to go home and change to something more appropriate for this occasion. He explained to me that we wouldn't want someone to lose focus on the message of Christ because they were focused on how we were dressed. I went home and changed into khaki slacks with a dress shirt and we went to the nursing home to share the gospel.

We had to drive about fifty-five miles to attend this mission church. Money for gas was an issue, as we had to make this trip Sunday morning, Sunday night, and on Wednesday night as well. I wasn't going to let this bother me today, because it was a privilege to attend church with Rosalba and my friends. We arrived at the mission church at 9:00am for the Sunday school service. At this time, we were still having services in the American church, or the mother church as it is called. We had about sixty members in the mission at this time, and the pastor Ramon Alemon was really dedicated to God and always really prepared for the Sunday school lessons and the sermon. I really had to focus on his words because he was from Cuba and his Spanish was a little different than what I had learned. I tried to follow his words, but many times I was lost from the beginning to the end. Many times, I would just read my Bible during the lesson or during the service, because I couldn't understand anything he said. This was all right for me, because Rosalba could understand everything, and I had to thank him for everything he taught her.

Rosalba really enjoyed being with our brothers and sisters in Christ, because she could talk about Christ and her life with them and they could understand her as well. She always sat up straight and really revered God and the church. I could see her parents had taught her well about respecting not only God, but the temple of God. After the service ended, Sergio and Leanor Ortega invited us to their home to eat dinner with them. I was glad to spend the time with them because I could get to know them better and we could have a conversation, because Sergio knew enough English to translate for Rosalba and me. We ate dinner and the conversations continued through dinner. Sergio translated for me about what was being discussed. This helped me learn more Spanish every day in the real world, and it helped Rosalba learn about me and living here in the United States as well.

Sometimes when I couldn't understand the conversation and nobody was there to translate for me, I would get very sleepy and bored and I would find myself dosing off. Many times, my friends and Rosalba would think that I was tired and always offered me a bed to sleep in. It wasn't because I was tired, but because I couldn't understand anything.

We spent the afternoon together visiting and remembering everything about the mission trip, and pretty soon it was time for us to go to the evening service. I was totally immersed in the Spanish language, and I did my best to learn and understand what was being sung and taught by the pastor Ramon. Some of the songs I knew by the music, and this at least helped me know the songs were from the same hymnal I had used in my home church. The service ended and we began the hour-long drive home about 8:00pm, which meant we would get home about 9:00. By the time we arrived home, we were exhausted and we had no trouble falling asleep. As always, though, we spent time together praying before we went to bed.

The following Thursday, the alarm woke us and it was time to go back to work. Rosalba seemed to be adapting to her new life better each day. We prayed and I gave her a kiss goodbye, reminding her that it would be a short time before I returned home for lunch with her. I went to work and my mind strayed from what and where I was to how I could and should prepare for the wedding on Saturday, which was three days away. We had Rosalba's dress from the wedding in Mexico, but I didn't have a tuxedo to wear to the wedding, so we had to make another trip to Enid to prepare for the wedding. I had no clue about how to prepare for a wedding and had no support from my family for this, but my pastor Robin Cowan and the brothers and sisters in Christ in my home church were wonderful, taking care of all the details for me. I didn't even know about it at the time. This was not going to be easy for Rosalba, either, because none of her family would be able to attend the wedding here for various reasons.

Before I knew it 11:30 came and it was time to go home and be with Rosalba again. I was glad because I knew she was also preoccupied with the wedding without her family here. I knew she was concerned about what everybody was going to think of her and the fact that she was from Mexico. Would my friends and brothers and sisters in Christ accept her as she was? I wasn't concerned about this as much as her, because these were wonderful people and I knew they had a passion for Christ. Churches like this one didn't leave their comfort zone to go to an unknown land to preach the gospel of their own accord without the Spirit of God motivating them to go. Once again, I came home to the wonderful smell of a home cooked meal, which of course was wonderful as always. I didn't know where or how she learned to cook so well, but I was sure her mother Maria was most likely the one who taught her so much about these dishes. The food was perfectly spiced and always served hot, and I was getting spoiled by this wonderful lady. We tried to communicate, and I found a way to convince her to speak slower so that I could process everything she was trying to tell me, and it seemed she understood me. She spoke to me a little slower and spoke clearly every word so I could process her words in my mind easier. I was excited because at least now we were beginning to have simple, short conversations that left me always wanting more every time we were together. As I said before, I really wasn't someone who had a lot to talk about, but with her I always found something to talk about.

It was now time to return to work. I kissed Rosalba goodbye and encouraged her to be patient during the next three-and-a-half hours for my return. I went to work to finish my day, always thinking of her and the wedding to come on Saturday. Now the roles would be reversed, because I would understand everything but she would understand nothing. Nobody in my church spoke Spanish, and how was she going to get through the wedding if she couldn't understand anything? How was she going to be able to say "I DO" if she couldn't understand the questions? Many questions and very few answers, so once again I asked for God's help in a situation where I had no control. I couldn't translate for her because I didn't know how, and I had to pay attention to what the pastor was asking me. I was going to be nervous also because this would finalize my promise to God to care for her and teach her what He wanted her to know from the Bible. I was also going to promise her that I would love her to the end without knowing anything about the end or when the end was going to come. This would be difficult for anybody because we want to have control over our futures, but I knew God had His own plans and He didn't have to share His plans with us.

Before I was aware, the siren sounded and my time at work ended. With my mind preoccupied by many other things, the time seemed to have passed faster than normal. I went home and gave Rosalba a big kiss. I was excited due to her beauty and the fact that Saturday was now only two days away. I was going to be married to a woman God had provided me and how could life be better than this? Her lips were so soft and full, and it seemed like I was closer to heaven every time I kissed her. I wondered how far away heaven was every time I could embrace her and kiss her. I wasn't actually in heaven, but I couldn't imagine anything that could compare to being in her arms and feeling her lips on mine. I asked her if she would like to go to Enid and help me find a tuxedo for the wedding, because the time was getting closer. I wanted to be as handsome as I could be, standing beside such a beautiful lady. I still remember her in her dress in Monterrey. She was gorgeous, and I knew she would be equally beautiful on Saturday.

We loaded up in the pickup and drove to Enid, to look for this tuxedo. I had no idea where these stores were. I drove around the city looking for places that rented tuxedos, and realized I should have looked in a phone book before leaving home. We finally found a place in downtown Enid that offered this service, and I began the process of trying on tuxedos. Rosalba wanted me to wear a white tuxedo so that I would match her dress and show that I would be coming to the ceremony as pure as she was. I liked this idea. I had never thought about it this way, but it was true because I had worked very hard not to place myself in compromising situations.

I had had opportunities to compromise my purity, but I had seen in my own family what happened to people who tried to obtain in their own power what God wasn't offering. The consequences were ours because they resulted from our choices. I had seen what happened when someone committed to a physical relationship before God intended it to happen. I had seen in my own family what happened when someone looked for a

Christian husband in a bar. There was something very wrong with this picture. I wouldn't be looking for a future spouse or friend in a bar to begin with. I doubted that God hung out in bars. I had seen what happens when a girl became pregnant and her family sent her to another state to get an abortion and the baby's father had no choice in the matter. I had seen with my own eyes how hard this affected the lives of people I cared about. I had seen someone get married, and find out three months later that his wife had given herself to a man who was not her husband. I had seen the pain that comes when we do these things our own way and they always go wrong in the end. I didn't want to be part of these statistics because these situations were not good places to end up.

We found a tuxedo that Rosalba liked and I got the size that they measured me for and entered the dressing room to try it on. I finished and came out to model myself for the love of my life. Her eyes lit up to see me in this white tuxedo. I knew this was the tuxedo she wanted me in as I gave myself to her in God and made my promises to her and to God. I paid for the tuxedo and we left to do other things, including eating. I was hungry because now it was about 6:00pm and my stomach was growling, but what should we eat today and what did she want to eat? This was always a difficult decision to make, because she was thinking about what I wanted and I was always thinking about what she would like to eat. We went to BRAUM'S. I hoped that she liked hamburgers. I didn't know if she had ever eaten one other than the one she ate on our way home from Mexico, but I knew they were good and BRAUM'S also had awesome ice cream to finish off the meal. Everything in one place and good things as well. You couldn't go wrong with that. I asked Rosalba what she wanted to eat and she viewed the menu hanging above the counter and pointed to the number one package. So, I ordered the meal for both of us and paid for it as we waited for the order to come. In a short time, our meal was ready, and I took her to get her drink and the condiments she wanted. We found a table to eat our meal. I realized that all the tables were bigger than the one we had in the restaurant in Monterrey named VIP'S. I know that God used that small table in VIP'S to get us together, even if we could only make faces to each other. We finished our meal as I tried to find the words in Spanish to say, "Did you enjoy your meal?" I still didn't know enough to find them. We gathered our trash and placed it in the receptacle provided for it, and we left for home.

We got home and said our prayer before we went to bed. I was excited as I realized that now we had only one day before we made this union legal once and for all. We prepared for bed with the same arrangements as before. I was glad, because now even with a small bed, I was beginning to enjoy being with Rosalba even with the pillows in between us.

CHAPTER 10

A PROMISE TO LOVE AND OBEY

The day finally arrived for this special occasion. I was really nervous, not only for myself but because none of my Rosalba's family would be there to encourage her or witness this wedding. She had to be really nervous because she didn't really know anyone at my church or any of my friends, and I could sense it in her emotions. She would stand up and marry a man of a different country, culture, and customs in front of his family and friends who she didn't even know. All the watching eyes would seem to penetrate to her very soul as she stood with me and everyone silently asked the multiple questions yet to be spoken and heard. I saw she was tense from the moment we awakened and prepared for the big day. Both of us had yet to learn exactly how God had been preparing the sacrificial hearts of my church family and friends at the First Baptist Church in Okeene, OK.

We prepared breakfast even though we really were not hungry due to our nervousness, but we didn't know when we would get the chance to eat later. We looked at each other and smiled nervously, but with an excitement at the same time. We had planned this for quite some time, and Rosalba could finally see this was real and legal and I wasn't going to use her as many had told her in Mexico.

What do you really say to each other on that day when you are about to make one of the most important promises you will ever make to another human being?

I tried to encourage Rosalba that everything would be great, but I don't know if she believed me at that time. She was so beautiful and I didn't want her to put unjust pressure on herself, especially for things out of our control. This whole relationship had been out of our control since we met each other during the mission trip. God had been leading us through doors, corridors, rooms, and many different valleys and mountain tops. We couldn't see any of these or where they led, but we took one step of faith at a time and now we were here in Oklahoma, getting ready to make a promise of faith to God and each other for a lifetime.

We dressed casually as we prepared to go to the church for the wedding. I was glad because it was hot and I couldn't imagine her in the big dress and me in the tuxedo before it was time. I needed to speak to Pastor Robin Cowan before the service to cover other questions that had been passing through my mind since the mission trip.

When we step out in faith, we sometimes need to be convinced that we are not making a wrong choice. *Am I capable of taking care of this wonderful woman? Can I carry the cross God has given me in this marriage? Do I know enough about Christ so that I can love and serve her like Christ loved and served the church?* These were some of the questions that had been bothering me as I prepared to make this step in faith. This moment was very important to me because it was the last time I would make this decision in my life. I would take this promise with me to the grave and into eternity, where God would hold me responsible for teaching Rosalba His ways and serving her as was Christ's example. I would be compared to Christ and He would be my standard.

Rosalba sat quietly and I was sure she was wondering what I said to Pastor Robin, but the discussion didn't last very long. Before I know it, it was time to suit up and prepare for the wedding service.

This was not going to be a normal wedding service. I had no groomsmen and she had no bridesmaids. There was no caterer with a meal provided and we didn't even have a wedding cake to serve to those visiting. Rosalba didn't even have anyone to help her with her dress, makeup, doubts, and fears. She didn't even have any of her family and friends with her to encourage her and calm her fears as she prepared to step out in front of so many strangers' eyes. She didn't even know my family or friends and she must have really been stressing out at this time and wondering where her family and friends were. Why didn't they come from Dallas for the wedding? Many questions, and very little answers in return. Now what?

Rosalba was trying to put on her makeup for the wedding, but she was really nervous and didn't listen to me tell her she was beautiful and she didn't need to paint her face. It didn't help and she was really getting stressed out as she tried to put on makeup without a mirror. I asked Merthala, Jacob's wife, to please help her with the makeup. Merthala was also from Monterrey, but Rosalba really didn't know her yet. She had met Jacob and Merthala once together before and spoke to them, but she had not spent time with Merthala alone until today. Merthala agreed to help Rosalba with the makeup and I was glad, because I didn't think she was going to make it through this part without her help. They went into one of the choir rooms and prepared her for the wedding as I went to the other to get dressed myself. The wedding crowd arrived as we were getting dressed. I knew everyone there but they didn't know Rosalba and she didn't know them. I was wondering how would they accept her, being from another country and being Hispanic. Would they accept her as a sister in Christ and how would she relate to them? How could they relate to her when they couldn't even talk to her? How would she talk to them?

I was about to be surprised by the amount of love and sacrifice my brothers and sisters in Christ were willing to sacrifice for me and my bride. Rosalba didn't even have her father here to give her away. I was sure this was going to bother her, but I had spoken to my grandpa, Vernon Wilson and Rosalba about the possibility that he could give her away.

I remember my grandfather's reaction when I told him that I was going to marry a woman from another country.

He asked me, "Are you crazy or what? You don't know anything about women, especially one you can't even communicate with."

He wasn't about to give Rosalba to me unless he could see something in me that would convince him that I was responsible and willing to do everything possible to take care of this special little lady. She had stolen his heart and it was probably because he also knew about some of the difficulties she was going to have to overcome in this new world.

I always respected my grandfather and sometimes even feared him. He worked his whole life outside, and every time I saw him as a young child, I thought he was the devil. He had white hair, always crew cut, but his face was always really red from constant exposure to the sun at work. He was never mean or anything, it was only his appearance and I was a young child who had never really come to know him until the later years of his life. We would always go play golf together and I enjoyed being with him. I was proud that he finally agreed to give Rosalba away to me on this very special day in our lives.

Rosalba made her way to the back of the church for the service as Pastor Robin's wife, Joyce, came to me and asked me if I had planned someone to play the song for the wedding march. My response was, "Do I need someone?" She asked me if I had anyone to sing a special song for the wedding service, and my response was the same: "Do I need one?" Joyce Cowan was a lovely sister in Christ, and she told me she would be proud to do these things for me. I was now at a point that I started to realize how little I was in control of this moment, because I hadn't even taken care of the small details associated with a normal wedding. We had rehearsed briefly how we would enter for the ceremony and I was sure my grandfather wouldn't miss a beat as he walked this beautiful lady down the aisle. What I didn't know at the time was that she had panicked when she saw how her face was painted. She looked into a mirror and saw several shades of makeup were used on her face, so she thought made her look like a clown. She was really upset about this and had asked Sergio's wife, Leanor to help her fix her face before the ceremony. She looked spectacular as Joyce played the wedding march and my grandfather and my bride came through the double doors to the front. The two most important people in my life were walking arm-in-arm to me as I faced the moment to make the most important promise to another human in all my life. Not only my promise to her, but my promise to God. As I had discussed with my grandfather many times, I was concerned with my promise to both of them. How would I be able to fulfill my promises to both of them?

The music stopped and there they stood in front. All the others attending stood in reverence as the ceremony began. Annette, was a wonderful woman from my church who unknowingly is responsible for telling me that I would meet a young señorita in Mexico and fall in love. She now played the piano as Joyce sang a special piece, and it was beautiful. As the song ended, Pastor Robin began by asking who was giving away the bride. With a big smile on his face, my grandfather Vernon said, "I do," and he gave her to me. Pastor Robin spoke to us about the responsibilities of marriage in English, then to my surprise I learned he had also gone out of his comfort zone to learn how to say the same things in Spanish. What a pastor! He knew how Rosalba must have been feeling and presented her the ceremony in Spanish after he had done the same for me in English.

I said, "I DO," and Rosalba said, "SI." Pastor Robin finished the ceremony and invited me to kiss my bride. I was more than willing, because now it was official. I had fulfilled my promise up to this moment to honor her and her family by making it legal, and she glowed from the truth that I really loved her to the point that I was willing to promise God to cherish her as long as I lived.

As we left the sanctuary, I noticed that Brother Harley, Annette's husband was taking pictures of us, and I had not planned on pictures. I discovered later that another couple Brett and Lynn from our church paid him to take the pictures. We entered the kitchen and dining area and others asked me who I had to serve the cake and other things provided by the church family. I knew nothing about it and my answer was the same: "Do I need servers?" My Aunt Susan, my dad's sister, asked me if I had someone to write down the names of the people who gave us gifts, and once again the answer was the same: "Do I need someone?" As everyone realized how unprepared I was for this wedding, they volunteered one by one to help me with all the details. I loved these guys and all the sacrifices they made for us.

As we enjoyed the cake, punch, and the other things after the ceremony, my friends were up to other things outside with my pickup. I was so focused on the wedding and my new bride that I didn't even consider what they might be up to. I left the church with my new bride and went to the pickup. I opened the door for her in her big dress, and I was in my tuxedo, ready to leave for home, but the pickup wouldn't go anywhere. Of course, by now all of my friends were busting their guts in laughter. I discovered they had put halves of watermelon under each rear tire and I wasn't going anywhere. My pickup was small, and in a matter of minutes they lifted up the back of my pickup and removed the watermelons under each tire, and we were able to leave. There was no hurry. We didn't have a honeymoon planned either, because there just wasn't any money to go anywhere.

I enjoyed my family and friends and they were more than supportive of me and my new bride Rosalba Wilson. I knew things always changed once a person got married, but I hoped it would not change the relationships I had with my friends. We had been together through some difficult times, and without knowing it they had helped me get through my addiction to drugs and my past. None of this was a secret to my new bride, because I have written in all of my letters to her about my past and the obstacles I had to deal with to become who I was. My relationship with God and the Christian friends I had now have helped me mature and really understand my new relationship with Him and my responsibilities in this new life. I never had a father because he left us when I was five years old and never really had a father-son relationship with him. I don't say this for anyone to feel sorry for me, but only to enlighten others about the importance of God in my life. I had to learn from God what being a father was and how to do it, and I believe He guided me in how to do it. Now I was in another constant learning phase of how to love my bride the way Christ loved the church, which was only to be found in His word.

I didn't know how it was possible to be so happy and yet filled with fear at the same time. I was so happy to have my new bride Rosalba, but so fearful that I didn't know the first thing about the love Jesus shared with His bride, the church. I needed to learn so much more, and fast. I was driving home with my new bride and it was legal, but now what? Rosalba was mine and I was hers, but I still couldn't communicate with her properly and she couldn't communicate with me.

Our physical union had a difficult beginning. Usually people assume that would be accomplished on the honeymoon. It wasn't so easy for us because there were things Rosalba had never revealed to me before we were married. She had deep secrets too embarrassing for her to even repeat or share with me or her mother. I learned she and her sisters had been sexually abused by their father, and she had never been able to let go of these dark and damaging moments in her life. *God, how could I help Rosalba overcome these memories and help heal her scars from the past?*

I prayed to God about how a father could do something so perverse and damaging to a child. I couldn't fathom the pain and bad memories she was going through at that moment. She wanted to give herself to me, but the memories and fears of how her trust was used and abused wouldn't allow her to do so.

Now what, God? I married a woman who had issues I was not qualified to deal with. How did I help my new bride Rosalba deal with her past so we could start our future? I cried out to God to heal her pain and use my helplessness. I had seen this in my own family with our stepfather sexually abusing my sister, and it angered me to a point that I would drug myself to make it go away. It came to a point that day and night all I could think of was killing my stepfather for the things he had done to my sister. I had planned several times how I was going to kill him for the things he had done to her. I wasn't a Christian at this time and it was still totally perverse to me how someone could so abuse the daughter of the woman he had married. It seemed fitting and just to me that he would die for what he had done. Every moment of my life became totally focused on how to kill him. I thought about it many times and concluded that even if I killed him, it wouldn't change what he had done to her. We forced Mom to divorce him and get him out of the house where he couldn't abuse my sister anymore or my other sisters, but the desire to kill him remained and the drugs were not helping.

I spoke of my uncle in the first chapter but mention him again to emphasize the impact he had in my life. I had spoken to my uncle Leland about what was happening in my life and my plans to take this man's life. I always liked my uncle Leland. He was my aunt Carol's husband. Carol is my dad's sister. He told me what I already knew, but the drugs were my problem and I would never be able to control my thoughts and emotions while I was doing drugs. He offered me his home and support as long as I would keep myself off of the drugs that were leading me into the thoughts of killing this man. Could God have been letting me deal with this issue in my past to help me assist Rosalba in dealing with her past? I never had my father, but I could not imagine him abusing his daughter this way. I couldn't even begin to understand the perverse mind that would even contemplate abusing a girl this way. *How do I proceed now, God?* Here I was in one of the worst situations I had ever found myself. Rosalba had been abused sexually by her own father and never spoke to anybody about it. At the same time, I had to deal with my past and reliving the painful situation with my stepfather and sister. Now I was angered more than I had been before. I had fled the situation at home with my sister and never dealt with it. I found that deep within my own heart I had some un-forgiveness issues that I had never left at the foot of Jesus' cross. I couldn't help Rosalba until I was able to leave my own rage at His feet. I was now enraged toward my stepfather and Rosalba father, and I didn't know what to do.

I spent many hours in prayer because I didn't know what to do and I couldn't force myself on my Rosalba while she was dealing with this life-altering event. It had changed innocence to fear, and withdrawal from what was supposed to be pure and holy. Satan had used my stepfather and her father to remove from my sister and Rosalba the most sacred and designed sacrifice that a woman could provide for her husband. Rosalba told me she felt dirty and used, and she couldn't give herself to me knowing what her father had done to her. I didn't marry Rosalba for sex, but it was something I had been saving myself for.

Now what, God? How could I show Rosalba I loved her even though she had been robbed of her purity by her own father? I realized that I was dealing with Rosalba the same way Jesus has to deal with His bride, the church. Many people in church have been abused in some way or another, and Jesus has to deal with all our pasts and hurts to use us to complete God's plan. *How can you use me, God, to help heal my wife's pain and hurt?*

I had to come to grips with my own un-forgiveness before I could help Rosalba deal with her issues with her past. I spent many hours on my knees, praying for God's direction in our lives, because I didn't know what to say or how to say it. I was facing double frustration because I didn't know what to tell her and I didn't know how to tell her in Spanish. Here was a person who knew nothing about being a good father, trying to distinguish the differences between godly fathers versus what we had in our lives. Rosalba spent hours crying as she wondered how her father could do this to her and her sisters. I find myself crying even now as I remember her tears as she relived every moment of her father abusing her. I cried as she told me how and what he did, and she could do nothing. I cried as she told me that if she said anything, he would abuse her mother physically. I cried as I thought of her suffering as her own father did these things to her.

I can't heal her pain, God, I found myself crying out. *I cannot even heal myself of the pain that I endured as my brother and I entered the house to find this pervert abusing our own sister.* These memories brought up some of the things I had told myself in the past: *If this is God, I don't want anything to do with it.* This stepfather who had abused my sister would stand up in our Assembly of God Church, supposedly speaking in tongues, and the next day abused our sister sexually. *If this is God, my unsaved life is so much better, and I don't need a God who would allow or permit things as perverse as this to happen.*

All of my doubts about God and His ability to really save us was an issue I thought I had overcome. Rosalba had been abused, and years later she was still carrying the cross of an abusive father. I was carrying a similar cross of seeing how much a life can be devastated by such perverse abuse. I knew what I had seen and what had happened, but I didn't know what to do or say now.

Now what, God? We are both in a valley now, and You have given me the responsibility to lead Rosalba as her new husband. How in the world am I going to lead her when I don't even know where in the valley I am? I am hurting deep inside now because I have no idea what to do. I love my new bride, but I cannot help her, and I cannot make her commit to me physically until I find a way to help her get rid of these demons of past abuses.

I decided that only fasting would help me find healing for myself and direction from God on how to lead Rosalba to the place where she could lie down besides the still waters. *Where is this place, God, and how do I get her and me to it?* I needed the still waters as well, because even though I had shared all my past evils with her in my letters, this one had overcome me to the point that I doubted my own relationship with God. Every moment that I wasn't working I was on my knees, praying to find some kind of direction or guidance from God in this situation.

Rosalba was now preoccupied because I had not eaten anything for a week, but she didn't understand that an evil as great as this could only be overcome by prayer and the angels of God guiding our steps. The Spirit of God is the only comforter that we have to help us overcome evils such as this. He is the only one who can provide a peace that overcomes our own understanding of such perverse actions. Food was not an issue to me at the time, because I could see the fear and hurt Rosalba had to deal with.

Something pure and wonderful had been stolen from Rosalba and she would never be able to get it back. Something so evil and perverse happened that God's creation was compromised by the actions of her own father. God is not hurting as Rosalba tries to overcome this abuse. God cannot even understand how this young woman feels as the memories and pictures come back to her mind over and over again. God is supposed to be holy and He doesn't think of things as perverse as what her father did. God is not the one remembering how it felt, as her father touched her and performed physical abuse on her. God did nothing as her father did this to her. Where was He when His creation became so perverse? God, how in this world are You going to be glorified by something as perverse as this?

As you can see, I had so many thoughts I had to address before I could understand why such perverse things were allowed to happen to such beautiful people. I asked many times the same thing: *God, why do You allow things like this to happen, and then You put people like me in the middle to lead when we ourselves don't know where we are going? Now what?*

CHAPTER 11

HOW TO HEAL AND FORGIVE

T he thought of how the past has altered and even stunted the lives of so many people reminds me of how perverse and sinful we have become. I know God had nothing to do with the perverse things that Rosalba's father had done to her and others in her family, but He didn't prevent it either. In His Word, He has said "It would be better for them to be thrown into the sea with a millstone tied around their neck than to cause one of these little ones to stumble." (Luke 17:2) I didn't see this happen to Rosalba's father, and I can't do it for God. I really don't understand the depths of God's love because at a later date her father excepted Christ into his heart and was forgiven, but the consequences remain from his perverse choices to abuse Rosalba and others in his family. The sins of one man have had a big and terrible impact on so many people besides my wife Rosalba, and I didn't know how to deal with it. *How do I help my wife and your daughter, God? Other than being born into a sinful world by man's own choice, Rosalba has done nothing to deserve such evil in her life, nor have the others.*

How would I lead Rosalba to the place that surpasses our own under-standing? We are very limited on what we can do as humans because that is the way God has left us since we decided we wanted all the knowledge of good and evil. I tried so hard to do what God wanted me to do, but how did I deal with an evil such as this? How would I help Rosalba overcome this when I couldn't even imagine the level of evil that would be in such a person who would decide to sexually abuse members of his own family? In the Old Testament, it says that a person such as this should be taken out-side the city limits and stoned to death, but we cannot do this today and it wouldn't change the past. He might be dead, but the results of his abuse would still remain in her life and the lives of many others.

Now what, God? This is supposed to be our honeymoon time. A time to join each other as one body and a union in peace with YOU, but there is no peace. There was no way I could ask Rosalba to commit herself to me physically with all this hurt and abuse that had damaged her thoughts about physical relationships with men in general. Even husbands had been included in her category of abusers because her dad was a husband and had no respect for the family God had provided him. I was the husband who had to deal with the consequences because her father had done nothing to heal the abuse. What could he say or do to heal the sins of his past with Rosalba or others in her family? Somehow, hearing "I'm sorry" didn't seem to be something that she would want to hear, and I didn't believe she would've believed him to begin with.

I asked Rosalba why she didn't say anything to her mother or others in her family, and she said her father had told her, "If you say anything, I will physically abuse your mom." Rosalba really loved her mom and would never do anything to hurt her, and for this she didn't do anything to stop the abuse that she was dealing with. I was sure she asked herself many times how it was possible that her mom didn't know what her husband was doing to her daughters and nieces. How was it possible that she didn't know?

With my mom, we told her what happened. She admitted she knew and would deal with it, but didn't do so until we told her we would deal with it by telling the police or killing our stepfather ourselves. This was the only reason she divorced him, but she never pressed charges on him for raping my sister. Why not?

Just because we were born into a sinful world, did we have to permit evils like this into our lives? I wonder why we do. How could we cover up or excuse such abuses within the family? Before I could help Rosalba deal with her past and embrace the future with me, I had to find answers that were beyond my grasp. Even to this day, I have trouble imagining how a young lady like Rosalba had to deal with all the mental, physical, and spiritual consequences of what her father did to her. I knew the answer, but I hated it at the same time. She would have to leave it at the foot of the cross Jesus died on, but how could I even understand how she was supposed to do this? As humans, how did we let go of something that altered our lives so dramatically? I was sure she was thinking at this time how many more of her nieces and neighborhood girls were abused by her father. Even to me it seemed impossible to forgive someone of their sexually abusive past. Chances were good they were continuing to abuse others. How did we forgive someone for what they had done to us when we knew they continued doing the same to others?

I had to commend Rosalba for her courage in telling me what her father did to her, because it was probably the most embarrassing and degrading thing she would ever have to confess to me. She did nothing wrong, but the past had left her feeling dirty and used, and she had trouble giving herself to me when something so nasty and disgusting had happened to her. How could she give herself as a new and innocent bride when she felt so used and abused? She knew her loss of innocence wasn't of her choosing, but nonetheless she felt so dirty in her own mind.

Rosalba knew her father no longer could abuse her, but her mind was set in the past and in the future knowing her father could be abusing other girls the same as her. Physically she was now free, but was still trapped in a cage of past sins of another's choosing and she didn't know how to escape mentally or spiritually. I saw her and the cage she felt trapped in, but I didn't know how to set her free or convince her to leave it at the cross. I continued to pray for guidance from God, but had not found the answer, though I knew her freedom was coming.

Even five months after we married, because of this sin we still hadn't had any type of physical communion because of this sin. I was still human, but not focused on the time we could spend together. Instead, I focused on how to get her to see that physical relationships were great when done as God planned. I was waiting on God's time, and His time would come for us to spend this time together, but for now I had to help Rosalba find healing from the past. This wasn't a problem a psychiatrist could resolve because this hurt went to the deepest parts of the heart and the mind. This problem could only be resolved by the hand of God, because only He knew the depth of the pain and hurt suffered by those who were abused by someone who was supposed to be willing to give his life to save theirs. It was alien to think that a father who was charged by God to instruct and protect his children would willingly do the opposite.

I had no time to analyze the perverse mind of one who chooses to sexually abuse his children because I had to focus my time on how one who had been abused could be set free. I didn't have the answer and this drove me a little crazy, because there was no clear answer in the Bible, other than leaving it at the cross. The human side of me didn't understand this concept, much less possess the ability to convince someone else to believe it. I could see myself saying something as true but humanly stupid as "leave it at the cross." It sounded so simple but so stupid, because as humans we couldn't let go of the past for whatever the reasons might be. We couldn't fathom the ability of God to help us overcome the past and become better people after something like this had happened. We only saw the fact that someone charged with protecting and loving us had abused us in the filthiest way possible. How could this be in a world that God created and called good? We didn't focus on the fact that we invited sin into our lives many years after Adam and Eve chose knowledge of good and evil over God Himself.

It seems convenient to us to believe that God should always intervene and stop all evil from happening. This truth sucks! We live in a world we warped into a place of our own interpretation of good and evil, and now we are suffering the consequences. We eat all the sweets in the world and blame God for diabetes. Somehow, it's easier to blame God for the sin in our lives rather than understand our culpability. Don't misunderstand me, because I'm in no way blaming Rosalba for the choices her father made. Evil was not her choice, but it affected her life because someone else practiced it and this was her father.

I knew the truth but I didn't know the answer. What could I say or what could I do to help Rosalba find an escape from this cage of abuse? How could I convince her that evil abused her but it doesn't define her? Her life would not be defined by her past, but rather by the choices she made today. It sounded easy, but would not be so for her or her family, because leaving the past at the cross meant being willing to let it go and not return to use it to get even or for revenge.

Many people use sin like this to define who they are going to be the rest of their lives and they're happy living like this. I couldn't permit Rosalba to live her life like this because this was not the woman God provided me with. She was so much stronger and so much more intelligent than to permit the choices of others to define her life. Rosalba had always been a fighter and she would not let the past define her future. She was going to overcome the negatives in her life and define her own future. This was one of the reasons she stood out above the other women I had met, and I knew she wasn't going to go silently into the night as another abused person who had no control over the life she now lived. This was the only direction I could lead her to because many things in life happened to us that we had no control over, and we couldn't let these things define us. It might be a natural disaster or a medical problem, but these were issues we had to address, yet they did not define us. The choices we make after these things are what defines us. What were we willing to do to avoid these choices that would prevent us from living and being who God wants us to be?

I had finally found what I could say and believe when it came to helping her: *Rosalba, you cannot let the past define who or what you are in the future. We cannot change what has happened in the past, but these things were not of your own choosing and they are not who you are. Good things are twisted by the devil on a daily basis, but somehow God uses them to make us better people, parents, or Christians. All that matters is how we use the past to motivate us to become better people and the best people God created us to be.*

I had seen in many people how evil had dragged them down to the depths of despair because they allowed it to. Rosalba was so much stronger than this, and I knew this because she was such a great fighter and her goals in life were more than honorable. She wanted to be the best Christian and wife she could be, but the past had its hold on her life, and somehow, she had to let it go or she would be defined by the choices made by other people. Forgiving her father was going to be very difficult, but not as difficult as the choice she had to make to not let the past define her future. I was a sinner, but this was not going to define me because I trusted in God every day to help me make choices that glorified Him as much as possible.

Even with our language barrier, I asked Rosalba to join me more in our prayer time because she needed to know I was also angry with her father and with God, but I needed to trust in God so my future was not defined by the choices of perverted people who chose to use me. I did my best to pray in Spanish because I wanted her to hear me pray. I wanted her to hear me say that I was angry with her father and I was angry with God because He allowed this to happen to her and others in her family. I wanted her to see that I was hurting myself because of the choices made by my stepfather when he abused my sister. I wanted her to see that I was not humanly willing to let go of the choices made by evil people, but I was going to trust in Him to show me if and how I could do so. I wanted her to see that it was not going to be easy, but it could be done. There was no way she could be the best she could be if she allowed this past to define her future. Every day I prayed the same way: *God, please show me how I can let go of these memories before the memories make me a victim for life and not victorious.*

It sounded easy to some, but it was not easy for either of us because it would mean we would have to forgive the past and allow God to begin to create our future together. I didn't want to be married to a lady who allowed the past to define her or give her an excuse to not try to be a better person than her father or the stepfather and mother I had to forgive. Don't think that I am talking about forgetting the past, because there was no way I would ever leave Rosalba alone with this pervert ever. I was angry with her father and I still didn't know how I ever stopped myself from unloading on him every time I saw him after that. I was angry with her mother for not knowing over such a long period of time, with all her daughters and others who suffered the abuse by her husband's choosing. I also had to be careful and not let this define the husband God wanted me to be for her.

Every day we would pray in the morning, afternoon, and at night for God to intervene and not let the past sins define our future. It seemed that little by little it was helping both of us. I didn't know if Rosalba mentioned her past to other women in the church, but it seemed like her hatred for her father and the past were less severe. Before long, she was praying for God to help her learn how to forgive her father and how to overcome the past to become what God wanted her to become. I was proud of her because I saw with my own eyes how she was learning to let go little by little every day. I knew this had to be very difficult for her. She couldn't be defined by the choices of other people. She was so special and so beautiful for more than the physical side of her, but rather in her spirit and mind. Her desire to be her best motivated her to be better than the past, to be better as a wife and as a partner in a marriage than the example she saw in her own family. Rosalba used those memories, as ugly as they were, to be a better wife, friend, and partner.

Little by little, Rosalba was able to let go of the past and start embracing the new future. She was married to a man of God who was willing to wait for her to overcome the past hurts and cope with the changes she had to make. I knew with her strong determination and motivation she would make the right decisions to make her future the best it could be. I was proud of her and I let her know every day that she was making the right decisions, and soon she would start feeling a release from the bad memories created by a perverted father. This was a huge burden on my shoulders and our marriage because I was a new husband and I had no experience with teaching others to leave such profound things at the feet of Jesus. I didn't know if I could do it, but I was more than willing to wait and trust in God to help me and Rosalba.

The time had come, and God had helped us both overcome the past and spend time together. Without details, I learned how great a creator God was because God's plan for our physical relationship turned out to be much more than I could have ever imagined. We were now one, physically and spiritually in Christ, and I was totally bound by God to take care of Rosalba just like Jesus cared for the church. I needed to study the Bible more than ever before because this was a new experience in my life. How much does Jesus love the church and how does He do it? These were very big shoes for me to fill, and I didn't know if I would ever get it right. I was going to do my best to talk to God and read His Word for the answers.

It wasn't long before family relationships were put to the test and this was going to be another challenge. Rosalba worked as a seamstress in Mexico and she was really good at it, but I didn't have a sewing machine at home and I knew nothing of the machines she used in Mexico. She told me she needed a commercial machine like she used before. I looked up those machines and found one that was called commercial and cost $2,000, but I didn't have this money to buy it. My uncle Leland asked me if he could help purchase it for me as a gift to her. I paid half and he paid the other half. Rosalba was extremely happy, because now she saw a way to help me pay our bills. I made enough money for what I was accustomed to as a single guy, but the cost of marriage was more than what I was making to cover my debts and her needs.

One of my cousins was going to get married and asked Rosalba if she would sew her wedding dress. She agreed to do so, but told her it would cost her $100 for the materials and the labor. This was a very cheap price to pay for the dress she wanted, because it involved a lot of details and labor. Rosalba finished the dress and gave it to her, but my cousin didn't pay her. I made the mistake of asking my uncle Leland what to do, and I put him in a difficult position. He now had to defend his son or the wife of his nephew. He chose his son, of course, and began verbally attacking me and Rosalba by trying to tell her hateful things about my past. Little did he know that she already knew about my past and he was only showing her how mean he could be. I quickly went to the bank and borrowed the $1,000 he paid for half of the sewing machine, and gave it to him. I might have owed him my respect, but Rosalba didn't owe him anything.

The big problem now was not the $100 for the dress, but instead how mean my family appeared to Rosalba through my uncle. Rosalba initially liked them, but now she was trying to protect me and she could only see my uncle as a mean individual and didn't want anything to do with them anymore.

Once again, abuse had come into her life, this time through my uncle's mean words, and she was going to do anything she could to avoid more by not being with them. The worst part was that now she viewed my family as abusive, and what else could she see? Something was offered to her as a gift to make money, but the person who helped buy the gift wanted her to work for free and buy the material for the dress for free. She worked about 100 hours to make this dress perfect and now she only had grief to show for it. Once again, we had to learn to leave something else at the feet of the cross of Christ, because we didn't know how to deal with this.

Sad to say, a close relationship with my uncle was now limited because I wasn't going to put Rosalba in a continued situation where he could tell her hateful things about my past, which Rosalba already knew. I didn't want her to see anymore how hateful my family could be, so we stayed away from this part of my family on purpose, so we could leave it at the cross. I wasn't sorry for this decision I made because I was responsible for my wife to God, and He was not going to hold anybody but me responsible for her. I needed Rosalba to accept me as I was and not how someone wanted to program her to think. I had no secrets from Rosalba, and she knew all about my use of drugs when I was younger and the fact that I didn't do them anymore.

With this problem now out of the way, we enjoyed our seclusion from them and focused on our new Hispanic church family in Hennessey. These are wonderful people, and pastor Ramon Alemon was really in step with the Word of God. I still had trouble understanding his sermons, but I understood more every day. He preached slower and didn't use difficult words in Spanish, which made it easier for me to learn.

Now that I didn't spend time with my family, I started spending more time learning to play the guitar. I needed to spend time praising God and this was something I liked to do. Once in a while I learned a love song in Spanish and serenaded Rosalba when I got off work. I loved her and even if I didn't understand the words to the love songs or Christian songs in Spanish, I knew she loved them. One time when I was working the evening shift, I got home at 1:00am and got out my guitar and started singing to her. Rosalba woke up and looked at me and told me to be quiet. Ouch!

What I didn't know and realize at the time was that Rosalba was still terrified to be home alone in the morning, but three times as much when I worked at night. She would open all the blinds and turn on all the lights while I was gone. Every insect or animal sound would frighten her and she would hide in the bedroom until I got home. She couldn't sleep at all until I got home from work, and this night all she wanted to do was sleep once I got home and started taking a shower. When I got out of the shower and dressed for bed, she had fallen into a deep sleep and was frustrated due to her exhaustion. My heart hurt a little bit because it seemed she rejected my serenade, but that would be okay. I put my guitar up, read some of the Bible, prayed, and went to bed.

The mornings were great when I could wake up and know she was beside me in bed. I enjoyed being with her during the day and at night, and this was all that was important to me. I enjoyed being with her.

This enjoyment was about to change our lives further before we even planned on it. I had been praying for God to do with us as He desired, but also to provide Rosalba a way to overcome the hurdles she had to face in this new world. She wanted to start taking classes in Spanish with a lady named Mary. Mary Ester was a retired missionary that lived in Fairview, OK and gave free English classes to students. She spoke fluent Spanish. The classes were in Fairview, OK and about 17 miles from where we lived. The main problem with this was that she doesn't know how to drive. I had to teach her how to drive so she could get her license. I took her out to the quarry at work where she would be able to learn how to drive a standard without injuring anybody but me. As I drove the pickup in the quarry, I showed and explained to her the do's and don'ts of driving and operating a standard. I asked her if she understood my Spanish and my instructions, and she confirmed that she did. I parked the pickup about halfway up on a hill with a pond at the bottom. I told her that if she didn't learn how to clutch, then we would probably roll into the pond. You might call this cruel, but I call it motivation because sometimes the most difficult thing about learning is overcoming the fear in the situation you are facing.

CHAPTER 12

THE BIRTH OF OUR DAUGHTER

Throughout the next six months, we enjoyed our time together and Mary Ester and I continued to teach her English as Rosalba helped me with my Spanish. She had learned how to drive our pickup and needed to go for her driving tests. She was nervous for the obvious reasons, but more so for her lack of understanding the English language. We drove to Enid for the tests she would have to perform. When we arrived at our appointed time, we found the officer who was to give her the test was a very large man. She was nervous to begin with, but now she is scared. The officer was polite and this helped as Rosalba began the testing. He handed her the test with the questions she had to answer, but much to her surprise all the questions were in English. She had been told by a lady at church that she would be able to take the tests in Spanish. She looked at me for help and the officer saw this and told me I could do nothing to help her. Now I was nervous for Rosalba. It turned out that the test was a multiple answer type and this meant all she had to do was understand what she was reading. She didn't have to write anything in English, and this seemed to ease her fears a little. She was nervous, so in her panic her understanding of English wavered as she read the questions. The officer must have noticed her nervousness and felt sorry for her, because as she began to circle the letter a on the first question, he asked her, "Are you sure?" He repeated this until she picked the right answer. She made it through the written part, but still had to pass the driving part of the test. The officer wouldn't allow me to go with them as she performed the driving test, and maybe this made it easier for her. She passed and now all she had to do was complete her photo and get her license to drive. The officer must have seen in her the same inward beauty that I had seen in her and fell in love with her character as I had.

God used this officer to help her pass this test, but another test lay around the corner. Rosalba woke up one morning and she felt nauseous, so when I returned in the afternoon from work, we drove to see the doctor. We found out that she was now pregnant, which was causing the nauseous feelings she was experiencing. I had been praying for several months for our future family and had asked God for a girl first. If she had to go through the nine months with being sick, in pain, and the compromising things happening to her body, then she should have a girl first. Having a baby was a big learning curve for both of us because of the emotions and cravings for the weirdest food at the strangest times. I still cannot understand some of the things we experienced together during these nine months. I'm sure most parents can relate to some of the things that we did during this time.

This moment in time was scary for me as well. The problem was the fact that I knew nothing about being a parent, much less a loving and caring father. I really had no example in my life because my mother and father had separated when I was five years old. What's the difference in being a "sperm donor," a casual convenient father, versus a real loving father? This was a big issue for me because I knew now I was going to be responsible directly to God for my own life, my relationship as a husband to my wife, and now a father. Was this now triple jeopardy? I had immersed myself in the Word of God, and I couldn't find anything written concerning the relationship between a father and daughter. Could I use the same guidelines that God gave me concerning the relationship between a father and son?

Rosalba continued to experience nausea from the pregnancy and frequented the bathroom on a regular basis. There was very little I could do to help relieve the symptoms she was experiencing. Thank God, I had a strong stomach and I could at least hold Rosalba's hair as she did her thing. I felt so helpless and I could see those beautiful brown eyes staring deep into mine as the unspoken question burned into my brain. *Why did you do this to me?* I was guilty, of course, but it was through a pure and blessed method that God had created, and I was just doing my part. I didn't know if she saw it this way, but I hoped she would. We were both old enough and mature enough physically to make this decision, and it was holy according to God, so I felt good about this part. I still was struggling with the extra responsibility coming my way. Spiritually I prayed continually for God's direction about being the child of God He wanted me to be, the husband God wanted me to be, and now the father He expected me to be. I felt so lost even though I was now twenty-nine years old.

Whoever says they are ready to be a parent should really consider God's definition of "Father." I felt so inadequate at this moment. It hadn't been that long since I had to face the fact that financially I was not prepared to be married, and now I was going to be married with a child on the way. I prayed to God and asked for His guidance concerning this, and I had to consider the things I had and the family I was getting ready to receive from

God. I already sold my brand-new Bass boat to pay for the wedding and costs. Now, I had to choose to sell the 1965 Ford Mustang hardtop or the 1965 Ford Mustang convertible I owned. My wife was scared of the water because she didn't know how to swim, so deciding to sell the boat earlier was the easiest of the three to sell. The cars were a tougher choice for me. I love the 1965 Mustangs. The money from the sale of the boat helped me pay our utilities, and by now my wife had learned that dollars are not pesos. We were okay as a married couple. We lived week to week on my income and she would occasionally make tamales or enchiladas for me to take to work and sell for extra income. Rosalba was driving to Fairview three times a week to study English with Mary Ester and she was learning every day. She continued to watch "Plasa Sesame" every day to help her learn how to pronounce words in English. She was so driven to be the best she could be. I had rarely seen anyone try so hard to be the best Christian, American, wife, or mother as she did.

Seeing all that Rosalba sacrificed to be all this motivated me to sell my 1965 Ford Mustang convertible. This money would help us pay for the doctor and hospital and future diapers. I felt a little more financial freedom even though I lost a part of me in the car, but it was worth it. As the nausea continued, I helped Rosalba follow the doctor's direction concerning the morning sickness. I fed her crackers and Seven Up to help her, but she wanted her normal diet of Mexican food with the hot peppers and every-thing else. As she found out on her own when I was at work, this did not help her situation.

I had always thought Rosalba was so beautiful and couldn't be more beautiful. I was wrong. She had a glow to her now that seemed to radiate her beauty. She was now not only my wife but the mother to our daughter. I always presumed she was more beautiful because she knew she was going to be a mother and not just a wife, and this would help fill her time at home and ease her fears of being alone. This beauty was more than that. She was a product of God blessing my life, and inside her was something also of His creation. She now had a wonderful growing and breathing force of life that only God could perform so perfectly. She glowed with a beauty that I never will forget.

I had always known the child Rosalba was carrying would be a beau-tiful girl. I never doubted this since I began to pray for it. God had chosen to say "yes" to my prayers, but Rosalba always believed she would give me a son first. It was so like her to always put her desires behind what she thought I wanted. This always made it easy for me to go all the way to make sure she continuously knew I loved her with all my heart.

When we had the first ultrasound performed on this creation growing in her body, Rosalba was scared but also excited. I sensed it in how she breathed and fidgeted around the house. I held her close to me and shared my excitement and reminded her of all that God had helped us overcome just to arrive at this moment. I drove her to the doctor in Okeene for the test. Our doctor could sense her nerves, and his bedside manner was so perfect. He was gentle with his words as well as his touch. He shared her excitement as he asked how she was feeling and her nausea, diet, and exercise program. He gave her a complete check-up and then called in the specialist to perform the ultrasound.

I saw the results of the ultrasound as it was being performed, and I didn't know what Rosalba was watching more: the tool being passed over her abdomen, the screen, or my face? I believe she was watching my face to see how I would respond when I found out it was a boy. To her surprise, I knew and the specialist performing the tests knew it was a baby girl. Now it was my turn to watch her face to see how she would respond when she heard it was a baby girl. Would she be disappointed to know she hadn't given me the son she believed I wanted first? Would she be ecstatic to find out it would be a girl she could teach to be the beautiful woman that God had created her to be? Would she see a girl she could spend her time with, fixing hair, sewing dresses, painting fingernails, etc.?

That time came and the doctor came in with the pictures of the ultrasound. Rosalba's anticipation was growing because she couldn't get me or the specialist to comment on what we had seen. The doctor put the picture on the lighted screen and showed us everything on our baby but the sex. As the excitement continued, he looked into Rosalba's big brown eyes and told her, "Rosalba, you are going to have a healthy baby girl."

Rosalba glanced at me as if to say, "I'm sorry," but her look was radiant when she found out God had given her the desire of her heart. We had always believed that if we were obedient to God, He would give us the desires of our hearts. Obviously in her heart she wanted a daughter, even though she wanted to give me a son. God is good all time, and all the time God is good. I remember she looked at me and asked me, "Is this all right with you?" I told her that all the time I had been praying for God to give her a daughter so she could raise her in a safe environment, something that she didn't have as a child. I prayed God would give her a daughter so she could enjoy the things that all mothers and daughters enjoyed together. These are things that boys and fathers simply don't understand or appreciate.

Once Rosalba realized I was okay with a daughter, her face was illuminated with joy and we thanked the doctor and left. I knew she couldn't wait to call her mother, family, and friends to share the test results. I was so thankful to God that He chose to say "yes" to my petition for a baby girl first. Now don't misunderstand me, because I did want a son as well, but since she was going to carry the child and take care of her, it only seemed the right thing to ask of God.

I felt a peace in my heart because the place where I worked was so close to our home and Rosalba. I couldn't wait to get home and hear her explain to me how our baby girl was moving in her. She would look into my eyes with wonder and gently grab my hand and place it on her abdomen and say, "Do you feel her?" At first, I could feel nothing, but she would encourage me to be patient and wait. Before I knew it, I could feel the baby moving around. It was such a blessing to experience this creation of God and the awesome privilege we were experiencing to be a part of it.

I began a practice from that moment. I would get my guitar and sing songs to our baby girl. I waited to see if her mom could feel her moving. Sometimes she would move more with one song versus another. It was a blessing to experience this knowledge that from the womb, a child could hear or feel your love. Sometimes I would get a book and simply lie beside Rosalba and read to our baby girl, and I would get the same response. Our baby seemed to like the upbeat stories more. She would continue to move as I read the story of **Beauty and The Beast**, or **Cinderella.** Sometimes I would simply lie next to my wife and place my hand on her abdomen and talk father to daughter. The baby always seemed to move when I talked to her.

We continued to go to the doctor on the appointed times during the last three months and everything went well. Thank God. Rosalba was getting more nervous as that ninth month approached. She had no family near to be with her as the time approached. I noticed this and arranged for her mother Maria to come and stay with us as this time neared. I told Rosalba I would do everything I could to make this moment the best that I could. I knew she feared the moment of birth and the pain that came with it, and I didn't think she wanted to hear me tell her it was all going to be all right. What did a man, including her own husband, know about having a baby? This was a very good question. The correct answer is: NOTHING. All I could do was continue praying, talk to her, soothe her, and occasionally give her a foot or back massage. Was this enough? I felt useless as the delivery time approached, and I was sure Rosalba knew this as well. Once again, she spent more time encouraging me that everything was going to be okay and she was okay. What a beautiful woman and person. Even though she was scared of what was to come as she gave birth to our daughter, she was more concerned about me than herself. I had truly been blessed by God.

Once again, I found myself in a life moment when I was totally helpless and lacking the knowledge or wisdom to do or be what I needed to be. How could I learn to put God first, love, appreciate, and care for my Rosalba second, and love, care, and cherish my daughter third? How was I supposed to know how a father and daughter relationship was supposed to be? I was nervous myself. I wasn't sure if I had my personal relationship right or my Christ-to-bride relationship correct at the same time. Now I was about to have the father and daughter relationship coming around the bend. I found myself asking that familiar question once again. *Now what, God?*

I loved my talks with God. He might not have responded as I desired, but He always gave me peace when I approached a "NOW WHAT?" moment, whether in a Word of God moment or that still, calming peace that came as I prayed and trusted in Him. This might seem strange to others, but once I found out the perfect father to son relationship in God, it has become more real to me every day.

How could I comfort Rosalba during this beautiful but scary moment if I doubted Him myself? She needed Him more than me at this moment, and it was important for me to realize this all the time. I was not God, nor would I ever be. He could know, do, and see things that I would never be able to experience. I would never know the mother and daughter or mother to son relationship. How could I teach her something I would never know? I would never know the experience of carrying a child inside me for nine months. God could see inside her heart and her body at the same time and take care of them both, and this was what I needed now. I was not ready for this moment.

Rosalba is so beautiful. If she gave birth to our daughter and the baby turned out to be as beautiful as her, how would I love them and protect them? I knew she would win my heart as did my God and Rosalba. How would I share my heart with them when I was supposed to give it all to God? I needed to spend more time with God because I didn't know how to do this. Love Him with everything I was, but love them at the same time. This was when I wished I had a Christian father or even a normal father to advise me. *How do I do this, Father?*

I knew this would require me to change my prayer time on a continual basis because my Rosalba would need me more and now my daughter was waiting to wrap me around her beautiful finger as well. Mentally and physically I thought I was prepared to be a father, but spiritually I was in want. Later I would find out that I was lacking mentally and physically as well.

Rosalba's mom Maria arrived and I was glad. Her mom is such a beautiful lady in all aspects of a Proverbs 31 woman. She had given birth to eleven children, and Rosalba was her youngest child. There seems to be a bond between the first and last child born to most woman. I cannot explain it, nor do I wish to try. Rosalba had always had a special love for her mom, and it provided me a peace that I cannot explain just to have her there with us. Her mom was in her seventies but she was always moving. She helped with the cleaning and cooking that Rosalba was highly focused on.

Extremely focused on! Nothing could ever be out of its place or she could not rest. Even when she was supposedly at rest, she would be knitting or doing something else with her hands. Her mind was never at rest, and I was sure she was wondering if I was going to be a better father to our daughter than her father was to her. She was thinking of all the things she was going to do with our daughter when that time came. She was hoping more than anything else that our baby would be born a healthy child. I was sure she was also worried about the pain that comes with childbirth.

Rosalba would never discuss her deepest fears or thoughts with me, maybe because she didn't want me to worry over her. This was difficult for me many times because it would affect my prayer life. How could I ask God to care for her or provide her peace if she never would share her deepest fears or thoughts? I thought about this and realized that God already knew. I didn't know, but He did. I guessed I would have to live with this whether I liked it or not. It seemed strange to me, because I'd always tried to be as open as possible to her. Maybe I had it wrong and she had it right. We were supposed to take our problems up to God, but somehow, I felt left out. Something seemed out of order because this was supposed to the chain of command that God established. Wife goes to husband and God, while the husband goes to God for himself and his wife. This was something that I would have to figure out when God allowed me to do so.

I snapped out of my thoughts when Rosalba told me the pains had started and we needed to go to the hospital. I had prepared a suitcase with her clothing and personal care items for this moment, and now we had to go. I wasn't the panicky husband like some we had witnessed, but I did take care to help her to the car with her mom so we could drive the twenty minutes to the hospital. We didn't have cell phones at this time, so I called from our home phone to advise the doctor that we were in route to the hospital. We arrived at the hospital and they checked us into a pre-delivery room until the doctor declared it was time for delivery. It took about twenty-three hours for that magic but painful moment to arrive. For Rosalba, it must have seemed like an eternity, but also an eternity she was willing to wait to avoid the most painful part of the delivery. We both were glad her mom Maria was there.

That moment came. Our beautiful daughter no longer wanted to wait for her first glimpse of the outside. As the labor pains increased, I held my Rosalba's hand and tried my best to encourage her that it was about over. I still don't know if this helped, but I was trying my best to help. I didn't know a lady so small had that much strength in her body. I thought she was going to squeeze my hand off at times, but I knew it was nothing compared to the pain she was enduring. I wondered how long she would have to endure these birthing pains, and prayed to God for help as she went through this.

Before we knew it, the doctor advised her to push one more time, and as she did, we heard the cry of our precious daughter. While Rosalba recovered from such a painful experience, the doctor and nurse made our daughter more presentable. Rosalba's mom Maria was asking me, "What does she look like? What color is her hair? Is she okay?" I could only hold Rosalba's hand and remind her that I hadn't seen her myself and the nurse would bring her shortly. The moment came and I couldn't believe my eyes. She was so small but beautiful, with these same big brown eyes as her mother. I was a little jealous as they handed her to Rosalba for the first time. To this day I'm not sure of the tears flowing down my wife's face at that moment. Were they tears of happiness? Were they tears of finality? Maybe they were only tears of praise as she saw God had given us a healthy child. I believe the tears included all three of these.

Rosalba took our daughter in her arms ever so gently and talked to her in Spanish. Who knew how long she had practiced all the first things she wanted to tell her beautiful daughter? Now was the time and I was wondering if I would ever get my time to tell her the first things I wanted to share with her. Our daughter had other ideas in her own little mind, because she was hungry and looking for that source of milk that she somehow knew was hers. No directions or anything. She squirmed until she could find that source and then she was happy. I would have to wait some more before I could hold her in my arms. In a way this was good, because I was nervous that I would break her or something. She was so beautiful but so small. For the time being I was happy to see her clinging to her mom's breast and getting that much-needed milk.

I took the time to kiss Rosalba and remind her that I loved and admired her for everything that she was and had become. In my mind and my heart, I thanked God for this awesome privilege to be a part of His creation. What a miracle God had given me with this opportunity to be a part of it, witnessing the whole thing with my own eyes. I looked at my wife and daughter and they both were sleeping. They both were exhausted after this nine-month journey and I decided to wait for that moment to hold them both in my arms. I just wondered what we were going to call this beautiful girl, because Rosalba never spent much time thinking about girl names. For a long time, she was waiting for a boy. God would help her decide on a perfect name.

CHAPTER 13

THE BIRTH OF OUR SON

The next two hours, I just watched in silence as both wife and daughter slept, until Rosalba had to go to the bathroom. This was my chance to hold this sweet princess in my arms for the first time. Rosalba got out of bed and handed our daughter to me, showing me how to hold her and assuring me that I wasn't going to break her. I wasn't as sure as she was, but I wasn't going to let this "first" pass me by. I cradled our girl's head in my left hand and the rest of her body in my right hand. She was so small and so beautiful, with a head full of thin brown hair, and as she looked up to me with a smile, my heart melted. I wasn't sure why she was smiling, though. Was it because I was lighter in color than her mom? Was it because even now she was planning on how to wrap my heart around her little finger? Maybe it was just because I was funny looking to her. It didn't matter, because her laughter reminded me of Abraham and Sarah in the Old Testament. I remembered the story of how Sarah laughed when the angel told her she was going to have a child in her old age. I imagined that Sarah would be a beautiful and fitting name for this small and beautiful bundle of miracle God has provided us. The name Sarahi is of Hebrew origin, meaning "PRINCESS" and falling into the category of royalty.

I looked into her big brown eyes and whispered the name, "Sarahi," and she laughed and seemed to jump in excitement. As Rosalba returned from the bathroom, I suggested the name SARAH and Rosalba added the "I" on the end to give us the name "SARAHI." "KIM," her middle name, means "leader" and "keep it moving." This fit her personality perfectly and she has lived this out throughout her life. The Koreans define the name "KIM" as golden, precious, and rare.

So, with the name now determined, we filled out the birth certificate and the doctor checked my Rosalba and Sarahi one more time before they dismissed us from the hospital. It was a blessing to have Rosalba's mom Maria with us, and it really helped Rosalba during this trial and birthing period. It helped take a large load of uselessness off of my shoulders. We all went home and planned to now be a family in God, and with clear evidence from the beginning to know that He had been with us all the time. It was hard to return to work with both my queen Rosalba and my princess Sarahi at home, but the bills had to be paid and there were now more mouths to feed. Not to mention the price of diapers and formula as time went on. I held Sarahi on my chest for the longest time. She would just lay there and enjoy being with me, or just listening to my heart beat. I didn't really know why, but she enjoyed this spot and I enjoyed her being there. Before too long, she was walking and trying to help her mom in everything.

After this first year of Sarahi's life, my Rosalba once again had the nauseous feelings she had before. At first, she didn't share this with me until it became more frequent and she couldn't hide it. I made an appointment with our doctor, and when that day arrived we found out we were going to have another child. I had never shared with my wife my private request to God for a son. I wanted this to be a personal request from me to God. I wanted to live out a father to son relationship. I wanted to experience a love for a son with no boundaries or limits. Clearly, I didn't have the awesome power of God, or the ability to be everywhere, and know everything as He did, but maybe I could experience loving my son above and beyond human limitations.

My lovely Rosalba was now wondering if I was going to make her like her mom. She had no desire to have eleven children like her mom Maria. She didn't even want to have one in the beginning. To avoid the pain of childbirth, she was leaning towards adoption, but changed her mind once we were married and praying for a family. She was okay with one and only one. Fair or not, my prayers to God had not changed because I wanted the opportunity to share this father to son moment. Was it really possible to love my son the same as God loved His Son? Of course, I hoped my son would come without the hanging on the cross moment. I knew the child now growing in Rosalba was a boy, and I was excited but nervous as well. You know, some people say, "Be careful what you ask for because you might get it." Was my son going to be like Jesus was to God, or was he going to be a rebel as I was?

Time went on as I enjoyed my beautiful Rosalba and daughter Sarahi. I got more time with Sarahi as Rosalba dealt with her role as Christian, wife, and mother. I had absolutely no problem with this, because I had all kinds of ideas of what we were going to do together. Sometimes I would read to her, play with her, or we would go outside and I would show her the wonderful things that God had created. She was always inquisitive and willing to learn as I spent time with her.

Rosalba was sure she would have another daughter because most of her sisters had all daughters and few sons. I knew all the time that God would give us a son, but I kept this to myself until that time came. The doctor continued to monitor the progress of the pregnancy as the time got closer. When it was time for the ultrasound, I was probably more nervous than Rosalba. Was I going to shout in excitement as the doctor told us it would be a boy? Was I going to look into my wife's eyes and gauge her reaction when she found out it was indeed a boy? Was she still as excited to give me a son as she initially wanted to do before Sarahi was born?

I watched intently as the technician performed the ultrasound on my wife's abdomen. Would I be able to see what was needed to determine if it was a boy or not? As the instrument passed over her body, I could see God had answered my prayer. We were going to have a son to go with our beautiful princess Sarahi. I didn't shout out, dance, or do amazing feats of gymnastics, but Rosalba was studying my reactions and I knew she could tell this baby in her body was a boy. Without hearing anything from the technician or the doctor, she looked into my eyes and asked me if I was happy. My response to her was, "I'm happier." I didn't think it would be possible, but I was indeed happier. I now could experience a father to daughter relationship and a father to son relationship. Maybe now I could understand how God could love His daughters and sons so much that He would give His Son to die on the cross for me.

I had already learned so much about the wonderful feeling of walking hand in hand with my Sarahi. I looked forward to it every day. I waited to have her look into my eyes and ask me questions or to show me something. This melted my heart every time. I couldn't imagine it would be any different with a son, and I was looking forward to this moment to see for myself. I continued to thank God for our son, and asked Him to continue to bless Rosalba and our son as His creation process continued.

Once again, I arranged for Rosalba's mom Maria to be with us during the birth of our son. She was such a blessing for us during the birth of Sarahi, and she was a necessity for Rosalba now. The time came and the labor pains commenced. I believed Rosalba was more scared now than before, because now she knew from personal experience the pain she was going to go through. All I could do was the same as before. I asked God to be with us and help all of us during this creation moment. I held her hand as before and encouraged her that hopefully it would be over soon. As the delivery commenced, the doctor noticed a potential problem because the umbilical cord was wrapped around the baby's neck and pulling him lower in the birthing canal. The blood pressure of both of us rose at the same time, and I lifted my face to God for help. *Now what, God? Did You lead us to this point to have a problem like this?*

The doctor saw the concerned expressions on both of our faces and assured us that everything would be okay. He would have to manipulate our son's body so the umbilical cord could be moved from around his neck. He completed this procedure, but told us the position of the baby's body was low in the birthing canal and would require a procedure to fix the damage that occurred during birth. Within a few minutes, our son's head popped out. Due to the doctor's need to repair Rosalba, the nurse cleaned the baby and placed him into my hands. I don't know now if I felt elated or guilty because I got to hold him before Rosalba. Due to the circumstances, I had no choice because Rosalba needed further attention from the doctor.

Just as with Sarahi, this moment was so special. I wasn't as worried that I might break this one as I was with Sarahi, but I was very careful and gentle. Our son also had his mother's deep brown beautiful eyes and he had her deep black hair as well. He was his mother except for the mouth and the slight tilt of his eyes, which he got from me. I studied him as he studied me during this time. I told him I loved him and welcomed him into this world just as I had done with Sarahi. The doctor finished his procedure with Rosalba and they brought her back to the room. I gently handed our son to her so he could be near the person who had cared for him the last nine months.

I asked Rosalba which name she wanted to give our son. She looked into my eyes and stated she wanted him to have my name. I asked her why and she said, "I hope he will love his wife and family the same way you love us." My heart melted, not because of the name but because my wife knew without a doubt that I loved her and our children. This meant so much to me, because this was the beginning of my journey as a "father" and a continuation of "groom" to my wife. The two most important things I wanted to experience the most in this life. How did I compare to God's love towards His Son, and how did I compare to Christ's love for His bride the church? The name John means "God is Gracious."

My thoughts returned to the present moment to see my son John Jr. had also found the source of nutrition at his mother's breast. This was such a beautiful reminder of God's creation. It seemed he got his fill and began to cough up the milk he had consumed. This concerned me because it wasn't normal. We later learned that he had difficulty breathing as he swallowed the milk and was suffering from a mild case of bronchitis. We had to feed him formula and I got the privilege of milking Rosalba with a breast pump. This was a little awkward but necessary for her and for John Jr. He needed his mother's milk for the antibodies to help him overcome the bronchitis and other potential illnesses and she needed relief from the pain in her breasts from the built-up milk that was not being used.

For the following three months, we battled with this bronchitis problem and it seemed to get worse. I found myself asking that same question: *Now what, God? I have never ceased to pray before or during this trial and YOU have yet to answer me.* During this time, I began to have pain in my abdomen and had to leave work to see a doctor. I went to the clinic early and had to wait on a doctor to show up for work. I woke up in a hospital room and learned I had passed out in the waiting room as I waited on the doctor.

When I felt better because of the pain medication they had given me, Rosalba walked in with our John Jr. in her arms and Sarahi by her side. Rosalba was crying and said the doctor wouldn't look at our son John Jr. He had difficulty breathing. I asked her why they would not examine him and she told me it was because I was on a "black list." I was up to this challenge, feeling invincible because of the pain medication, and I went to the office in my hospital gown. I wasn't concerned with what might be showing in the back side at this moment. In my medicated state, I asked what this "black list" was all about. They told me I had never paid for an EKG examination performed on me a year ago and the bill was $172. I asked them to look at the file and examine the age of the patient and their social security number. The name John Wilson is a very common name and I was sure that was the problem. They opened the file and found that this patient on the "black list" was a seventy-two-year-old John Wilson who lived in Hennessey, and was a friend of mine. They apologized and removed me from the "black list." I recovered enough to realize my behind felt a cold breeze and quickly closed the back of my hospital gown.

I composed myself and took Rosalba, Sarahi, and ill son John Jr. back to the clinic for evaluation. The doctor dismissed his illness as an allergy and tried to dismiss us. I told his nurse we were not going to leave until the doctor further evaluated the problem. I told the nurse John Jr. could barely breathe, and I could feel his body rattle as he tried to breathe. The nurse told the doctor that this child is not all right and he needed to pay more attention to his diagnosis. He ordered an x-ray on my John Jr.'s lungs and found he had pneumonia. Soon my son was in the same room with me, in an oxygen tent and on medication to remove the phlegm that had filled up 75 percent of his lungs.

Rosalba was a fighter, but now she needed help because her husband and son were in the hospital together. She wanted to be with us, but needed someone to help with Sarahi. Her sister Gloria brought her mother-in-law from Nebraska to help her with Sarahi as Rosalba spent time with us in the hospital. They had diagnosed my problem as an ulcer, but they were wrong about that as well. It turned out to be my gall bladder, which had to be removed at a later date at a different hospital. John Jr.'s lungs eventually cleared up after many days and nights of placing him on our legs and patting him on the back to move out the phlegm. At eight months, he overcame this problem, but missed out on most of the breast milk he needed. Thank you, God, for helping us during a very difficult time. Once again, I had found myself in a situation that was above and beyond my control and God stepped in and helped us. Finally, we were all home as a family and I appreciated my relationship with God, Rosalba, and our children. I thanked Gloria's mom for all her help as she left for Dallas with her family. She didn't even know us but was there to help us.

John Jr. formed a relationship with me that couldn't be explained. One day, Rosalba called me at work and told me that he had been crying all morning and nothing her or her mom Maria had tried could calm him down. It was lunch time and I drove home and held him in my arms. Within five minutes, he fell asleep. Much to Rosalba's disgust and gratitude, John was now sleeping and comfortable. I returned to work and finished the day. While working, I reflected on all the times I would be going through a difficult time and many people who cared about me offered their advice. The advice was good many times, but it would not calm my mind or my fears. Only after spending time with my Heavenly Father would I find the peace that surpassed our understanding. Was this what my John Jr. had just experienced? Just being with his earthly father provided him with the assurance that he needed to know that everything was going to be okay?

I really enjoyed being a part of a family. Even though the responsibilities increased, God never left my side. Sometimes I imagined I heard Him say, "This is all I want from you. I want you to desire to be with me as I desire to be with you." I began to live in this moment, and even though there was more to do, I couldn't wait to spend more time with God. I sang hymns and choruses with Rosalba and studied the Bible with her. This helped me learn more about God, even if I was reading in Spanish now. Before bed, we both would go spend time with our children and read Bible stories and answer questions. We would also make up imaginary stories and allow them both to create their own characters. Before long, they would be in a deep sleep with smiles on their faces. The world seemed to be good at this moment. Rosalba seemed to be happy and both children seemed to be secure with their parents.

I enjoyed spending time with both of our children, and playing games with them was always something I enjoyed. It didn't matter what we were doing as long as they knew I always wanted to be with them. It didn't hurt when I had to sell my 1965 Mustang Coupe to help pay for my son to come into this world. The cost of diapers, formula, and me being in the hospital left me little reason for having a car like this. I sold the car and paid the hospital and had extra to cover the cost for four people now instead of only one. It made my life easier as well, because now I only had my family to care for. This was now my life in God, and I was more than willing to do my best to get it right. I had had many examples in how to do it wrong.

I remember walking with my Rosalba and our children one night. We were passing a herd of cattle near the house. I would "moo" at them and they would "moo" in return. All of a sudden, the bull ran up to the fence and gave me an earful. I didn't know what I said, but Rosalba and kids didn't want me to repeat it. It was scary for all of us. After a couple of days, I had convinced the children that I really could not speak to the cows. I'm still not sure they believed me.

I realized just how lovely Rosalba was as a mother as well. I would come home and both the kids would be playing in the dirt and as happy as could be. When it was raining, she would bring a little dirt into the entryway in the house and let them play with the dirt there. Once they finished playing, she would give them a bath and clean up the dirt off the floor. While doing all this, she managed to prepare the next meal for the day. This had to be heaven on earth with a lovely, talented wife, a great mother, a great manager of her home, and two beautiful children. I actually enjoyed being alive for the first time in my life. I actually felt like I was useful for something. Rosalba wanted to be with me and both the children couldn't wait for me to get home from work.

I wondered if this was what God looked for in us as well: a bride who wanted to be with Him, and His children waiting in anticipation for Him to return to spend time with them and talk to them. I spent a long time reflecting on this, and I believe this was what God was trying to teach me through Rosalba, Sarahi, and John. All I had to do was try my best not to screw it up.

This wasn't easy, because the hospital bill came for my son and for me. I had lost a week of work and the insurance didn't pay very well. I still had to pay for the deductible for both of us and this used up all the money I had left from selling my car. It always seemed to happen this way. We seem to reach a learning level in God and another test came our way. *Now what, God?*

Although I believed in God, it didn't mean I made godly choices. We had to get another vehicle for our family and the safety seats for the children, but my two-seat Toyota truck wasn't the answer. We went looking for another car that would accommodate all of us, safety seats and all. I knew at the time I couldn't afford the car payment and insurance at the same time, but I needed something dependable for our family. The car we bought wasn't new, but it was new to us. The Toyota Camry wagon was a good vehicle for our family. Now all I had to do was pay for it. We were not getting any extra time at work and my checks were smaller than normal. It was very difficult to do my best and still fall short in my efforts. I began to ask God, "Where are You?"

I put myself in this situation and somehow now it was God's fault? I asked for a family and I bought the car, but somehow it was now God's fault I couldn't pay my bills? I tried my best not to let Rosalba see this was bothering me, but she could read me like a book. She tried her best to help me by making Mexican food for me to take to work and sell to the people I worked with. She was very helpful as she made the household function with little extra money. I didn't know how she did it, but without her I would have been lost.

I felt sorry for myself while forgetting that I had a great God, Jesus who died to save me, a beautiful loving wife, a princess for a daughter, and my own son. I had a prince in John Jr. God gave me who would eventually carry out my legacy. What kind of legacy was I leaving now for my son? Would I give up and feel sorry for myself every time life got difficult?

I read the Bible in my quiet time and asked God what He was doing in my life. He simply showed me that just because I followed Him, that didn't mean life would not be difficult at times. I learned something that I had to share with my wife and children. I first had to learn it myself. This was going to be difficult, because I really didn't want to hear that I served an all-powerful God, who knew everything, and could be in all places, but would let me figure this one out on my own. As a new father, I could never imagine not jumping in to help out my children in every difficult situation. It didn't matter if it was their fault or not. I wanted to be "Super Dad." It was very difficult for me to accept the fact that God wasn't going to help me out the way I wanted Him to.

What I didn't know at the time was that this was a lesson I should have paid more attention to. *Now what, God? You have given me a family and I can't teach them this kind of "tough love." I love them too much and I cannot say no.*

118

CHAPTER 14

THE CHILDREN LEAVING FOR COLLEGE

The time came that Rosalba and I had been preoccupied with for eighteen years. It's strange that parents spend so much time doing our best to prepare our children to be independent and motivated, and when it's time for them to do so, we wonder why we did so. In our minds we want them to grow up and have lives of their own, but in our hearts, we don't ever want them to leave. We cherished the times growing up with Sarahi and John Jr. As they grew up we were able to enjoy their passions with them. We would always play games with them, share story times with them, help them with homework, and attend their sporting events. Everyday was wonderful as we left them at school but not without praying together first. They both excelled in school and developed their own strengths and weaknesses. It was a blessing just to be with them to encourage them as they grew older. As they grew we had to deal with the normal bumps and bruises. We had to deal with racism because people love to hate and not practice the love God teaches us. It was difficult for Rosalba, Sarahi, and John Jr. as they faced this problem. The only answer I could give was, don't worry about it. God created us all and saw that it was good. We had the same trials as most parents. Sarahi and John Jr. both had friends that liked to party thus making alcohol and drugs a topic that we were challenged with. Sarahi handled this better than John Jr. After the 7th grade John Jr. decided that he was happy just being average. He would make all A's on his tests at school but never wanted to do his homework. The harder we tried to motivate him to be his best he was happy with average. Sarahi seemed to have her focus on school and friendships in a totally different way than John Jr. Her friends were motivated as well to continue improving and being their best. John Jr's friends were more rebellious and less motivated to become anything. It seemed that they were happy just existing. Just don't get in their way or try to stop them from their endless pursuit to be average. God has just revealed to me how my life was before I ask Jesus Christ to come into my heart to forgive my sins. God loved me but couldn't force me to listen to Him or follow His Council. He couldn't make me want to be more than normal or motivate me to do more than exist. This father son petition that I ask God for is now a daily challenge for me and John Jr. and God with me.

Sarahi was preparing to leave for college and Rosalba began the normal discussion most parents have: *Why don't we move to the city where she is going to college? Why don't you quit your job and find another one in the city where she's moving to? What if she never calls? What if she never comes home?*

Then when our daughter was at college, the questions changed to: *I called her and she didn't answer and I wonder if she's okay. Is she okay? What if she has trouble making friends? What if she meets a boy that doesn't know Christ?*

More questions existed than I could perceive, much less an answer. I found myself asking one question only: God, *You gave me eighteen years to teach her your ways. I wonder, did I do it right? Did I teach her all that You wanted me to teach her?* I could understand all the questions milling around in Rosalba's mind but I had no answers to give her. I asked that same question once again: *What now, God?*

I had enjoyed the time God gave me to spend instructing Sarahi, but a part of me didn't want her to leave either. I enjoyed being a part of her adornment. That ring wrapped around her finger that others could see and know without a doubt that her father loves her. I knew that she knew without a doubt that we both loved her with no reservations. I liked the fact that she could show her friends her dad's love wrapped around her finger and let them see that he was indeed her father. I found comfort in knowing that in the future she wouldn't have to struggle with the same questions that I had to deal with: *What is a father? Why did my father leave us? Does my father love me? Did I do something to make him not love me?*

As I wrote this, I realized that these are the same questions many of us ask of God. The reason we do so is because we haven't taken the time to know Him. My daughter took the time and she knew my love for her was real. Not because I was her father, but because I wanted to be with her. I wanted to spend time with her. I wanted to talk to her. I wanted to be involved in her life. I cared about what she was thinking, planning, and scheduling. Every time I had the opportunity, I wanted to be with her in everything she did.

This made it harder, though, as the time came for her to leave for college. It was hard for me personally to not have her here with me, but when I would hear Rosalba cry, just thinking about that moment, made it that much harder for me. It was very difficult for me to find peace from God during this time, and somehow I had to show that peace to my wife and her mother. *How am I going to do this Father God? I don't have the answers. I have barely had a chance to learn how to be a father and now I've got to learn to trust in YOU and remember that Sarahi has always been Your charge, not mine. I can say it and write it, but how do I live it and teach it to my Sarahi and Rosalba?*

Many nights I could hear Rosalba crying and I had nothing to say. I would just wrap my arms around her and ask God to help us during this difficult time. Learning to really let go and learning that God was really "all-knowing," "all-present," and "all powerful."

Life is really difficult at times because we don't ever know God's side of the story. We only know what we experience in our own lives, and many times this has very little to do with God's world.

I had to trust in Him and know that before Sarahi was born, He was there. While she was living with us, He was there. When she left for college, He would also be there. These were three very important things for me to remember, but it still did very little to dry the tears from her mother's eyes. I had no words to keep Rosalba from crying, so I held her close and just whispered for God to help us. I say "us" because inside I was also crying because Sarahi was leaving, but also because I could see her mother's heart hurting so.

The last several weeks went by as we attended the awards ceremonies and the high school graduation. God allowed us to see how He blessed our daughter and allowed us to see how she has taken an interest in her own success. This was what He wanted us to do in her life.

That day came and we loaded up her clothes and other items she needed to begin her college life. Rosalba was busy running back and forth, making sure Sarahi had every little thing that she might need to live in the dormitory. I knew inside she just wanted to go to her room and cry, as they gathered all the little things here and there that had been a close and personal connection between a mother and daughter. I never pretended to understand the bond between a mother and daughter, but I knew there was a lot of pain going on during this process, and the only way Rosalba could avoid the tears was to keep busy.

We left our home to take Sarahi to her new living quarters at college, and the whole trip was very quiet. I knew that if anyone said anything, someone was going to start crying. During this time, I was just asking God to help me be strong during this transition in our lives. I was losing my daughter from my home, but I wasn't losing my daughter. She was still living and breathing. She was just going to fulfil her desires to be a more educated individual.

I could deal with a more intelligent daughter. My biggest concern was her future relationship with Christ. It's very common for most young people to stray from their mom and dads' God and plant their own seeds in life. How would she deal with this transition? I asked God: *How am I to teach her when she's not here. Have we been a good example to her about YOUR grace and love? Will she want to follow the God her mother and I have been following?* I asked God to help me. I asked Him questions in my mind that I already knew the answers to, but I hoped He would change His truths for me. *God, I know You only have sons and daughters, but in my case will You accept granddaughters?*

We finally arrived on the campus and tried to locate the dormitory where Sarahi was to live. The busyness continued so the emotions wouldn't overwhelm any of us, and we carryied boxes full of things and clothing. My lovely wife was so dedicated to organizing everything that I knew this would be an all-day process. She discussed how to move the furniture, the color of the curtains, and even painting the dorm room. She wasn't happy with the small size of the room and the fact that there was no refrigerator, microwave, or stove. How would this skinny daughter of mine survive without all of these amenities? I could see Sarahi's eyes as she looked for some type of salvation from this situation, and suggested that we go to Wal-Mart and buy what we could to help her survive. We made the trip to Wal-Mart and we must have traveled down every aisle in the store, pondering if our daughter would need this or that. Eventually we checked out with two or three carts of things that she couldn't live without, according to her mother. We returned to her dormitory and now we had more things to carry up the stairs to her room. Now we had a new problem. Her room was now smaller than before because now all these things we just bought had to go somewhere.

We toiled for a while as we tried to find a place or way to organize all these things. I had to remind them that we had a schedule to keep so we could take the parents tour of the campus. We had more walking as a student took us through all the facilities that all new students needed to know. I knew Sarahi very well, and I knew she was sad for us as she left, but her excitement for the future was more overwhelming to her at this moment. I believe it is common for most young people to have the desire to leave home and find their own new and exciting world. *Surely mom and dad don't know all that stuff that they have been telling us for all these years. Life is easy and exciting and I don't see all these potential dangers that they have been warning me about for all these years.*

I continuously prayed for her, for God to protect her as she saw the world with her own eyes. I wasn't as concerned with what she saw as I was with all the things she couldn't see. There is a constant battle for our lives and souls that happens all around us that we cannot see. This was where I always found myself asking God: *What do You want me to do now?*

We finished the tour of the campus and now it was dark. The time I had been trying to avoid had arrived. We had to say goodbye to our first born, our daughter. My heart burned and I had difficulty breathing because I knew I was going to cry if Rosalba started crying. She did and so did I. It seemed like the only one not crying was Sarahi. She put her arms around both of us and gave us a hug and told us it was going to be all right. This was strange to me, because as her father I was supposed to be the one holding her as she cried, and encouraging her that everything was going to be okay. We turned to leave and I felt Rosalba resisting my hold on her hand. I had to encourage her that God was in control and He knew much more than we would ever know. He could be there for Sarahi when we couldn't, and He had the ability and power to do anything to keep her safe.

We got into our van and waved to Sarahi as we drove away towards home. It wasn't easy. I felt the emotions stirring in my heart and all the thoughts going through my mind. It wasn't easy because Rosalba was going through the same, and as we got further away from Sarahi, her tears only increased. I felt so useless once again because I didn't know what to do or say to make her feel better. How would I ever know the bond between a mother and her daughter? How would I ever know the fears in her heart that came from her past? How would I ever help her reach a place of trust in God, that He was in control, when it appeared in the past that He wasn't in control? How could God protect our daughter when He couldn't protect me as a child? My wife didn't tell me these things, but I knew her mind and it never rested. She was constantly reflecting on these things, and I knew this because I heard her praying to God all the time for the answers. Many times, I had the privilege to pray with her, and sometimes came home to find her praying for all of us. There is nothing as pure as the prayers of a mother who really loves their children. *God, You blessed me with a PROVERBS wife and mother. Thanks.*

One child now gone, and our job remained as parents. Our daughter would need our guidance and support as she challenged herself in college. She would look for and expect our encouragement as she faced life in her own way. As a young woman, now she would choose how to accept the advice that we gave, and if it was what she wanted to use in her life. Meanwhile, we still had our son John Jr. to focus on.

As a parent, I made the mistake most parents made. I presumed that we had the parenting down to a system as we raised our daughter. I was totally wrong when it came to our son. Rosalba constantly reminded me that having another child was my prayer to God, not hers. I don't say this in a bad way in any sense. Every child had their own personalities from the day they were born. John Jr. had his mom's personality but my stubbornness.

I remember even when he was a young child, he had a very strong will, which I remember my mom has always said that I possessed. I didn't know what she was talking about, but I've come to accept that moms usually know their children best. She must be correct. So here I was. I was raising myself. Now, I knew me, and this would be a daunting task. *What am I going to do, God? I'm a grown man and I still do things that are not pleasing to You. How am I going to teach my son to do the things that please You when I haven't figured it out myself yet?*

John Jr. was completely opposite of our daughter. I tried to teach him to read and he would have no part in it. If it didn't move, crash, or make noises, he wasn't interested. It took a great kindergarten teacher, Mrs. Houck, to motivate him to read. Sarahi was reading when she was three years old and she loved it. Not John. After he finished kindergarten, he did love reading and would want to read all the time. I remember at bedtime we would have make believe stories and everyone participated. I would start the story with a bunny and Sarahi would say "The sun was shining and the bunny made friends with a squirrel." John's turn came up to continue the story and he would say, "The aliens came in their spaceships and blew up the bunny and the squirrel." Sarahi would sleep all the time in the car and he never would. On long trips, Rosalba would give him cereal to eat and all I heard was crunching during the whole trip. Sometimes I would have to turn up the volume on the radio just to keep the crunching from irritating me.

I know that different is not a bad thing though, but I had to learn how to raise my son. One thing would never be compromised: My love for them both was real. I might have to love them in different ways, but it would always be real. My mom always told my wife this about me: "It's John's way or no way." Rosalba always reminded me of this as we raised our son. This made it hard for me because I was this way until I got married at the age of twenty-eight. *How am I going to teach my son to be submissive to You, God, when I'm still learning it myself?*

Throughout elementary school until the ninth grade, John was making straight A's in everything and it appeared that he liked school. In the ninth grade, the father's genes must have kicked in because he lost interest in school. It wasn't what he thought it should be. This caused him to lose interest in education and focus on other things that interested him.

He would be interested in all sports until it didn't happen the way he thought it should, and he would quit. Despite all the motivating from his mother, father, and coaches, he would give up. His interest in school diminished as well. It wasn't because he didn't know the material, because he would make straight A's on all of his tests, but he never turn in his homework. After many discussions with him and removing many of his privileges, he just didn't care. I asked him if he was satisfied with his efforts and he told me he was "satisfied with just being normal." I asked him if he would be satisfied with an average father, policeman, firefighter, or doctor, and his answer was always "yes."

I prayed about this for many days and years, asking God to help motivate John to be the best he could be. My eyes were opened to the painful truth about my own relationship with God. His response to me was like this: *John, you and many others are just as stubborn with ME as well. You want everything in this life exactly the way you want it and never consider if it's the best thing for you. You give average responses to ME and to the situations you find yourselves in. You are happy being average Christians. Now I have given you an opportunity to motivate someone you love to be their best when they are happy being average. I can't motivate you to be your best. I can only teach you to be your best and be here to help you when you decide to try. I want the very best for you and I want you to succeed in MY plan, but I cannot make you or anyone else to do so. This is something everyone has to decide to do on their own.*

Wow! This was difficult for me to hear, but I couldn't debate that it wasn't true. I spent more time focusing on how to make my life, my wife's life, and my children's lives better than I did focusing on how to make God's family better.

Here comes the ever-popular question once again: *Now what, God? I haven't figured it out myself and now I have asked You for a son when I don't know the answers. I can't make my son do his best. I can't make him see the importance of doing his best. I don't know what his best is. YOU and my son are the only ones who know what his best is. What do You want me to do now?*

I found HIS direction in the Bible. "Start children off on the way they should go, and even when they are old they will not turn from it." (Proverbs 22:6) *Okay God, I'm good with this. Now, could You tell me at what age is old? Is it seventeen, twenty, thirty, or when?* John finally finished high school and he didn't even have the interest to attend graduation, take senior pictures, or attend the awards ceremonies.

Rosalba and I tried to find guidance from the brothers and sisters at church and received none. This frustrated me because I believed the church should provide hope in all situations. Maybe the church didn't have the answer, but they should have been there to offer hope, encouragement, or even a prayer. I often remembered all of the brothers and sisters who helped disciple me when I was a new Christian. I still remember the guidance and direction that they provided for me as I grew in Christ. I needed this now in my own life, but more so in my son's life.

The story of the Prodigal Son came to mind as I prayed for God's direction. God once again showed me that I waited for twenty years to ask HIM into my life, and at fifty-three years of age I still hadn't given HIM 100 percent of my life yet. If HE couldn't make me decide to love, trust, and follow HIM 100 percent, how was I going to be able to show my son how to love, trust, and follow HIM? *You cannot make your son love ME and you cannot make him love you. It's free choice and when he realizes that he is living, smelling, and eating from the pigs only he can make the choice to turn around and go home. Only he can decide to do his best because only he and I know what his best is.*

With all this in my mind, Rosalba convinced John to go to college for one year. If he didn't like it, he could decide what he wanted to do next. Get a job, join the military, or attend a trade school. I didn't know what he wanted, but I encouraged him to do his best at whatever he chose to do. He finished his first year in college and accomplished his goal of being average. His only desires were for material things. Now he had to work to pay for the "thing world." He was not lazy and he was very responsible when it was time to work, but he was in a difficult situation. The time it would take him to pay for all the things he had purchased was time that he could have finished college or whatever type of education that would have guaranteed him a better future.

It was hard to let Sarahi go when she went to college, but it seemed harder to let John go. Our daughter seemed to have a direction in her life, but I had yet to figure out what direction my son desired to go. This was a great concern for Rosalba and me, and we were on our knees, praying for both of them. This world was so distracting for this younger generation. There were so many things that turned their minds away from what was really important. John had no interest in God or the church, and most of the advice and encouragement we gave him came from what God taught us or what we were still learning in HIS Word. How could we teach it when he didn't want to hear it? *What do You want us to do now, God?*

Many times, I would come home from work or wake up in the middle of the night to find Rosalba praying for our children. I would listen to her praying for our son and noticed the desperation in her words for God to help us guide him. She would ask God to give me and her answers for our son. *What are we to do or say to help him understand that YOU love him and only YOU can give him the answers that we cannot?* I would kneel down beside her and hold her as she continued to weep for God's direction. Once again, I was in a situation that I wasn't prepared for. Understanding the love of God for HIS children compared to the limited, non-powerful, and inadequate knowledge situation that we were now in. *What do You want us to do, Father?*

John was a good kid and his problems were not with his mother and earthly father. His problem was his lack of understanding of his Heavenly Father. He was working and paying for the choices he had made and we encouraged him that God was there and He was still in love with him. I knew John would glorify God when God finished working on his heart. I knew my love for him will never diminish and I could only imagine that the love of God for him hadn't diminished either. God was working in his life just as He was working in mine even today. He wasn't finished with me and I knew He wasn't finished with our son, either. He had something planned for John and this phase was only something God was going to use to make him a better Christian, son, and future father himself.

God, I find myself in a useless position. Please use me in whatever way You desire to lead John to a better relationship with You. I know when I take myself out of the situation and let YOU do YOUR desires, everything works out for YOUR glory.

CHAPTER 15

LEARNING OF MY WIFE'S CANCER

I avoided writing this chapter for some time. I could blame my job for not having the time to complete this chapter, and I would not be lying. Writing this chapter meant I returning to the point in my life where I was planning to enjoy twenty-five years of life with my wife and learned the next six months would be the test of our lives. The ultimate test for her, because she was fighting pancreatic cancer and leaving this world to begin her life walking side-by-side with Jesus Christ. Meanwhile, I had to remain here and try to figure out how to live without my best friend, wife, lover, helper, and mother to our two children. Here goes a tumble through the hell on earth that we had to carry our crosses through.

We were preparing to celebrate our twenty-fifth anniversary on April 22, 2014, when Rosalba began to complain of abdominal pain. I took her to our doctor and he set up tests at the hospital to check her gall bladder. It turned out her gall bladder had to be removed. I was concerned but not fearful, because I had undergone the same procedure four years earlier without any problems. The surgery was performed and Rosalba began the healing process. The doctor said she would hurt for a couple of days due to the surgery, but the pain would eventually go away in a few days. This, however, was not the case, because the pain stayed the same and eventually got worse. Nine days later, Rosalba called me at work, from Enid, and said she could not tolerate the pain any longer. I told her to go to the emergency room there. I left work to meet her there, which meant an hour drive for me to get there.

I arrived to find that she still had not been attended to. This really made me upset, and I insisted that she be attended to. On a pain scale of one to ten, she was at a ten. She had given birth to two children and she knew pain. She told me her pain now was worse than when she gave birth to both children. Rosalba was hurting so much that she was curled up in the chair in pain. I finally convinced the nurse in the emergency room to bump her up to immediate status and she put us in a room for the doctor.

What could I do as my wife suffered this horrible pain? I was constantly asking God for help, but would He say yes and take her pain away? We were not so blessed. I held her and tried to convince her everything was going to be okay and I would never leave her side. I had to ask God to forgive me because I lied to her. Everything was not going to be okay, and although I never left her side, God took her home. The doctor finally appeared in our room and he gave her an injection to help with the pain. He ordered the hospital to conduct a CAT scan. In about twenty minutes, a young man came to take us to the room to perform the scan. I waited outside the room only because they wouldn't let me enter the room during the scan. I was really concerned because the only thing I loved more than Rosalba was Christ, and she was suffering. I loved my children as well, but it was not the same.

I needed answers now and I was really impatient at this moment. The young man wheeled Rosalba out of the scanning room and I asked him if he saw anything we should be concerned about. He told me he could not respond to any of the tests and the doctor would be in shortly to talk to us. The only thing that kept me calm at the moment was the fact that my wife was no longer in severe pain.

We sat in the room, waiting for the doctor to come in for about thirty minutes. During this time, I held Rosalba close to me and tried to convince her everything would be okay. There I went again, lying to my wife. The doctor came in and brought up pictures of the scan on the computer screen and stated: "This is the ugliest thing I have ever seen in my life." He might as well have hit us both in the head with a baseball bat, because the news he gave us really hurt us both deeper than anything either of us had ever experienced. My wife looked into my eyes with a sense of fear I had never seen before in her. Could I possible tell her another lie and tell her everything was going to be all right?

God, I cried inside with the loudest internal voice I had ever raised in my life. *What do we do now?*

My wife had always feared cancer in the past. Every time she had a bump on her body, the first thing she would say to me was: "What if it's cancer?" I had a history in the Pentecostal church, and I had been taught not to confess things into my life, and now these thoughts were going through my mind. Did my wife have cancer because of this? In all honesty, I had never felt so anxious in all my life before. *Where are You, God? We have followed You with all our lives inside our home and outside. Why are we in this crisis now?*

In all the previous chapters, I stated how I couldn't do what needed to be done without God. Now I was totally messed up mentally, physically, and spiritually, and I wasn't the one with cancer. How could I be strong for my wife when I could barely find the strength in my own legs to stand? I could also see who I loved the most, because the most selfish thoughts went through my mind at the same time: *What am I going to do without her? What do I tell the children?*

I should have spent all my time holding her close to me and enjoying the last moments of her life, sharing with her how great a person she had always been. I should have spent more time convincing her that I would never cease praying for God to heal her. We were both numb and couldn't say anything. The doctor informed us that he couldn't do anything for her cancer in Enid and we would have to go to Integris Baptist hospital in Oklahoma City. They wanted to send her in the ambulance, but Rosalba wanted me to drive her there. They would arrange a room for her as we were on the road. I contacted my employers and fellow Christian friends to update them on our crisis. I was relieved to find that they told me to do whatever I needed to do. They would work with me as I tried to find out exactly what was going to happen to us. We arrived at the hospital and a room had been set up for us. Thank God, I didn't have to go through all the paperwork again. The information had already been transferred by computer.

The floor doctor arrived in our room and advised us concerning the tests that he had ordered. Blood tests, CAT scans, biopsy, and fasting. She wasn't allowed to eat anything that night because the tests were to be performed in the morning. She was hungry, but she could only drink water. The next morning came and they never came to get her for the tests. I asked what happened to the testing and they told us that they couldn't fit us in. Now I was angry because my wife was suffering the trial of her life and hadn't been allowed to eat in twenty-four hours. I asked them to bring her some food, but they told us that she couldn't eat because the tests were going to be performed the next morning early. I just got angrier, but what could I do? My wife lay in bed, trying not to think about dying, and dying with hunger.

During this fast, the nurses would come in every four hours to get more blood samples. It was frustrating for both of us because she had to endure the discomfort and I had to witness the nurses sticking her several times, just trying to find her veins. She would look at me for help, but what could I do? I finally asked if there was a nurse who could find the vein the first time if we had to do this process every four hours. I was so anxious that when my wife finally fell asleep, I would wake her up to make sure she was okay. If I said this was probably the only time in our relationship when my

131

wife was more focused on herself than she was on me or the children, I would most likely be wrong.

My wife never was very open when it came to serious matters of her heart. This was very serious and it was all of her life. I found myself asking God to heal her because I couldn't live without her. Once again, even my prayers were selfish. I should have been praying for God to help her as she carried this cross. I couldn't imagine her cross because I was too busy looking at mine. *What do I do now, God? Did You give her to me just to take her away from me like this?* My mind was racing and logically trying to find the answers. Human logic and God's grace were not compatible.

My wife finally fell asleep and so did I, due to exhaustion. When I woke up, I would panic and wake her up again to make sure she was okay. I felt so guilty because I fell asleep and wasn't watching over her as I promised I would. I asked God, "Why am I watching over her and YOU are not doing anything?" I had never felt God so far away and so distant in my whole Christian life. *God, can You even hear me when I pray?*

My wife was very observant and she could see I was having a very difficult time even breathing at this point, due to the anxiety. During the most difficult time of her life, she was now trying to console me. I felt like a real idiot. I was supposed to be comforting her and it seemed I was the patient, not her. *God, I don't know how to deal with this. I can't even breathe.*

The technicians come in the next morning to wheel her to another CAT scan. Once again, I had to wait outside while the scan was being performed. During this test, I used the time to contact our pastor and Christian friends to ask for their prayers. I prayed to God, asking Him to make the tumors disappear, but either HE was not listening or HIS answer was no.

The test finished and they wheeled Rosalba back up to her room. I told them to bring her some food to eat. She told them what she wanted to eat and they brought it. My wife had a very strong mind and it often controlled her body and life. Now that she found out she had three tumors, the food tasted different, and there she began the process of wasting away. This was really frustrating to me, because how could I encourage her to eat when her mind said everything was too sweet or too salty?

The doctor came in with the results of the scan and confirmed what the doctor in Enid told us. My wife had three tumors: one ten-centimeters tumor on the head of her pancreas; one ten centimeters and the other seven centimeters on each of her ovaries. This was confusing to me, because only two months earlier she had a well woman exam and the doctor couldn't feel anything on her ovaries and the ultrasound didn't reveal anything either. The doctor said a surgeon was coming in a couple of hours to discuss with us the details concerning a biopsy.

My wife was very strong emotionally, and kept her fears to herself most of the time. Now she looked at me and began to cry out of control. I had been with her for twenty-five years and I had never seen her cry like this. I held her as I cried out to God for help. She trembled in fear and so did I. *What do You expect me to do now, God? Why are we in this situation? How can I help her stop trembling in fear when I cannot stop myself from trembling? Why her, God? Why not me? Can You take me instead, because she is a much better Christian than I am? The children need her much more than they need me. Why don't You let me carry this cross instead?* Silence was all I heard. God was not talking to me. He was not leading me along the "still waters." He was not laying me down in green pastures. *Where are You, God?*

I held my wife and we were both on our knees, crying out to God for deliverance, but no answer came. Another night came, and the anxiety only increased for both of us. Every four hours the nurses came and went, constantly draining all of my wife's blood. They did these tests for pancreatic cancer tracers, but all of them came back negative. I was really frustrated with our medical system at this point. She had eight blood tests for pancreatic cancers testing and eight negative results. She didn't have pancreatic cancer, but she has pancreatic cancer. The white blood cell counts were good, which also showed cancer shouldn't be there, but she had cancer.

The following morning came and I tried to encourage Rosalba about the negative blood tests and the good white blood cell count. In walked the floor doctor, and I brought up these tests and asked him for a potential positive outcome. Maybe the tumors were not cancerous? He looked at both of us and in an irritated voice said, "You have cancer."

Bring out the baseball bat and hit us in the head again. Where is the proper bed side manner these days? Do you have to be so blunt and cruel? Can't you see our crosses are heavy and you just put more weight on them?

I was really frustrated with our medical technology and professionals. So many tests performed and so many different outcomes and different responses. *Why are we here, God?* The doctor then informed us that my wife couldn't eat again all day because the biopsy would be performed in the morning. Once again, the thought of not being able to eat irritated Rosalba. I didn't know why, though, because when they brought her the food she wouldn't eat it. She hadn't eaten very well in a whole week, and I could see it affecting her body now. I knew the night was coming and I now feared it. Everything was quiet, including God. I didn't want the night to come. *Please, God, take the night away!*

I now feared the night more than ever before and I didn't know what to pray. I continued to pray for God to help us and I couldn't even feel His presence. I prayed Psalm 23 and the Lord's Prayer, since God didn't seem to be listening to any of my words. Maybe He would when I prayed those prayers given to me from a man dear to His own heart or the words of His own Son. I had never felt so alone and helpless in all my life. This was the only time in my life that I wished somebody would come and be with us so we wouldn't have to face the night alone. I sat next to the love of my life, yet I felt so alone. She didn't want to talk about anything that she was now dealing with. I didn't know if she decided this for herself, for me, or for both of us. *God, the night is coming. Where are YOU?*

I held my wife's hand as she lay in bed waiting for something to happen. I repeated many times that I loved her. At this point, this was the only thing I was sure about. I loved her since the first time I laid eyes on her and that hadn't ever changed, and I had never doubted that she was the woman God gave me. I just couldn't understand now why HE would take her away from me. Did I not treat her as HE expected or desired me to? Was HE testing me to see if I really believed HE was God? Was this a test for her or for both of us at the same time?

I sat there in the darkness, trying to breathe as I watched my wife suffer and wondered why God seemed so far away. The anxiety and fear seemed to overwhelm me even as I read God's Word and listened to hymns and choruses. She lay there, quiet, as I tried to catch my breath. I wanted to wake her up so I could have someone to talk to, but I couldn't. I finally fell asleep, only to awaken as I fell out of the chair, and shortly afterwards in came the nurses for more blood samples.

They arrived every four hours and did multiple probes, trying to find the veins to get more blood to test for a cancer that she had but didn't have. They came and got her at eight in the morning for the biopsy, and I held her hand as we both hoped these tumors were not cancerous. I had to wait outside again as they performed the biopsy and my mind was everywhere. *What are we going to do, God, if they are cancerous tumors? What do we do if they are not? I know YOU say we are all going to die, but why like this? Why her and not me?*

I made several calls to inform our families about what was going on and where we were at. It was good to hear somebody else's voice at this time because it helped slow down all the thoughts flying around in my mind. What did you say to someone going through this? Everyone was doing their best to encourage and support me, but what did you say and what could you do?

They brought Rosalba out of the room and she was finally really asleep. This was probably the first time she had slept since we were hit in the head with the cancer statement in Enid. All I could do was hold her hand as she slept after the procedure. *God, I love her so much. Please don't take her away yet.* This was my prayer over and over again while she lay there sleeping.

She woke up a couple of hours later and said she was hungry. I quickly asked the nurses to bring her something to eat and drink. I was just glad now that she was awake and I could look into her eyes again. It seemed I could see deep into her soul when I looked into those deep dark brown eyes. She didn't seem to be in fear at this moment. There seemed to be a peace in her soul, but there was no peace in mine. She did her best to eat her food, but because of all the medicine the food was either too salty or too sweet. She took a couple of bites and discarded the rest.

The doctor came in and gave us the results of the biopsy. The tests from the tumor on the pancreas were not sure and he would like to perform a biopsy on the ovarian tumors to see if the results would be better. He informed us that this hospital couldn't do anything with the ovarian part and we must go to OU Medical Center, where they could address both the pancreas and the ovarian tumors. So, we were transferred to our third hospital now. *God, what are You doing to us? I pray to YOU asking for guidance. Help direct us to the right doctor and the right hospital. YOU can use whomever to save her, but YOU'RE not helping. What do You want us to do?*

We checked into a new hospital with the same routine. Rosalba was fasting again so another test could be performed in the morning. My wife was once again without food or drink for another twelve hours for another test. In came more nurses to drain more blood every four hours. While my wife slept, I was glad to have my niece Natalee in the room with me to keep me company as the evening arrived. I didn't know it at the time that Natalee had to address breast cancer herself. She must have known the fear and thoughts that we both were experiencing and just wanted to help us. When she was younger I would spend time with them as I visited my brother Jay. I would read stories to them and play with Natalee and her younger sister Allissa, It must have been tough for Natalee, since I began asking her all the questions that had been going through my mind. These questions had no answers and I knew this, but they poured out of my anxiety-laden mind. *Why her? Why now? Why not me? What must my children be thinking about God now? What do they think of me? Where is my faith in God now? I cannot win in any way right now. God doesn't seem to be listening. I don't have a clue how a test of this magnitude is going to help my wife, me, or our children. God, how are You glorified through cancer?*

I tried to be strong, but I couldn't. My strength came from the LORD, and it seemed that HE was not there. The night was quickly coming and I was just glad I had some family there and I didn't feel so alone. I could leave the room to go clean up, which I really needed. I didn't want to leave Rosalba's side at all during this time. I was so scared that when I left she would go and I wouldn't be there with her as I promised. It felt good to be clean, but I was in a hurry to return to be with Rosalba. She was my life and she was the evidence that God did give us the desires of our hearts even when we didn't know it. *God, why did You give me so much if You only desired to take her away from me?* Even driving back to the hospital my emotions were in control of me. I couldn't get them under control and this was very strange to me. I was not a man driven by emotions, but now I found myself crying and anxious every moment.

The morning came and they took Rosalba in for another test and I waited outside alone once again. The test finished and I walked on one side of her bed as they wheeled her to her room. She was once again asleep due to the medication and I prayed for her life in a totally different way than I ever had before. Now I really prayed for her life. Not God's will. Not what I wanted. *Just save her life, God, please.*

She woke up and we had several visitors during the day. They asked to pray with us before they left, and of course I wanted all the prayers we could get. The night was upon us again, and I didn't want to face another one alone. My wife was in her own thoughts, prayers, and exhaustion, and did not communicate with me, and I didn't feel the presence of God.

As we awaited the evening, I read the Bible to Rosalba and sang her some of her favorite hymns. I just hoped God's presence would fill the room and provide us the peace that surpasses understanding. As I hoped for this, a female doctor walked in at nine in the evening and sat on one side of my wife's bed.

She took my wife's hand and looked at her and said: "I'm so sorry to tell you this. You have pancreatic cancer and it has moved to your ovaries. We can do nothing to remove the pancreatic cancer, but we can give you chemotherapy to reduce the pain. I'm so sorry, but without chemotherapy you have three to four months to live, and with chemotherapy you have six months only."

Then she walked away and once again we were alone. *God, where are You? Will You not let this cup pass from us?*

I had never reached a pit of despair like this. How was Rosalba feeling right then? We were both crying more profoundly than we had ever cried before in our twenty-five years together. I took her hand and asked her to pray with me. Maybe God wasn't listening to me when I prayed alone. Maybe HE would listen when we prayed together. HE had always answered our prayers in the past for each other or for our children. Surely HE would listen when we prayed together.

We prayed and we cried for most of the night until the exhaustion defeated us both. Rosalba fell asleep in bed and I fell asleep in the folding chair. The rest of the next day would have to wait to abuse us because we were both totally spent mentally, physically, and spiritually.

CHAPTER 16

WAITING ON GOD'S HEALING

The next day arrived and I woke to find that we were not having a bad dream. We were still in a hospital and Rosalba still had cancer. God still had not answered and I still didn't feel HIS "peace that surpasses our understanding." My mind, body, and soul hurt and I couldn't even imagine how my wife was feeling now. I leaned over her bed and kissed her ever so softly because I didn't ever want to be the one who hurt her. I told her that I loved her and I was sure God was in control and HE would heal her. I imagined those wonderfully deep dark brown eyes without hope and thinking about everything that had gripped her body so quickly. She was so strong and she had always been so. Even when there didn't seem to be any answers to our previous tests, she remained positive and hopeful. Now she needed me to be positive and hopeful for her, but I don't know if I could tell her what I wanted to tell her, because I might be lying to her. I didn't want to ever lie to her and I couldn't honestly tell her that everything would be okay. I didn't feel the presence of God even though I had prayed most of the night while she lay still at my side. *God, how can I tell her everything is going to be okay when I don't have a clue about what we are suffering?*

I looked deep into her eyes and told her once again that the only thing I was sure about was that God loved us and I loved her with everything that I was. I really didn't know if that helped her, but at this time I had nothing else to give her. Without God's intervention, my wife was going to die. I knew all the verses in the Bible concerning God's promises about healing His people. I had been reading them and praying them over and over again before this situation occurred. When I was sick, when the children were born, when they were sick, and when we faced family members who were suffering sicknesses as well. I had been very fortunate because God had answered our prayers most of the time. When He didn't, those family members were well into their lives. The family members I had lost in death were all over eighty years of age and even though I missed them, I knew where they were and that they had lived full lives. Not my wife, though, because she had to deal with the death of her older sister at the young age of twenty-two due to tuberculosis, and a brother at the age of one to hemophilia. Her dad passed away several years ago due to bronchitis and prostate cancer in his late seventies. She had to see others suffer immense pain and suffering, and now I could only imagine her thinking that now it was her time.

I was sure she was thinking about me and the kids at this time because that was the way she had always been. Thinking of others before herself was her life and her way of life. It didn't have to be a family member only, because many times she would prepare a meal, clean a house, visit with the sick or elderly, hold the hand of one in despair, kneel and pray with others in need, or just take time to constantly be positive when only hell seemed on the horizon. She is the reason I am the man I am today. God molded me and used Rosalba to help do so.

At this point, I didn't know what I was anymore. I couldn't seem to say, do, act, or even pretend in a way that seemed to make this situation any better. I found myself thinking, *What would Rosalba do or say if it were me lying in the hospital bed with cancer? How would she act or respond as she looked into my eyes? Could she look into my eyes and tell me honestly that everything was going to be okay? Would she be able to say that God was going to heal me and we would spend the next twenty-five years together?*

I knew Rosalba, and she couldn't lie either, but somehow she would find a way to be positive in this situation. I just couldn't seem to find or see how she would do it.

Once the morning was over, I asked her what she desired. *What do you want me to do to help you? What can I do for you to make you feel better physically, mentally, or spiritually?*

She looked me in the eyes and she said, "Just let me go."

You could've taken a knife and pierced my heart at that moment, because this was the last thing that I wanted to do. I had difficulty breathing again. Was she giving up? How could I fight this with her if she was already giving up? I had fought so many battles with her and she had never given up on anything in her life with me. Where was the positive wife of twenty-five years who was constantly encouraging me that everything was going to be all right? Times when I was ready to give up, she was always so strong and so positive. I didn't have any idea how to face cancer, but if she wasn't willing to fight, what could I do? Was she really asking me to just sit there and watch her die? I couldn't do this. It was just not possible, because my God didn't give her to me just to take her away so quickly.

There's got to be an answer. We just aren't looking hard enough. Maybe we just need a second opinion or a better group of doctors.

She looked into my eyes, knowing where my mind was going, and she said the same thing. "Let me go. I don't want any chemo or radiation." My spirit was crushed because this would mean she was willing to let go of me and our children.

She knew where she was going to end up when this nightmare would end. She was in love with CHRIST and many times she would tell me that I was her second love. I could be her prince, but never her KING. This was the most important thing for both of us to know at this time, because without CHRIST in our hearts there was no hope here in this hospital room or later in eternity. *This is great, but other than what the BIBLE says, I don't know anything about eternity. I've never been to heaven and I've never dreamed of heaven. I cannot see, touch, smell, taste, or hear heaven. I can see, touch, smell, taste, and hear this woman YOU gave me for the last twenty-five years. I don't know how to deal with eternity. I don't even know how to deal with today. I pray and I trust in YOU, GOD, and I let you take care of every second of every day. I want her today. I want her with me now. How can she be a helper You provided for me if YOU take her away from me now?*

If I had these difficulties dealing with her wishes, I couldn't even imagine how our children were dealing with it now. I remember my John telling me, "How could GOD let this happen to the best mother and Christian that I know?" How did you answer your son with a response that he could accept in this situation? I didn't know the answer, as we both had been looking on the Internet for the best doctor, hospital, care center, or some "magic pill" that would remove these three tumors and the cancer that was destroying Rosalba's body. God didn't seem to be listening and we had to find an answer on our own.

Sarahi was just like her mother in that she remained positive even when the situation seemed grave. I really didn't know what she was thinking, because she was also like her mom in this area. Almost a year later, she still hadn't spoken to me about what she had been thinking or feeling. This was the same with John. He hated hospitals and he hated seeing people suffer. This was more difficult when it was someone close to his heart, like his mom. This made it more difficult for me because I knew they were watching me to see how I would respond. I knew they would be looking to see if I really believed in this GOD I had been teaching them about their whole lives. *In a storm, what does my dad really believe?*

I had never felt so alone in all my life. My GOD was all around me, but HE was not talking or answering me. My wife was next to me, but she was dying and now giving up to cancer. She wasn't talking to me, as I was sure she had many more things going through her mind other than how I was feeling. She was dying and I was still thinking about me. I couldn't open up to our children about my doubts and fears because they were looking to see GOD in me. I couldn't talk to the doctors because they just told us to go home and enjoy the time we have until Rosalba dies. I was looking for hope in a hopeless situation, as I saw it. I had never contemplated what happened when GOD said "NO," even if it was only one time in my life. *How will Rosalba deal with a "NO"? How will my children and I deal with a "NO"? If GOD says "NO" I lose a friend, wife, lover, sister in CHRIST, and the children lose a mother who really loves them.*

The next morning we were discharged from the hospital and sent home to die. Wow! How did we deal with this? I always looked forward to going home, but never looked forward to watching my wife dying at home. How would I tell my family or her family? When they called, how would they accept the news of "go home and die"? My children knew I would do anything possible to keep my wife and their mother alive. What would Rosalba's mother, aunts and uncles, brothers, sisters, and nieces and nephews think of my effort? Would they believe I did everything possible to save her? This weighed heavily on my soul. It was already troubled because it seemed to me that GOD was saying, "NOT YET," or worse yet, "NO." How would they see my faith and view my testimony as their loved one said, "Let me go"? I dreaded any phone call now because I felt like I was fighting alone and against the best satan can give. (This is my personal decision not to capitalize this name.)

The phone rang and the questions began. *Are you sure it's cancer? Are you sure there is no other option? No other doctor? No other procedure? No magic pill? Why is she giving up? Doesn't she believe God can heal her? How come you let her give up? What are you going to do now? How is she feeling? Can I come see her? Do you need anything?*

I didn't know the answer to any of these questions, except that I would like them to come visit us. The other questions needed to be directed to God. This was HIS decision, not mine. I didn't pick the date of her death before she was born and I wasn't happy with it now. I wasn't the one who said, "Let me go." My mind was going in many different directions and my best friend was not talking to me. The only thing she said to me after hearing of the cancer was, "What else can we do?" I didn't blame Rosalba for not talking to me, but I did miss my best friend.

I was also frustrated because the Bible tells us we are all going to die someday, but it doesn't say anything about how to die or how to grieve when someone we really cared about died. It tells us not to be anxious about anything, but doesn't tell us how to do it when our best friend, wife, and lover began to waste away due to cancer. How could I not be anxious when my only GOD and my best friend were not talking to me? *Where are You, God? How can I "just let her go"? Are You leading us to another miracle, doctor, hospital, procedure, or magic pill? What are YOUR designs for her life? What are YOUR plans for our lives? What do YOU want me to do now? How do YOU expect me to sit still and watch her waste away and not be anxious about anything? How can I help her when I can't even help myself? I find it difficult to breath, eat, sleep, walk, or even exist in the middle of this storm, how can I help our children when YOU'VE given me no direction? How does one die? Where are the answers in YOUR Bible?*

(I took a month break since writing the first half of this chapter, due to the extreme emotions that arose within me from remembering all that we went through. Now that I'm back, I really wish I wasn't because those memories are still fresh and raw.)

At home, it was difficult for us as well because I had to work to maintain our insurance. This was hard for me because I wanted to be with her every moment so I could do whatever to help her. Some of her family volunteered to come from Dallas to stay with her while I was at work, and I thanked God for them and for their love towards her. I continued to work even though my mind was always stuck at home with her. I would call several times each day to make sure Rosalba was okay and to see if I needed to bring something home on my way from work. She tried to remain positive in a very difficult and scary situation and I called Hospice services to begin what my wife requested. "Let me go." These ladies were very kind and compassionate in a "hellish" situation. It takes special people to work in this field. How could you take on a job where you knew the only service you provided was making death less painful? I filled out the appropriate paperwork to enter Rosalba into the program and a schedule was started to monitor her vital signs and symptoms three times a week. Rosalba's family was so helpful and I couldn't imagine going through this without them.

We were now into the second month of the cancer, and God still hadn't answered my prayers as I wanted Him to. Now that I have reflected on the situation, He was answering. He provided me with the grace that I needed during a very stressful situation. He provided Rosalba's family to help me with her care while I went to work. How many families in America would sacrifice their time to help an aunt or sister? I had an employer who gave me the freedom to take care of the emergencies that arose.

They say that stress can cause many strange illnesses during situations like this, but I didn't believe it at the time. I was wrong. Whether it was due to lack of sleep, not eating properly, stress, or whatever, I noticed that my eyesight had suddenly changed overnight. I woke one morning to find out that everything was double vision and blurry. This was scary to me, but I didn't mention it to Rosalba because she had enough to think about as it was. I put it off for a while because I wanted all my attention to go to her, but it was problematic for me because I would have to close one eye to drive back and forth to work. When I had both eyes open, everything was double vision and made it impossible to focus on the road or oncoming traffic. I continued to work and come home, waiting on some promising sign that God was healing Rosalba, only to find that she continued to lose her appetite and the pain continued to increase.

Her family came to visit and convinced her to get another opinion, and on top of this Rosalba asked me to let her stay in Dallas with her family as she went through this. So, I prayed some more, asking God to provide us the answer we needed. The right doctor, facility, cure, or magic pill. At this point, I would have taken anything to help get rid of this cancer attacking my wife. Rosalba's brothers and sisters agreed that they would take turns taking care of her if she came to Dallas. This would make it easier for her and for them, because they had family to take care of as well their jobs. It would be more difficult for me because I would have to make the six-hour drive to Dallas and back every weekend. I could live with this, though, because I knew her family would take good care of her and I had very few options here in Oklahoma.

Once again, I could see God's hand and grace helping us, even though it wasn't through healing her. My employer and her family were more than a blessing to me throughout this crisis. Many employers would tell you that this was your problem. You reported to work when you were supposed to, or find another job. God provided me the flexibility to complete the work required of me and spend as much time with Rosalba as was possible. There were things that had to be maintained at our home in Oklahoma as well as our two Siberian Huskies. Oh, how Rosalba loved to hold our female dog, named Luna. She named her Luna because it means "moon" in Spanish, and she was always fascinated by the moon. She would just hold her and Luna was half her size, but they both looked happy because they both were smiling. I also had to take on paying all the bills with Rosalba now staying in Dallas. This was difficult for me because Rosalba did such a good job of making the payments with what little money we had. She made it look so easy and God always supplied the money even in the most difficult situations. Whether I missed work for a sickness or lack of hours due to no overtime, she always had food on the table and the cabinets were full of healthy food for our family. I knew God was very instrumental in this as well and Rosalba proved that she was the helper that God knew I needed.

We loaded up her suitcase and ourselves and headed for Dallas. This was very difficult for me because I wouldn't see her till the following Thursday at night. I had to trust in God and her family to take care of her while I was gone. I knew this wouldn't be a problem though, because Rosalba's family was very different from most families I had known. I had worked in nursing homes in my youth, and I had seen patients who never had a visitor for two years. The families just hid the difficult people away from sight so they wouldn't have to experience what we were dealing with now. Thank God, again, for Rosalba's family and my employer who had helped me during the most difficult cross-carrying moment of my life. We arrived in Dallas at her sister's home in Haltom City, and I took Rosalba inside and returned for her things. Rosalba's older sister Estella had had heart surgery and maintained her husband, two daughters, one son-in-law, and four grandchildren. She was a busy lady and now she was volunteering to help take care of her youngest sister, suffering with pancreatic cancer and told to go home and die. I couldn't even imagine what went through Estella's mind as she encouraged Rosalba to eat, drink, and get out of bed when she really didn't want to. I sometimes wonder how selfish I really was when I thought I was the only one really suffering during this time. This would be the third time for Rosalba's sister Estella. The third time she would see a brother or sister she loved dying with a disease. I could only imagine how hard this had to be for her as well.

Sunday afternoon came too soon and I had to return to Oklahoma to work early Monday morning. I felt the crushing pressure in my heart and the tears welling up in my eyes as every second ticked off the clock. Even a year later as I write this paragraph, I can feel those same tears welling up, remembering how hard it was to leave her there. I went to Rosalba and gave her a kiss and she could see in my eyes those tears that I had been fighting so hard to hide from her. She looked into my eyes and told me everything would be okay and told me to be careful on the way home. I remember her telling me to, "Make sure you call if you're getting sleepy on the road and make sure you call me when you get home." I excused myself as quickly as possible because I could no longer hold back the sadness in my soul. I got into my car and the uncontrollable tears began. I couldn't stop them.

I drove from Haltom City to Oklahoma City and the tears never ended till then. I prayed while listening to Christian music on the radio and nothing seemed to stop the tears. I had never experienced this type of grief, sadness, or loneliness in all of my life. I was leaving my best friend and wife in Texas and driving home to be without her knowing, the cancer was eating away at her body. I asked the same questions as before: *God, where are You? Why haven't You healed Rosalba? Why are You letting her suffer so much? What do You want me to do now?*

I arrived at home around nine that night, and although I was exhausted I just could not sleep. I remained on my knees crying out to God for her healing until I couldn't keep my eyes open. I awoke to the sound of my alarm clock and began with prayer again, and once again that feeling that God just wasn't listening to me. What a desperate feeling. I had never felt like this before. I always felt better after praying in the past, and now it was like nothing was happening. No joy, peace, or guidance. I questioned what I could have possibly done that would deserve such a period of time when God would not respond to my prayers. I knew I was a sinner, but I didn't try to sin, and when I thought I had I was always on my knees, asking for His forgiveness. *If YOU are quiet because of my sin, God, why don't You let me carry this cross you have placed on Rosalba's back?*

I did my best to get off my knees and prepare to go to work, but it was very difficult. My only motivator was if I stayed at home, everything that made this home was Rosalba. All her decorations, blankets knitted, pictures, and even her aroma, but she was not here. I left for work and the tears continued to flow as I thought of all the years that I had worked for my family and now I did it just for the insurance to pay for the doctors to keep her alive. What motivation, but knowing all the time all I wanted to do was be by her side to help in every way possible.

I had to do everything possible to prepare my mind for work. I couldn't help Rosalba or my family if I got hurt or died in a car wreck getting there. Everything I did at work was based on using my mind, but now I wasn't sure how focused I could be. My employer was helping me in a very difficult situation and deserved my attention on the tasks that I had to complete. I would do my best, but I prayed I could.

I tried to show how God had always answered our prayers in difficult times in the previous chapters, and HE had in this chapter as well. HE hadn't answered my prayers the way I wanted HIM to answer them. I wanted HIM to heal Rosalba now so her family wouldn't have to deal with this cross as well. I wanted HIM to heal Rosalba now so that my mind could be focused on my job and safety. I wanted HIM to heal her now so that our children wouldn't have to see her suffer and die. I wanted HIM to heal her now so that I could hold her in my arms and tell her that I loved her. I wanted HIM to heal her now so that I could see, touch, taste, smell, and hear her at home with me now. I wanted HIM to heal her now so that when I got home I would have a reason to get there.

Maybe that was the problem I had to deal with. Everything was about what I WANTED and it was drowning out what was more important. WHAT DO YOU WANT, GOD?

CHAPTER 17

REALIZING THAT GOD IS NOT GOING TO HEAL HER ON EARTH

I wrote this on October 19, 2015. Three days short of the one year since God took Rosalba home. I have been trying to resolve these conflicts in my heart concerning God saying "NO." I wasn't used to Him not answering me in some way or another. It had always been "yes" or "wait" but never "NO." The more I prayed, the worse Rosalba became. Slowly and painfully she was dying before my eyes and the eyes of our children. Many questions are circulating in my mind about God and they were not good thoughts. How could a God of love allow His daughter Rosalba to suffer so much? If He wanted to take her to heaven, He could have done it quickly. Why didn't He? The words from my John echoed in my mind over and over again: "Why would God let something like this happen to the best Christian lady and mom that I have ever known?"

We were carrying this cross for four months and I continued to make my trip every weekend from Oklahoma to Fort Worth to spend the three days I had to spend with her. I contemplated which was more difficult of the two situations: Going to see her, hoping that she was getting better, or leaving her there to go to work, hoping she would get better when I returned. Both scenarios included her getting better, but none of them addressed the fact that God was saying "NO" and Rosalba was not getting better.

I arrived in Fort Worth on Thursday night around nine at night, hoping she was better. I knocked on the door and my brother-in-law opened the door for me. I gave my greetings and excused myself to go upstairs where the love of my life lay in bed, waiting for me. As I entered, Rosalba's eyes sparkled with excitement and she did everything she could to show me she was doing okay. She was such a hero to me because as she went through the most difficult time of her life, her desire was to convince me she was

145

okay. I was more than eager to hold her in my arms and give her the kiss of my life. I held her, only to find that the pain had increased and her whole body hurt. Now I was fearful to embrace her because I didn't want to hurt her. This was totally opposite to what I had been able to do in the past. When things were going poorly and there didn't seem to be a way out, I could hold her as we prayed and everything seemed to be in reach. After praying together and embracing one another, we just knew God was taking care of the situation.

At this moment, I was still waiting for God to respond to our situation, but I could see Rosalba was not getting better. Her sister came in with breakfast and Rosalba tried her best to eat it, but as soon as she did her body resisted and it all came back up. Rosalba was hungry and she tried her best to eat and drink, but her body wouldn't let her. Everything she ate or drank came right back up. The doctors gave her all the new nausea medicines, but they didn't keep the food or water down. I did my best to help her, but what could I do? We brought her the food or drink she requested, but nothing stays inside her beautiful body. She wanted to enjoy the food and drink and she did her best to enjoy it and always said "thank you," but nothing stayed in her body. Within minutes, everything she ate or drank came right back up. Rosalba knew this wasn't a good thing, as did we all, but we never gave up.

Many days and nights were spent praying alone. Many days and nights Rosalba's whole family spent time praying with Rosalba. All of the churches and mission churches were praying with us as well. I confessed the promises of God, including, "For where two or three are gathered together in my name, there am I in the midst of them," Matthew 18:20. I knew this verse addressed discipline, but it also enforced the power or God's people believing together. I had always believed in the power of prayer, and I knew this fight was not my own, but it appeared nothing was happening. How many people were needed to pray healing into Rosalba's life? I know for sure there were many more than two or three. *Where are YOU, God?* At this time, God was saying "NO" to all of us. How many promises were there in the Bible that addressed when God says "no"? Where in the Bible did I find out what to do when God said, "NO"? I knew that God said "NO" to King David when his child died due to the consequences of his sin, but God didn't tell him what to do. He just got up and continued with his life, but I'm sure some of the same questions were in his mind as well.

Rosalba and I prayed together as I held her hand and we pleaded for God's mercy and healing. I asked God to guide us to an understanding of what He was leading us through. He was my refuge and strong fortress and I didn't feel very strong right then. I knew Rosalba didn't feel very strong either. *What do You want from us, God? What do You want us to do, God?*

This is not just Rosalba and me, but all of her family, my family, and all of our church family. We finished praying, and as I helped Rosalba off her knees and into bed, I wondered if God even heard our prayers. Usually I could feel His presence after praying, but now I felt nothing. *Do You not answer me, God, because YOU know the answer is "NO," or do You not answer me because of some unknown sin in my life?*

I laid Rosalba down and lay next to her, remembering all the things that we had enjoyed for the last twenty-five years, and I saw them slipping away one by one. I would usually place my arm around her waist as we fell asleep, but now the pain wouldn't permit it. I would hold her close until the sleep overcame us, but now I couldn't even do that. I missed the times that we were able to embrace each other until sleep came. *God, what's going on? Why do You give me twenty-five wonderful years of embracing Rosalba, but now YOU'RE taking her away from me in such a painful way?*

She finally fell asleep, but as I watched her she continually winced in pain and never truly slept. I set an alarm clock on our phone so we wouldn't miss the regimen of medication for her pain. Every four hours I had to wake her up to take her medicine, and this was very difficult because sometimes when the alarm sounded she had finally fallen to sleep. If I missed the timing of the medication, then the pain became more intense and harder to get under control. We had reached the point where the medication wouldn't allow her the mental capacity to maintain the proper schedule and sometimes she would forget and the pain would get out of control. This was not a good sign for me, because Rosalba was always very sharp mentally and schedules were her thing. I didn't know what to do anymore. Rosalba was always the one who helped me train my thoughts and what I wanted to say. Rosalba was the better part of me, and as I saw her condition worsen every day, I knew my life was worse as well. She was the best thing I had ever had in my whole life, with the exception of God. If I had not accepted Jesus into my heart, I would have never met Rosalba to begin with. Rosalba was the one I could see, touch, smell, taste, and hear. God was there, I knew, but I could see and experience Rosalba every moment and every day, and now I wondered if God even listened to my prayers.

As I write this, the date is January 27 2017. I have been avoiding this part of the story because of the pain of remembering the details and the doubts that crept into my mind concerning God and His promises. I don't apologize for this truth, because it is very real and anybody who has gone through this themselves will confess the same if they are willing to be truthful to themselves and God.

The first of September 2014, my sister-in-law, Mayela, volunteered to come from Florida to help take care of Rosalba. She flew in from Florida to Oklahoma to help us. This was a huge blessing from God because now

Rosalba could come back home to Fairview to be with me. I wouldn't have to drive to Dallas every weekend to see her. This also meant that every day I would see Rosalba get worse. This was a huge sacrifice for Mayela to make, because she would have to leave her job, husband, four daughters, and the grandchildren. This was also a wonderful blessing from God, because it wouldn't have been possible for me here alone in Oklahoma. Sarahi and John had their own jobs and were just starting out in their careers. They came during the weekends and did all they could do to help, but it was also very difficult for them to see their mother wasting away a little more day to day. Having Rosalba's sister here helped a lot, because when I had to work she could care for her, and when I came home I could relieve her. It wasn't easy for her sister either, as she witnessed with her own eyes the cross of cancer that Rosalba was carrying.

We did our best to help Rosalba find comfort mentally, physically, and spiritually. Many members of the community came to encourage us, as did all the members of the mission churches. We would gather in the house or outside on the patio and worship God together. We would praise God, singing all the favorite hymns or choruses that Rosalba always enjoyed. I wish I could have known what Rosalba was thinking during this time, but once she found out she had cancer, she hardly spoke to anybody. She liked to talk about things that were not very important, but these types of things were very personal to her. I just wished that she would have opened up to me, her husband. This might have just been a selfish desire on my part, but I always enjoyed talking to her. In her defense, what could she tell me? Was my desire for communication more for my sanity and comfort or for hers?

We spent September to October 2014 working together to help comfort her, and now God's healing would really have to be a huge miracle. Rosalba weighed 154 pounds when this cancer started and now she was less than seventy-five pounds. She was mostly skin and bones at this point. My heart hurt and my soul was shouting out to God for a Lazarus moment without her dying. *Just give me the miracle. Just provide us with that magic pill or treatment that could destroy the evil of this cancer. Where are You, God, as my wife and I walk through this dark valley? Why have You taken this approach toward us? How does this evil of cancer glorify YOU in any way?* So many questions and doubts, as I watched the love of my life for the last twenty-five years wasting away in front of my eyes, and I couldn't do anything to save her. I doubted myself on many different levels during this time. *Do I really love God? Have we done something evil to deserve the crosses that we are now burdened with? Is there something I could have done or should have done to prevent this evil of cancer? Did I research all the possibilities out there to heal or treat cancer? Did I do everything I could to show her my love and does she feel my love for her now? Does she know how much I really love her and hurt for her?*

I never had a fear of death in my life, but now to be truthful, I did. Watching Rosalba suffer, and seeing that God was not doing anything to heal her allowed fear to enter my life. I now understood what Jesus said on the cross before HE died. "My God, my God, why have you forsaken me?" I knew this life was temporary, but seeing Rosalba suffer hurt so much.

Why are You making her suffer so much, God? Why are You letting this evil of cancer kill and destroy everything You have created? Your birds, fish, animals, and humans are suffering with this evil of cancer and You promised to deliver us from evil. Remember the Lord's Prayer, my God: "Lead us not into temptation but deliver us from evil"? Can't You see how we are hurting as we witness my wife and my children's mother suffering like this? How do YOU expect me to accept this "no" as a promise fulfilled? What about all the prayers of my own and all of our brothers and sisters in CHRIST? Were these wasted prayers? Did all this praying accomplish anything, or did they just go into the heavens and linger there, unheard and unanswered? You say we don't receive because we don't ask, and that the door is not opened because we don't knock, and we don't find because we don't seek. What is the truth, God? I've been asking, knocking, and seeking, but YOU are nowhere to be found.

The pain and nausea had reached a level now where hospice and our efforts were no longer helping Rosalba. She knew and now feared what she could see with her own eyes. She was dying and she was not eating or drinking anything. She looked at me with tears in her eyes and begged me to take her to the hospital. She told me that if she didn't make it to the hospital, she was going to die. Rosalba told me that if the doctor didn't give her fluids intravenously, she would die. She told me she needed fluids. Her sister and I discussed this with the Hospice nurse, and she agreed to help us, but also confirmed that the location would not stop this evil from taking Rosalba's life. She then told me in private something that hurt my heart. She told me Rosalba's body was starting to shut down, and if we gave her fluids intravenously this would only delay her death and make the pain and nausea harder to control.

We took her to the hospital. Mayela and I rotated our time at the hospital with Rosalba. We had help from a sister-in-Christ, Estela who relieved Mayela from 10pm to 6am the next morning. Both of these women were a blessing. Mayela was a super individual and helped us in so many ways, and I thank God for her. I couldn't have done this myself. I was in a very difficult position, as I was still seeing everything as I wanted to perceive it. This was very difficult for me, as I only focused on the fact that my wife was dying. I hadn't taken the time to see how many ways God had blessed me with our family, God's missions that we had been working with, and our church family here in Fairview.

I felt so useless because I couldn't save Rosalba, and at this moment I was of no help to our children. I didn't have anything left to help them with. All of their lives, I had told them my God saved and healed His people, and we were all watching Rosalba die a little every day. My children didn't challenge me concerning my beliefs, but I was challenging myself and I imagined their voices in my head, asking, *where is this God that you have always believe in and taught us about? Is this God's example of love to us? His love is letting our mom suffer with so much pain and misery.* I could hear them ask in my mind, *Why would we want to follow a God who can't even keep His promises?*

The doctor and Hospice nurse told us on October 10, 2014, to gather all the family for her death was near. I called the families and told them what I was told, and they gathered with us as the time approached. We gathered as always, singing, praying, and trying to encourage Rosalba during every moment. On October 13, 2014 Rosalba lost her ability to respond to conversation and eye contact. I wasn't even sure if she realized we were present. I was told that the last thing a dying person loses is their hearing, and I hoped she heard me as I held her hand and told her I loved her and encouraged her that it was all right to let go, and we would be okay. I never wanted to say we would be okay without her, because I didn't know this. (Two years later and I still don't know this.)

The final moments of October 22, 2014, Rosalba had several mini strokes due to the level of pain medication she was receiving. She stopped breathing on this earth at 5pm and started breathing a second later in the arms of my Lord and Savior Jesus Christ in Heaven.

So, I ask the questions I have been avoiding for two years: Where is the hope? Why dare to obey now? Why obey a God who let your wife suffer for six months with such a painful evil like pancreatic cancer? Why serve a God who doesn't answer your prayers? Why serve a God who doesn't keep His promises? How are your children going to perceive this God of yours now? If a level of faith is the determining factor in God not healing Rosalba, how did I mess up so badly? If cancer is evil, and many preachers say Christians cannot die from evil, why did Rosalba die of cancer?

So where is my story? If you dare to obey God, is this or some other evil all we have to look forward to on this earth? Hope: "In a flash, in the twinkling of an eye, at the last trumpet. For the trumpet will sound, the dead will be raised imperishable, and we will be changed (1 Corinthians 15:52." I find hope in this truth. 2 Corinthians 5:6-8 tells me and you, "Therefore we are always confident and know that as long as we are at home in the body we are away from the Lord. For we live by faith, not by sight. We are confident, I say, and would prefer to be away from the body and at home with the Lord." I agree with this because God made us a creation of feelings. Senses of sight, smell, hearing, sight, and touch. If you are losing someone as I have, then you would agree that the most difficult things we deal with are related to these five things. I cannot see, touch, hear, smell Rosalba, or taste the wonderful meals she prepared with her own hands. I have been created this way by my God and I've never experienced this Heaven thing.

Why should I dare to obey God after going through all this? My answer is this: My mind is delirious with doubts. My body is weakened by the grief and stress. These are important things to care for, but not what concerns me most. What concerns me most is that my soul is suffering and I don't know what to do. There are many things provided for mental grief advice and many diets to help us physically, but these are the easy things to deal with. I'm struggling with not wanting to think and not wanting to eat, because right now a large part of me is so sad that I don't want to live anymore. I've always felt like I don't belong on this earth. I ask my God: Why didn't You take me with Rosalba?

When someone loses the desire to live, many say this a mental issue, but I disagree. In my life, this is a spiritual problem. I'm being tested in the truth as it really is. This is God's world and God's creation, not mine. Psalm 119:28 tells me, "My soul is weary with sorrow; strengthen me according to your word." I am mourning for myself, not Rosalba. She is not suffering anymore. Her time of carrying her cross is over and she has crossed the finish line of life on earth and she now is enjoying her reward in Heaven.

So, why God and why cancer? It feels sort of lame now, serving a God who allowed Rosalba to suffer and die of cancer. So where is the answer and where is the hope? First of all, name me one person in the Bible who didn't see death or experience death and suffering. God Himself through Jesus His Son faced more suffering and pain than Rosalba experienced. He suffered the mocking, hatred, betrayal, pain, torture, and death, and He committed no sin. How then could I expect things to be great for Rosalba or me when it was never promised to us to be free of sufferings here on this earth? The last thing coming out of my mouth during this cancer were the words: "Praise God, Rosalba is suffering with cancer! My wife is going to be with God!" I never stopped believing or praying, but now I must face the truth that she is happier in Heaven than she would have been here with me and our children. I've always wanted the best for Rosalba, and now I have to believe that God's way is the best way even though it wasn't the best for me. It doesn't take away my pain or loss, but it is comforting knowing that she will never suffer again and this evil of cancer has been destroyed in her body and her life. She is happier now than she has ever been with me here on earth. I can't see, touch, smell, hear, or taste Heaven, but I believe in it.

151

Why obey God if these prayers were unanswered? I don't know, except to say that my God sees and knows things I may never know. I never would have written this book if I didn't experience the death of Rosalba. If I could have found some book in the Christian bookstore about grieving for the death of a spouse, I might not have written this book. There are many challenges I must overcome, and I cannot do this without God's help. How do you experience twenty-five years of physical intimacy with your spouse and lose it in six months? How do you cope with this truth? It's not written in the Bible, and only God knows the answer to this, and His answer for me may be completely different for another man grieving and dealing with the loss of his wife. How could God use my testimony if I chose to obey Him during this trial? Where else could I learn to practice real compassion for those who are or may be suffering the same cross?

Why serve a God who doesn't keep His promises? Numbers 23:19 states, "God is not human, that He should lie, not a human being, that He should change His mind." Does He speak and then not act? Does He promise and not fulfill? Three things that God never promised us. The first is, He will not deliver us from His justice for our sins until the Heaven and Earth are remade without the curse of sin. The second is, God never promised us a life of comfort even though many pastors falsely tell us we will have an easy life. He told us just the opposite, that we would suffer hardship and persecution from the world, and even correction from His hand (Hebrews 12:7). The third thing is, God never promised us instant change. Paul tells us, "Therefore, since we are surrounded by such a great cloud of witnesses, let us throw off everything that hinders and the sin that so easily entangles. And let us run with perseverance the race marked out for us.." (Hebrews 12:1)

How do my children perceive this God I claim to love after seeing their mom suffer and die? I don't know, but I know God has given us His grace in different ways. Through Jesus, we have learned that it is okay to cry (John 11:35). God has encouraged us by saying kind words will cheer you up (Proverbs 12:25). It's okay to discuss what you're feeling with Christian friends and family. God also tells us that true companions are "born for when there is distress" (Proverbs 17:17). We can also pour out our hearts to God. This is not just a feel-good act, because we are appealing to "the God of all comfort, who comforts us in all our tribulation" (2 Corinthians 1:3-4). These trials and pains will never completely go away until a new Heaven and Earth are made.

If a level of faith is the determining factor in God not healing Rosalba, how did I mess up so badly? I don't know yet. This is a quote from a pastor that helps me: "Examine my life and attitude in the light of God's works and words", (Pastor Robin Cowan). If my wife was still sick, there was a reason, and God would reveal it to me as I sought Him diligently. And seek Him I did. And yet, I often wondered -- did I have hope, not faith? Hope that she would be healed...faith in God doing the right thing? I became aware that I felt a pain in my chest when I would say the words of Jesus on the way to the cross, 'Your will be done.' I was afraid I couldn't convince God to heal my wife. I now realized myself, I could not persuade God to heal my wife against His own will."

In 1 Corinthians 5:7-9, Living Bible, God states: "7. Remove this evil cancer-this wicked person-from among you, so that you can stay pure. Christ, God's Lamb, has been slain for us. 8. So let us feast upon Him and grow strong in the Christian life, leaving entirely behind us the cancerous old life with all its hatreds and wickedness, let us feast instead upon the pure bread of honor and sincerity and truth. 9. When I wrote to you before I said not to mix with evil people. In this we return to one of the things that God never promised. He will not deliver us from His justice for our sins until the Heaven and Earth are remade without the curse of sin."

One of the five things you should never tell a person as they deal with a loved one suffering with cancer. "You just got to believe (or have faith)." Or "All it takes is faith the size of a mustard seed." I've had faith the size of a mustard seed. I still attended the funeral. So, was I not even able to muster up mustard seed-sized faith? Am I that sorry of a Christian? Everyone dies eventually and it's not because of lack of faith. One of my loved ones survives to this day and is doing well after cancer treatment. My faith was a lot less in that situation than it was on the previous several who passed away. It's not an exact science! Nor is it a spell that requires a pinch of faith. If we're being honest, it's actually pretty confusing at times. We live in a fallen world, and though we escape it in the next life, in this one we sometimes suffer along with it. Most people, like me, remember people they prayed for who died anyway, and in moments we don't like to admit, we wonder if God is 0 and 5. So don't tell me what the "magic recipe" is that will have God wanting to heal my loved one (or me). Hold your tongue and tell me that you love me and are praying for me (and /or my loved one), then do it. Tell me you're bringing dinner tonight so that I don't have to worry about it. But don't tell me to "just believe" or "just have faith." Just don't.

CHAPTER 18

GOD HAS TAKEN HER AWAY

At the time of this writing, it is March 28, 2017 and I'm preparing to address what I've gone through since October 22, 2014. This time was not easy for me or for our children. I was fortunate to have a loving niece/ daughter Natalee volunteer to arrange the memorial services for Rosalba. I mention Natalee like a daughter because of her love for me and my family. She is my niece but I wish she was my daughter. I couldn't and didn't have the mental or physical capacity to do so. I wanted to be alone to mourn, but at the same time I feared being alone. The questions and doubts were very present in my life at this moment and I was having difficulties discerning what was right and what was wrong. People would be talking to me and I could see their lips moving, but I wouldn't hear a word they said. I just wanted to escape and yell at God, but another part of me wanted to bow and thank Him for letting the pain end. A part of me wanted to hold on to Rosalba and never let her go, but as the director of the funeral home arrived with the doctor, I had to. They gave me time alone with her and I just prayed to thank God for finally taking her home. Home? The word had completely changed for me. Rosalba was never coming home again.

I still fight the tears as I'm writing right now, and have to stop to dry the tears and blow my nose. It's been two years now and it still hurts.

Our families gathered together at our home with the church families, but I don't remember the details. I was present, but I don't remember any of the details. It was like my body was present but my mind was numb and blank at this moment. So many thoughts and questions have flooded my mind for the previous six months, but then nothing. All my hopes and plans to retire and spend my life with my wife were now empty and void. I was planning to spend wonderful times with her and now I was planning her memorial. Everyone was trying to console me and give me hopeful quotes and I appreciated this. I just wondered what would happen when the voices left and I was left alone with my own thoughts and fears. What happened when the music faded and everyone slipped away?

My wife's family left the hospital and returned home in Dallas, Florida, and Mexico. The memorial was planned for a weekend at a later date. I tried to make it easier for all to plan their schedules. In all reality, I don't remember to many details after Rosalba passed away. I remember Rosalba's mother looked at me with tears in her eyes and asked me, "What do we do now?" This was the third of her eleven children she had witnessed dying before her. I couldn't imagine the pain she was experiencing in her heart. Rosalba was her youngest child. So many people involved in the life of Rosalba, and now there was one similarity with all of us. GRIEF! One five-letter word, but completely different to each of us. There was no way that they could grieve the same way as I did, and there was no way I could grieve the same as they did. How did you define the relationship that someone had with another? A husband with his wife was totally different from children with their mother. They were different but no less relevant.

I was so caught up in my own grief that there was no way for me to even evaluate how to help or encourage our children. At the moment, I was just hoping that all this pain would end. How come God didn't take us at the same time? The perfect ending for the spouse but not for those left behind. How would our children benefit if we both left at the same time? At the moment of Rosalba's death, I was of little help to anyone, including myself. A part of me just wanted to let go of everything. What was the use? Many days and nights on my knees praying, and the only thing I received was the death of my wife.

I found it difficult to be positive and hopeful at this time. People really were loving on me, but my heart was really conflicted at this moment. I wasn't seeing Rosalba suffer anymore, but there was no doubt she was dead and not coming home. I witnessed her taking her last breath, and even to this day I see it as I write this chapter. I woke in cold sweats, realizing I could not help her. I wipe away more tears and feel the lump building in my throat as I try to control the tears. It's real and if anyone tells you that this is abnormal two years later, then I'm guilty. How do you measure the love one shares with another? Who am I to determine the emotions and memories involved during a relationship and after a death? Right now, I'm just trying to catch my breath as part of me wants to quit breathing. The words of Matthew 5:4 are echoing in my mind: "Blessed are those who mourn, for they shall be comforted."

Once again, the doubts about God keeping His promises became very relevant. *Will He? When? Why not now?* I didn't feel comforted, and the greatest part of me just wanted to die. I had to be very careful, because I didn't want to become bitter towards life. What was more bitter than watching a loved one die as Rosalba did? This really didn't leave a sweet taste in my life and joy in my heart. Psalm 34:18 says, "The Lord is near to the brokenhearted and saves the crushed in spirit." *I feel crushed, God. Now's the time to do your God thing.*

A week after Rosalba went to be with God, I had to return to work. Everyone wanted to convey their condolences to me and my family. I appreciated their concern and love, but it was like I could hear the words but I wasn't there mentally. This worried me because I needed to keep focused on the things I was doing at work. I could hurt myself or someone else or make costly mistakes on the things I was working on. I finished the week. When I awoke to prepare to work on Saturday, I noticed my vision was blurred and I was seeing everything double. I would have to close one eye to maintain a normal view on the road as I drove to work. I used Google to open medical troubleshooting advice with my vision problem. Once I found their answer, I chose not to agree. Their advice was that I needed to seek immediate attention because I was having a stroke. I did decide to consult with my eye doctor. It really startled me when the first thing he checked for was a possible tumor behind my eye. Thank God it wasn't that. It did end up being one of the muscles in my left eye was not working properly. He explained that the human body suffers in many different ways while one goes through an extended grieving process. He provided me with a prism lens to place over my left eye to hopefully retrain this muscle to correct itself. Thank God, after three months the problem went away.

The time arrived for Rosalba's memorial and all the family and friends began to show up. I had to give special thanks to my niece, Natalee, for planning the memorial. This wasn't easy because the memorial was in English and Spanish, with two different pastors. As the memorial began, I tried my best to fight back the tears. I didn't succeed. Rosalba touched the lives of so many people and the evidence was that more than 300 people showed up to pay their respects. I stood at the doorway as the guests left and thanked everyone for coming. This wasn't easy, because at this time I just wanted to leave and let my emotions come out. At the same time, I hoped they would never leave. I now had a fear that Rosalba always shared with me. Her greatest fear was being alone. I was now alone. The children were working and away from our little town. We had taught them to be independent and they learned well. Now I was in a situation where they are worried about me and might be tempted to compromise their lives just to be with me. I was concerned for them as well, but I knew life never waited for us to pick ourselves up after this. The bills never stopped coming. The dogs never desired less of our attention. The house still needed to be cleaned up and the clothes still needed to be washed. I loved my children and they loved me. This truth would never bring my wife or their mom back to us.

Now the music of the memorial service faded and all had slipped away and I found myself on my knees once again. I didn't know how many

Kleenexes I went through every day, but at night was the worst for me. I was alone, and I hadn't experienced this for twenty-five years.

I saw all the wonderful decorations and pictures that showed just how unique Rosalba was, and the tears began all over again. I would stay awake late until I was exhausted, just to guarantee at least four hours of sleep without waking up eight to ten times a night with nightmares of her in pain or her last breath. I now understood Psalm 6:6 -- "I am worn out from my groaning. All night long I flood my bed with weeping and drench my couch with tears." This was where I had difficulty with people and their comments that, "You have an acceptable time to mourn. Now get up and get to work."

Can you tell me how God mends the heart? Can you tell me He mends all the hearts the same way? Can you tell me why He allowed the heart to break in the first place so He wouldn't have to mend it? If you can answer these questions in the lives of all the people in this world who were grieving, then I will hold back my tears.

The number one cause of death is from heart disease, but the number one need is someone to mend the hearts of all those who have lost someone they loved. I need the only one that can mend the pain of loss, loneliness, nightmares, and the loss of someone who all my senses will never experience again on this earth. Losing a spouse involves so much more sensual involvement than anyone else in our lives. As a couple made one by God, all our senses became as one. Our dreams, plans, activities, and time with God together changed in ways that I never experienced before. I had lost my grandfather, who was my best friend. I had lost both my grandmothers and my mom. I never felt the same level of loss as I did now. My heart didn't hurt then like it does now. They were gone and I missed all of them, but I never felt the level of loneliness as I felt and experienced every moment of the day and night.

While I tried to sleep, I would turn over to hug Rosalba as I frequently did in the past, and she was not there. I would wake up, concerned because she wasn't there and I would relive it all over again. So, I would turn on the television and listen to the Bible or other Christian programs. Sometimes I would sleep and sometimes I would be awake all night. During this time, I really thanked God for my job. Working took me out of my surroundings and kept my mind active on other things. People would ask me how I was doing and at the same time they really didn't want to hear the answer. So, I learned to shut up and not talk about it, knowing people didn't want to hear it anymore. Not because they didn't care anymore, but because they didn't know what to say.

I could understand this because there was only one God who can mend the broken heart. Many people say that it is time, a new house, a new job, traveling, and for some this might be their answer, but I needed something not as superficial. I needed something real. Everything I mentioned above was created by God, not me. God put Rosaba and me together, and God separated us. I didn't know the why as to putting us together or separating us, but He did. I needed to spend more time finding out who I was in Him. I thought I did, but obviously He changed my world and I needed to find out why and what I was supposed to do now. I was happy with my wife and family, but for some reason God chose to separate us from Rosalba. I knew where Rosalba was, and I knew she no longer had to worry about us or anything else. I did not have this privilege, though, because life was not going to wait for me to learn more about why God chose to do this.

So, the questions begin in my mind. *Why did God not heal her? Why did He allow her to suffer so much? What am I to do now? To who am I going to communicate my deepest thoughts and dreams? How am I going to deal with being alone without Rosalba?* She scheduled and paid our bills and she was good at it. Where were we at and how did I do this while I grieved? How would I deal with all the details of our married life that are ongoing? All the things we own were part of her dreams and plans. What did all this mean to me now? Her snow cone business, the basement, the carports, and her gardens. What about all the immigration papers that were still in process and now had changed due to her death. What did I have to do to get ahead of all this while I was still weeping and lacking any real desire to live, and pay bills? How did I do this, because at times I seemed paralyzed by the grief?

When I went to work, I would finish my day with no real motivation. I feared the time to leave because I would have to go home and realize once again Rosalba was not there. I feared the feeling of being alone. I feared looking at the same things that made her so happy and face the truth that God let her die. *What do I do now, God? There is nothing in this house that I care about now that Rosalba's not here.* I had to ask myself if I had indeed done the will of God or if I really was able to love this God who let her die. I felt for the psalmist who proclaimed in Psalm 42:3, "My tears have been my food day and night, while people say to me all day long, 'Where is your God?'"

I don't care who you are on this earth, you will face these questions from others but mostly from satan himself after losing someone you really love. I asked myself over and over again what I must have done wrong that would make God take her from me. *Didn't I love her enough? Did I love her more than You, God? Have I done something against You, God, that You need to punish me this way? Did I not love her as Jesus loved the church? You are aware, God, that I am not Jesus?*

Isaiah 57:1 tells me, "The righteous perish, and no one takes it to heart; the devout are taken away, and no one understands that the righteous are taken away to be spared from evil." *I take it to heart, God. It feels as if You are ripping out my heart right now. Are You telling me that something more evil than cancer could be found in this world? Are you telling me that there is something evil in my life or the lives of our children? What's going to happen tomorrow?*

This was the most difficult time of my life. Since I was twenty years old, my only desire had been to obey God and I dared anything or anybody to get in the way. Now the most difficult thing I had ever experienced was trying to get in my way. Why should I continue to obey a God who let Rosalba suffer and die like this? I now was facing my Job moment when he asked God in Job 10:2, "Show me why You contend with me." *What have I done to You, God? How have I offended You?* All my days with God had not been easy and we had met and surpassed our trials, with God intervening in many different ways, as I mentioned in previous chapters. *What's different now, God? Have You forsaken me?*

I pretended to hear the voice of Christ as He shouted from the cross, "My God, my God, why have You forsaken Me?" I would never pretend or presume that I was Christ, though I wanted to be like Him. If God wasn't there to save His Son, then why would He be there to save Rosalba? God had determined before the birth of Jesus that He was to die for the sins of all mankind. Rosalba didn't die for the sins of mankind, but God knew before her birth when she was going to die for hers. She had been forgiven for her sins because she asked God for it, but the consequences of those sins remained. Hebrews 9:27 tells us "It is appointed for men to die once, but after this the judgment."

I am writing this part of the book on May 4th, 2017. I have been stumbling over my emotions as I try to tell you the reader why you should dare to obey God as you face similar levels of grief and loss as I have. I'm looking for the easiest way to share the why without exhausting you with many Bible verses that you probably won't look for as you try to catch your breath or just try to breathe, as I did while I watched Rosalba wasting away and leave this world. The simple truth is that I continue to obey because I choose too. I cannot logically convince or explain to you or others why you should continue to obey a God you cannot see, touch, smell, taste, or hear. These are the things I miss the most about my wife. I cannot see, touch, smell, taste, or hear her anymore. I choose to obey because God proved Himself to me many times in the past. Many times, when no answer was available without God's intervention, He quietly stepped in and opened doors that to this day I cannot explain. My marriage would not have happened without Him. The births of our children were so miraculous and the process of life still astounds me. My personal salvation. Why would I choose to follow a God I cannot see, touch, smell, taste, or hear? Because

I ask Him to forgive me for everything that I am and for everything I cannot understand. I've never been to heaven or hell. I've never seen, touched, smelled, tasted, or heard either place. The Bible talks much more about hell than it does about Heaven. This must be important. Even when we plan a vacation, the details seem to be like hell concerning the bills and travel, but the beach is so beautiful.

Life is similar to this because it seems like pure hell as you watch your loved one suffer, but until you get to the destination you cannot appreciate how beautiful it is. I just know that now Rosalba is in Heaven because I know she loved Jesus. It's possible that she loved Him more than me! I choose to obey my supervisors at work, and many times I don't know where they're going or what they are trying to accomplish through me. I have no clue as to what God is trying to accomplish through me, either. I know that He has never let me down in the past even when it was difficult. He has led me to the most profound part of our relationship thus far. *Can you obey Me when I remove the most important person in your life?* I agree that many times I've wondered if I loved Rosalba or God more. I could see, touch, smell, taste, and hear Rosalba. I cannot do this with God. Now, I'm in a situation I have never been in before. I have a God I cannot see, touch, smell, taste, or hear and a wife I could see, touch, smell, taste, or hear. What do I do? Do I continue to trust in this unseen God or wait for my wife to return? Which do you think is more real? God, or my wife returning?

In the Bible, only a few people have been resurrected from the dead to live again. What happened next? They had to die again. I could never imagine being sick or in an accident and die, only to live again and possibly repeat that death. I cannot imagine Rosalba suffering with cancer for six months, then resurrected, only to possibly suffer six more months with cancer again. I believe for Christians, death is a release from these evils of cancer, diabetes, heart disease, and evils that we cannot even imagine, except to read Revelation. Somehow, I find comfort knowing that the events in Revelation will never be a problem for Rosalba. I hope they won't be the many evils I will possibly have to face if my relationship is not right with Jesus Christ. I cannot imagine an evil worse than cancer, other than what we have been told about hell.

I have now faced the loss of several people in my life, but I choose to see my life as blessed. So far, all the people I've seen cease to breathe have had a relationship with Jesus Christ and I have been comfortable with this truth because of the fruit they have shown in their lives. I do have loved ones in my life who do not know Jesus Christ as their personal Savior, and I do not know how I will feel when it's their time to go.

Why obey God? I choose to. What else can I do? I can see His creation. I can feel the love that I had with Rosalba when everything told me that it was all about me. She gave up everything she knew and experienced to leave Mexico and spend twenty-five years of her life serving with me. Many times, I'm sure she wondered why she chose to do this. At times, I'm sure what she saw in me wasn't God-like. I'm sure some of the things I said didn't sound like God. I'm sure that many times in her life she wondered if I indeed was following Jesus Christ in my own life. Was I spiritually qualified to lead her in our marriage? Could she trust me to lead her to Heaven? She needed so much more than me to help her carry the cross she had to carry during her cancer. This was so true because I could not see, touch, smell, taste, or hear the cancer destroying her life and body. I couldn't stop this evil. Neither the doctors nor I had a magic pill or procedure to deliver her.

I ask myself continually the same question: *Why should I dare to obey God if this is what I have to face as a result?* God has never changed from the beginning of mankind to this very day. All the people in the Old Testament and the New Testament died except for two people, Enoch and Elijah. They too will die in Revelation, only to live again mysteriously because God wants them to. So, God has not changed. From the moment you and I were conceived; our days have been numbered and we cannot change our end date. If we make the choice to believe in Jesus and decide to follow Him, then we will know Him as He is. This is a very big "if."

I find comfort in knowing that Rosalba is in Heaven, hugging her oldest sister who died of tuberculosis and was a Christian, and her oldest brother who died of hemophilia at the age of one. I'm sure she welcomed her second brother Armando into Heaven, who took a lunch break and died of a heart attack recently, on a curb in Mexico.

I'm sure that she is there to embrace my grandfather and grand-mothers and my mom. I'm sure that when it is my time, she will be ready to give me a tour of Heaven and show me how organized God really is. She will show me the awesome colors of the gardens that we could only dream about as we gardened together on this cursed earth. I'm sure that now she can praise God in a beautiful way she could only dream about here on this earth. I choose to believe God will give her the ability to sing on key and with a voice that resounds across the Heavens. I remember that she was always singing her favorite hymn or praise song as she toiled in her tasks at home or at work. I'm sure now she has the answers to the questions she had about Jesus and about God. I'm sure as a mother she had questions about Mary and how she dealt with watching her Son die on a cross for our sins, and wondered if God impregnated her with Jesus to let Him die that way. I'm sure she is talking to Mary about this situation. *How did you do it, Mary? How did you decide to keep obeying and following God after you watched Him die on the cross the way He did?*

CHAPTER 19

DEALING WITH THE FACT THAT GOD DIDN'T ANSWER MY PRAYERS THE WAY I THOUGHT HE SHOULD

I t is now January 8th, 2018, and I have been trying my best to find a way to address this question for myself. It has been very difficult for me to understand the question. God, did You set me up to fail? God, You have provided me all these promises of healing, strength, rescue, shelter, provision, and said YOU will never leave me alone. It appears that YOU set Mary up to fail. You give her the opportunity to go through the virgin birth and all the difficulties that came with a single girl impregnated with YOUR child and expecting everyone to believe this was even possible. After all this, YOU let her oldest son, JESUS, be beaten, cursed, betrayed, and killed on a cross like a criminal. We know now why because of the Bible, but she didn't know why. She must have felt so betrayed because YOU set her up only to watch her son die.

Why would she feel blessed as she watched her blessed and promised son die this way on a cross? I'm sure she was asking the same questions that most of us ask ourselves as we watch our loved ones suffer and die.

What about the disciples? They walked with JESUS for three-and-a-half years, expecting to be part of a powerful country with a powerful leader. Maybe another King David or King Solomon. A life and country freed from the tyranny of the Roman dictators. Judas believed this so much that he betrayed Jesus for silver when he realized Jesus was determined to die or talking about dying. All but one of the disciples fled and hid while fearing for their safety. God, did You set up the disciples for failure as well? We know the story because we have the Bible, but they didn't. They still had no indication how You would walk on the earth with them and hang on a cross like a common criminal after three years. Both Mary and the disciples were eventually blessed by witnessing the truth with their own eyes, but we here on earth now didn't experience or witness Your death or resurrection.

What about Lazarus? He was YOUR own friend when YOU received word from Mary and Martha that he was sick and dying. You did nothing. How did they receive the news from the messenger as he told them that YOU weren't coming? They knew that YOU were the only one who could heal him, but YOU decided to wait. I could only imagine what they were thinking as they watched Lazarus suffer and die before their eyes, knowing that YOU could have prevented his death. YOU have healed others, but now YOU allowed YOUR own friend to suffer and die. Why? YOU knew what YOU were going to do and You knew YOU had the power to heal him. YOU knew YOU had the power to raise him from the grave, but I'm sure they didn't fully understand this themselves. When YOU finally arrived, we see where Martha came running and I was sure she was not happy with YOU. For days, she had been waiting and worrying about her brother and YOUR friend. *Where are you, JESUS? Why aren't YOU here yet? What is more important to YOU that YOU'RE letting my brother suffer and die?* I don't even know what to think about what Mary was thinking, because she didn't even come to meet YOU when YOU arrived. I'm thinking that she was still pretty angry and disappointed with YOU.

Why did You set them up to fail? YOU gave them hope and they ended up preparing Lazarus for burial and placed him in a tomb. *Where is this awesome Jesus who has healed and rescued so many strangers but let our brother suffer and die?* YOU told Martha "he will rise again," but she was thinking about in the future resurrection of the dead. YOU told us, "He who believes in me will live, even though he dies: and whoever lives and believes in me will never die (John 14:12-14)." Memo, Jesus: Lazarus is dead! Once again, we know the story because of YOUR WORD, but they didn't. YOU finally arrived and you sent for Mary. Why? Did YOU think she was waiting to give YOU a big hug and tell YOU she loved YOU after YOU let them down? YOU told YOUR own disciples Lazarus was not dead but sleeping. John 11:11I could only imagine what was going through their minds when YOU said that. *Excuse me, we know what dead is, JESUS. We have buried many loved ones and friends in the past. Lazarus is dead, JESUS!* Thomas asked the other disciples to go with him so that they could die with Lazarus. John 11:16

It appears to me that all these witnesses up to now would agreed that Lazarus was indeed dead and YOU let them down. YOU built up all their hopes, and now nothing. YOU set them up to fail. YOU knew what YOU were going to do, but they didn't. We know because we have the Bible. As all of the family and friends were weeping in grief, we learn that "YOU wept." The Bible states that as YOU witnessed all the people grieving, YOU were deeply moved in spirit and troubled. Why? YOU knew what YOU were going to do. Why were You "deeply moved in spirit and troubled"? Why did you then "weep"? Did YOU weep because YOU really cared about Lazarus? Did You weep because they still didn't see who or what YOU really were? As they pondered YOUR every move, the questions continued. "Could not HE who opened the eyes of the blind man have kept this man from dying?" John 11:37

YOUR WORD tells us that once again YOU were deeply moved.John 11:38-40 Why? Were YOU contemplating the death YOU would eventually suffer on the cross for our sins? Now YOU had the disciples, Mary, and Martha trying to convince themselves the obvious had not happened. Not only was Lazarus dead, but after four days his body was decomposing because YOU waited too long to come. Now YOU wanted them to roll away the stone so YOU could wake him up? I'm sure as Mary arrived she was thinking about how YOU failed them. She even stated it: "Lord, if YOU had been here, my brother would not have died." John 11:21

YOU asked them to "take away the stone," John 11:39 and I'm sure Martha gasped at the thought as she replied, "By this time there is a bad odor, for he has been there four days." YOUR next question must have been confusing to her at the time when YOU asked her, "Did I not tell you that if you believe, you will see the glory of God?" John 11:40 Up to now this whole process of Lazarus's sickness and death had been full of questions and doubts. Then YOUR big prayer: "Father, I thank you that you have heard me. I knew that you always hear me, but I said this for the benefit of the people stand here, that they may believe that you sent me." John 11:41

If I would pray like this in public, people would call me prideful and arrogant. But then, I wasn't the one who called in a loud voice, "Lazarus, come out!" John 11:43 The people around me have never seen me command someone to come forth from the dead. YOU did it, though, to the disbelief of all those standing around YOU.

So, what are we missing in this story?

First, I have to manage my expectations. I am part of God's creation but not the Creator. God has explained this to us in HIS WORD, but those in the time of Christ only had the Old Testament. They probably had more questions than I do right now because of this. I have to believe that what God says will be completed and fulfilled. This means that life will be given and taken away here on this earth. We will witness with our own eyes the births and the deaths of those we love. Since Rosalba has died, I've witnessed the deaths of my grandmother, mother, and Rosalba's oldest brother. Death is real! Lazarus was dead! All functions of his body were finished, other than decomposing. If it wasn't for God's desire to show the truth to Mary,

Martha, their friends, the disciples, and all the Jewish people witnessing all that was going on, Lazarus would've still been dead in the grave.

I have to remember that Jesus died on the cross. The story of His power was recorded by many witnesses who spread the story to endless places on the earth. This was also the purpose for this miracle of raising Lazarus: So that many would see that Jesus indeed came from God and eventually would have total power over death, hell, and over the consequences of our sins on the face of the earth. In a way, Jesus was telling us what was going to happen to HIM in the near future. HE would die on the cross and it would appear to everyone witnessing HIS death that HE was truly dead! The blood, the spear, the last breath, HIS statement, "into YOUR hands I commend my Spirit." Luke 23:46 Everyone who witnessed JESUS' death on the cross believed indeed HE had died. Those who went to prepare His body later truly believed HE was dead. People wept and wailed. There was a funeral and a burial process. They believed that soon His body also would start stinking and decomposing. I'm sure the people who smelled the body of Lazarus and of Jesus would agree that they had indeed died, and this was important to fulfill the witness of the power of God.

It is important for them and for me to truly believe that the ones they loved and the ones we love are truly deceased. This is part of what God has promised us due to the sins in our lives and the curse on this world.

Second, Martha was not convinced that Jesus would perform a miracle here. I'm sure she was not expecting to see Lazarus come back from the dead after being dead for four days. Jesus tried to encourage Martha and us to believe and stretch our faith in HIS promises. Jesus had warned us about saying our prayers in public, but this prayer was an exception. This prayer did nothing for Jesus on this earth. In fact, it probably sped up His death on the cross. There were many who feared His ability to perform so many miracles that they could not. God performed this miracle through Jesus to show them and us HIS power. This prayer was for those around Lazarus and for us to see that God indeed listened to Jesus and for us to truly believe God sent Jesus to us.

How do we know this? We know and they knew because of what happened next. This was a clear case of "cause and effect." Jesus was the cause of Lazarus rising from the dead. Several things happened that we can relate to on this earth. We watched our loved ones suffer and die, or we got word of their death. We were there to witness their last breaths, as I was. We witnessed the doctor definitively proclaim the death and document the time. We were there as the mortuary arrived to remove the body. We looked upon the body as it was prepared for the burial or cremation. We were there to share with our families, friends, and acquaintances as the pastor delivered the final service. We shared the same tears with each other, just like Mary, Martha, and Jesus shared in this story. We saw the body lowered into the grave to apparently finish the process. What we haven't seen and they did witness was the rest of the story. Jesus through God has the power over death, hell, and the grave.

Third, we have to choose what we want to believe. Many in the time of Lazarus believed in the power given to Jesus by God and they proclaimed the miracle over and over again into many parts of the world. There were those who could not deny this miracle, but were fearful or threatened by this power to raise people from the dead. *If Jesus indeed has this power, what else is He capable of doing? Are all the other words of Jesus true? Can He convince all the people that His message is correct and our message is in error?* To prevent this possibility, many of the people conspired to kill Jesus because they felt threatened. I know this to be true because I also fear repeating death as Rosalba experienced it. I also fear what happens after death. I do not fear death or what happens afterwards in my conscience only because of my faith and personal relationship in Jesus. My mind is on a different level. I'm just like Mary, Martha, and the disciples on this earth because I've never witnessed a "Lazarus moment" or a "Jesus ascension" moment.

Fourth, God's plan will continue despite what we choose to do or believe. The religious leaders in the times of Jesus and Lazarus could not deny the evidence of the power of God through Jesus. They just chose not to except it as truth in their lives. If I choose not to believe it, then it must not be real, right? Even the head religious leader recited the word of prophecy, stating "You do not realize that it is better for you that one man will die for the people than that the whole nation perish. John 11:50" He repeated what we were told, but chose to ignore it because it did not benefit him in his pride and arrogance.

We see four responses in this story. 1) It demonstrates our Lord's power from God. 2) It strengthens the faith of those who believe in Jesus, especially the disciples, Martha, and Mary. 3) It brings many to faith in Jesus as the Messiah. 4) It provokes greater and more intense opposition to Jesus and a unified Sanhedrin, intent on bringing about the death of Jesus.

So, what about you and me? How many times have I asked Jesus the same questions as Mary and Martha? *If You had only come earlier, Rosalba would not have died. I thought YOU loved her. Were YOU so busy that YOU couldn't find time to travel such a short distance for YOUR friend?* The answer that I've found after more than three years is the testimony, the sharing of the story in their situation and the story of our faith in ours.

I remember the question Rosalba's mother asked me after she died. "Now what?" I told her the same as I've been telling myself for more than three years. "All we have, Mom, is our testimony to others. Our children and others will be watching us to see how we respond to Rosalba's death." Is it the end? Is it a beginning? People will see how much we loved them just as we can see how much Mary, Martha, and Jesus loved Lazarus. If we are truthful, those around us will know that we indeed loved them, but they will also see that we have a hope to be reunited with them with Jesus and God.

I often hear people state, "If only I had..." Had done what? I don't think I have ever posed this problem to myself. I have no doubt in my mind that the control of life or death is not in my power. In Rosalba's situation, there was absolutely nothing that I could have done to prevent this pancreatic cancer. There was nothing I could have done to make her find me or fall in love with me. It has always been a blessing to know that I'm not in control of anyone's life, not even my own. The breath that I breathe today is not guaranteed tomorrow. I have found for myself that second guessing what happens is not good. I would ask the question, "Why did Jesus raise Lazarus from the grave only so he could die again in the future?" Only God can answer this question because everything happens according to His will. I breathe because He wants me to breathe. With this breath, I can share His promises with others who are watching their loved ones suffer, or suffer and die as I did with Rosalba.

This story has helped me in dealing with the grief and the powers of hell chanting in my mind, "Where is your God now?" I have to remember five things again: 1) This has strengthened my faith as it did for Mary, Martha, and the disciples. 2) This story and Rosalba's story bring many to salvation through their testimony and ours. 3) These situations will cause many to leave the faith and actively lead others astray. 4) This and other similar stories have led to the persecution of many Christians in the past. Jesus was no exception. 5) As with the story of the Jewish church at the time, some will prepare the way for the betrayal of our Lord as with Judas or with us. God can use the same story for His will, whether I choose to believe or not believe. God is going to use me like Jesus or like the Jewish leaders who had Him killed.

There are two "ifs" that are recorded in this story. "If You had only come earlier You could have saved him" and "If only you believe" as Jesus spoke. I choose to believe although God didn't answer the way I wanted Him to. I wanted Rosalba here on earth with me for much more time. I choose to believe she carried her cross until God said she had carried it long enough. I believe Jesus wept for Lazarus, Mary, and Martha because He knew how hard it is to watch and understand something they had never experienced themselves. They had never seen anyone come from the grave until Jesus performed this miracle. I've never seen it with my own eyes and I'm not going to pretend to know what Rosalba experienced after her last breath on this earth. I wish I knew, and someday I will when my recorded time arrives.

I cannot presume that Jesus only wept because He was now human, and as God He feels nothing. It is recorded that God also shows emotions as God, not as a man only. He was angry, sad, jealous, and loved as God. It is also recorded that "He (Jesus) is despised and rejected by men. A Man of sorrows and acquainted with grief. And we hid, as it were, our faces from Him; He was despised, and we did not esteem Him. Surely, He has borne our griefs and carried our sorrows; Yet we esteemed Him stricken, Smitten by God, and afflicted." (Isaiah 53:3-4)

"So also Christ did not glorify himself in becoming high priest; but the one who glorified him was God who said to him, 'You are my Son! Today I have fathered you.' As also in another place God says, 'You are a priest forever in the order of Melchezedek.' During his earthly life he offered both requests and supplications, with loud cries and tears, to the one who was able to save him from death and he was heard because of his devotion. Although he was a son, he learned obedienceaudience though the things he suffered. And by being perfected in this way, he became the source of eternal salvation to all who obey him, and he was designated by God as 'high priest in the order of Melchezedek.'" (Hebrews 5: 5-10) I believe that Jesus became our sympathetic high priest.

There's one last thing that comes to my attention from this story and ours. "UNBELIEF IS UNBELIEVABLE.Or Unbelievable unbelief." I wonder how many of us, as well as those in Jesus' time, have fallen for the popular lie that "faith is believing the unbelievable," or as the little boy is said to have expressed it, "Faith is believing what isn't true." This is not true! The whole book of John was written so that we could believe Jesus is the Messiah, the Son of God, the Savior of lost sinners. In the time of Jesus, the Jewish people did not fail to come to faith due to a lack of evidence. They refused to believe in spite of a mountain of evidence. No one disputes that Lazarus died, or that Jesus raised him from the dead. Yet, while this raising brought some to faith, it was a "problem" that had to be reported to the Jewish religious leaders. It is the unbelief of these Jews which is unbelievable, not the faith of those who do believe. Perhaps we should come up with another word for our proclamation and defensed of the gospel, other than the word "apologetics."

I'm sure of several things. God told us that because of our sin ""Just as people are destined to die once, and after that to face judgment." Hebrews 9:27 Rosalba died due to this statement made by God. I believe she had no unconfessed sins in her life when she died. I believe she suffered and then she died. I believe Jesus also suffered and then He died. I believe when Rosalba took her last breath on this earth, her next one was in heaven at the side of Jesus. I believe when Jesus died on the cross and He stated "into YOUR hands I commend my spirit; deliver me, Lord, my faithful God." Psalm 31:5, Jesus called out with a loud voice, "Father, into your hands I commit my spirit. Whe he had sad this, he breathed his last. Luke 23:46 His next breath was at the side of His Father God. I believe the cancer cannot ever destroy the life of Rosalba again. She will never hunger, thirst, tire, cry, or despair ever again. I believe nothing on earth, heaven, or hell will ever take the life of my Lord again.

I believe even if Rosalba is not with me here on this earth anymore, she is in a much better place than you and I who remain. I believe Jesus told us "And if I go and prepare a place for you, I will come back and take you to be with me that you also may be where I am. John 14:3 He is busy at work right now. I believe I should be at work sharing this story and my story to those who are looking for some light in a dark and hopeless world without Jesus. Jesus is preparing a home for you and me to share with our loved ones who have arrived before us. We should be sharing with the others here on this earth the way to get there with us. I believe Jesus was waiting for Rosalba's arrival in heaven with His arms open wide to welcome her with the words, "Welcome, My good and faithful servant." I believe our loved ones will be there with Jesus as we arrive in His presence and also are greeted in heaven. I believe there are many more people waiting for hope as they face suffering or watch someone they love suffering. I believe Jesus waited as He suffered on the cross as He cried out, "And about the ninth hour Jesus cried with a loud voice, saying, Eli, Eli, lama sabachthani?That is to say,My God, my God, why hast Thou forsaken me?" Matthew 27:46

I believe that even as it was silent for Christ in this moment, His Father God was right there waiting for His Son in heaven, to greet Him saying, "Well done, My good and faithful servant!" I believe that through Jesus Christ I will have to carry my cross, as do you and others. I believe the same angels who comforted Jesus during His suffering will be there to minister to us. I believe that although the angels will not change the will of God and the crosses that you and I are given to carry, they will provide help and strength as they did for Jesus. I believe that as difficult as it is for Jesus to forgive those who continually say no to Him and those religious leaders in His day who eventually gave Him up to be crucified, Jesus asked His God and ours for the forgiveness of the sins of everyone.Jesus said, "Father, forgive them, for they do not know what they are doing. And they divided up His clothes by casting lots." Luke 23:34

I believe you and I must also forgive the doctors and nurses for all the painful memories and details we witnessed in the suffering of our loved ones. They didn't give Rosalba cancer. They were there to help her carry her cross the best they could. I remember a special nurse who tried and failed several times to draw blood from Rosalba in the hospital. In tears, she looked at Rosalba and me and asked us if she could pray with us. Of course, we agreed, and we all knew this cross and this burden could only be eased by the grace of God. It's the same grace that carries us now here on earth as we long to be with our loved ones as we carry our own crosses to that same finish line where Jesus waits to say, "Well done, My good and faithful servant!"

CHAPTER 20

HOW TO REALIZE I'M NOT ALONE WHEN ALL MY SENSES TELL ME THAT I AM

May 22, 2018. This has not been an easy topic for me to address. Every day I come home from work or church and I am indeed alone, based on what I can see, taste, hear, smell, and touch. So how do I tell others that after the loss of their spouses, they cannot rely on their senses? It is difficult to explain the way that God has created man in the same image as Him. We are created as a spirit, mind, and a body just like Jesus our Lord. We spend 90-100 percent of our lives in the mind and in the body, and therefore we understand very little of the truths of God. God is Spirit and only through Jesus Christ can we see the difference between our lives on this earth and what happens afterwards. Jesus walked on this earth for thirty-three-and-a-half years before He died and arose again. All the people who saw Him die and be buried experienced what you and I have experienced with our spouses. We saw how our loved one died and how they suffered until the end. Some of us had the chance to say goodbye and some did not. Jesus had time to tell His mom and disciples goodbye, and Rosalba had time to tell me and our children goodbye. We saw her suffer and die with cancer and we saw her take her last breath. We saw her carried away as the funeral home came to do their thing. We gathered as a family to remember her as a wife, mother, sister, and sister-in-Christ. These are the things we have similar to Christ and the disciples, without the fear that people were hunting us down to kill us too. So, what are we missing?

God and His Son, Jesus, know what happens next and the Bible tells us the same. I haven't seen it with my eyes and you haven't either. I never saw the spirit of Rosalba come back from the grave to tell me she was alive and that all the Bible says is true. This is why it is so important to understand what the Bible says about the words and actions of our Lord and Savior Jesus Christ. This is the only example we have in the Bible to show us the difference between the spirit, mind, and the body when our lives on earth are over. I myself have been hesitating on writing this chapter and finishing this book with a small fear that when I have finished, my time on earth will be over. Maybe God has allowed me to go through this trial only to finish this book and help others who have lost their spouses as well. I have a lot to learn as well because I have not experienced what the 500-plus people witnessed when Jesus arose from the grave as a spirit and showed Himself to them. We only speak from imagination and fantasy because we know nothing of the spirit world. We make movies, write books, and sing songs from imagination and fantasy because we don't know the truth about the spirit world. We spend so much time on the mind and the body without ever addressing the needs of the spirit. Maybe this is why we know nothing about the spirit side of ourselves?

This is a third of the creation God has made in us, and we know nothing about it. I know nothing about it myself, and only now am I spending more time in it. I now enjoy spending more time in prayer and praising God, even in the silence and the loneliness after losing Rosalba. I understand now the words of Paul the apostle when he encouraged us to remain single and focus on God. It's very difficult to focus on the needs of the spirit of the man when the needs of the mind and body are so evident. It's much harder when one is married and has children, because the needs of the mind and body are so demanding and evident. We can see these things very easily. We know the need to educate ourselves and our children, and we can see when they are hungry or sick. We know if they are clothed or if they are happy or sad. Our senses tell us these things. My question is this: What do you or I know about our spirit?

The spirit of man is never alone. God is always there and satan is also there as well. We are never alone, but we seldom are aware of it. Somehow, we continue to breathe, walk, talk, and continue to exist, and there must be a reason for this other than our minds and our bodies. God breathed life into us, and with that breath came the Spirit of God into you and me. So, the question is: If the Spirit of God is within us from our creation, how are we ever alone? I can almost understand how difficult it was for Jesus to try to explain this to His disciples and to us in the Bible. How do you explain something that we have never seen, touched, tasted, smelled, or heard? How do you explain to me or anyone else that my body and mind will die and pass away but my spirit will never die? I've never seen my own spirit, have you? It's there and God can see it, but I can't. Why not?

I have some things similar to you and others who have lost our spouses. I can still visualize her face and wonderful smile in my mind. I can still smell that sweet smell of her perfume and her hair after a shower. I can still feel her embrace. I can still remember how the body and the mind seem to go to heaven and return safely and go back again after spending time together physically. I can still smell the aroma of her great cooking in the kitchen and how it seemed to fill the whole house. Even if you weren't hungry, you just had to try what smelled so good. Did it taste as good as it smelled? As always, it did! I found out with Rosalba that a way to a man's heart is indeed through his stomach. But, how do you get through to his spirit? After almost four years I still have Rosalba's clothes and shoes here in the house with me. I haven't changed a single thing in the home since she went home with Jesus. There have been things that I've had to change, but not of my choosing. I've spent so much time thinking about how much I miss her mind and her body, but have a difficult time remembering how I remember the spirit of Rosalba. Did I even recognize it? How would I identify it? What does it look like? What did it do? Where did it spend its time? I know all this about her mind (10 percent) and her body. When does a man really know what a woman is thinking? But, even with a limitation on knowing what she was thinking, what did I know about her spirit? This has been the most difficult part of finishing this chapter. If I don't know my own spirit or the spirit of Rosalba, how do I recognize the Spirit of a God I have never seen before?

Loneliness is a real thing for all of us. We could be in a crowd of 10,000 people and still feel completely alone. We can have a spouse and children and still feel totally alone. Why? I believe it's because a third part of us is always ignored. Our spirit is deprived while we constantly tend to our bodies and our minds. This explains so much about our deficiencies in life, whether with ourselves, spouses, or our families. If you have four in your family and you're supposed to be twelve parts in all, with your spirit, mind, and body, but you're really only functioning on eight parts versus twelve parts, you have a real problem. A problem with yourself, spouse, and your children. The biggest problem we have is with our God. If He is Spirit, and you and I cannot even identify our spirits or His, who are we? What are we? Where are we? Why are we here? So, my biggest problem is that I don't know myself.

If God never leaves me or abandons me, why should I feel so lonely? I know that I can never explain this in a way where our senses would ever understand. Jesus couldn't do it either with His disciples. Rosalba reached the point where the mind and body were removed and only her spirit remained. To my embarrassment, I might not have truly known her spirit, but I have the confidence and faith to know our God did. I know she is with Jesus right now and she is spending time with all the loved ones who left this earth before us. If the spirit never dies, where does it spend its time? What do our spirits do on this earth? If the Bible tells us in John 4:24 that "God is Spirit, and his worshiper <u>must</u> worship in the Spirit and in truth," what does the word "<u>must</u>" mean? "The spirituality of the divine nature of God is founded on the necessity of the spirituality of divine worship; for the worship of God <u>must</u> partake of His nature: as His nature is spiritual, his worship, to be acceptable, <u>must</u> be so likewise. If we do not worship God, who is a Spirit, in spirit, we neither give Him the glory due to His name, and so do not perform a real and proper act of worship, nor can we hope to attain His favor, and acceptance with Him, and so we miss the end of worship. The exercise of faith and love, therefore, and of other graces, <u>must</u> constitute the true spiritual worship we owe to the God and Father of our Lord Jesus Christ, and which cannot but be acceptable to Him, wherever it is offered, in whatever place, and by whatever person." (Benson Commentary, Rev. Joseph Benson. Published By: T. Carlton & J. Porter. 1857, Internet BIBLEHUB.)

So, how do I simplify this to speak about loneliness? If the God who created us only with the purpose of spending time with us cannot, due to our sin and our inability to see, taste, touch, hear, or feel Him, what do we do? How can we avoid loneliness when our children are gone and our spouses have passed from this earth? Some of us have many friends and activities to keep our minds occupied, but that still doesn't address your spirit and its connection to God's Spirit. This just means we stay busy. If and when it becomes my time to carry this cross like Rosalba, what does "busy" mean to me? Even Jesus asked the powerful question of, "My God, My God, Why have You forsaken me?" The sins He took onto Himself from you and me separated Him from God's Spirit for that moment, and it was miserable for Jesus. Can I even discern when His Spirit is with mine or not? Jesus could, and that explains His question.

What I have had to accept is the truth that I have been blessed with a family and friends, but this was above and beyond what I was created for. It has always been a God-and-me relationship, just as it is a you-versus-God relationship. We were created to worship God. "And they heard the sound of the LORD God walking in the garden in the cool of the day, and Adam and his wife hid themselves from the presence of the LORD God among the trees of the garden." (Gen. 3:8) Do you really think God appeared to them in the garden only *after* they had sinned? I choose to believe God visited with them every day in the cool of the evening. What captures my attention is this: Why were they afraid *this time*? The truth then and now is not that God was walking with man every day in the garden, but that now man sinned and felt fear near the presence of God.

I don't think we are any different today than Adam and Eve were in the Garden of Eden. We want to be in God's presence once again, but <u>must</u> face the reality that with our sins we cannot anymore. They were in a wonderful place where they didn't have to worry about where God was because He was always walking and talking with them. They didn't have to worry about what each other was thinking, because sin still did not exist and they didn't know the difference between "Good and Evil." They didn't have to worry about sickness or death before the sin. They didn't have to worry about sex or pain during childbirth. Adam didn't have to worry about his job or if he made enough money to care for his family. Eve didn't have to worry if she looked fat in a new dress because they both walked around naked. They didn't have to worry about paying for a house, utilities, food, transportation, or entertainment to occupy their minds. They had God and this was fine with them, until the serpent came in and entered their minds and broke the spiritual connection they had with God when they took the fruit off of the tree of the knowledge of good and evil. Sin and separation entered and so did loneliness.

It's not God's design for the spirit of man to be separated with the Spirit of God. He still wants to walk and talk with you and me, but we chose the knowledge of good and evil. We only know it when evil attacks our minds and our bodies. We have no idea how our spirits suffer when evil separates us from God. I cannot tell when God is near me, can you? I hear people all the time tell me that they feel this or that, but this is based on feelings only. Many times, I can imagine feeling the caressing hands of my wife on my forehead or my back, or her breath on my neck or chest. I can still at times imagine the smell of her perfume or how it felt as I ran my hands through her hair. I can still imagine the softness of her skin and the beat of her heart as I laid my head against her chest. I treasure these memories, but she is gone. She's not here with me. I have sinned and God is not here in the midst of my sin and a sinful world. This is why He sent His son Jesus Christ in His place. This is why His last visit in the Garden of Eden with Adam and Eve was to address their sin. I wonder how His voice must have changed when he addressed their sin, or did it?

I still recall when I was younger and did something I was not supposed to do. I can still remember how I felt knowing I did something wrong. I remember I spent most of my time trying to figure out how to help myself mentally or physically, but spiritually there was nothing. Maybe a little guilty conscience and fear of my sins being discovered. I never felt my spirit hurting as much as my behind or my mind when I was punished. I wonder why I have never been sensitive to my spirit. Shouldn't it bother me that spiritually I never felt, saw, touched, heard, or tasted anything? We are in a different world now than the Garden of Eden. We've limited ourselves only to know good and evil, when at one time all we knew was good. We have also lost our ability to *know*. Now we are limited to knowing God through limited means:

1st: The inner witness -- The Inner Knowing. This is like when a child knows he did something wrong and he finally confesses he did something wrong, or like me when inside I knew my life was wrong and Jesus needed to be the Lord of my life. Like I feel right now, knowing God has things He wants me to do, but every day I feel like this earth is not my home.

2nd: We have the Word of God. This is something Adam and Eve never needed, but many years later and many sins later, we do. It has always been with God, but wasn't written down until God saw we couldn't do or believe it until we saw it written down. Still, the speed limit of 65MPH must mean 75MPH, right?

3rd: We have leadings. I felt led to the mission trip to Monterrey. I obeyed God and I went. I spent my last dollars for college and obeyed. This is a leading. I wasn't forced to do it. I wasn't guilted into doing it. I wasn't motivated by payment to do it. There was no fame or history for me. I didn't plan on meeting anyone or marrying anyone. I simply felt God leading me and I obeyed and He did everything else. Adam and Eve walked and talked with God and He did everything else.

4th: We have a check in our spirits. Our conscience and spirit is intertwined and when God speaks to us, we should know to stop and listen. Don't we have a check engine light on the motors in our cars? We might not know anything about motors, but we should know when that light comes on it is important and we should address it immediately.

5th: God gives us QUICKENINGS. What does this mean? I remember a pastor telling a story about something telling him to go upstairs in his house. He didn't need anything from up there, but the prompting continued inside him. He listened and went upstairs, feeling stupid. As he was standing at the top of the stairs, he heard the sound of splashing and found his son upside down in the bathtub. His son had floaters around his waist and had turned upside down in the water and was drowning. The quickening saved this pastor's son and wouldn't have happened if the pastor ignored his spirit working with the Spirit of God.

6th: We have VISIONS. I have visions of people going to hell as I'm there to direct them to the gates of Heaven. I see people falling all the time and constantly feel like I'm never doing enough to guide them. I still remember Rosalba telling me that I must not be a very good youth pastor due to all the poor choices the youth group was making. I can have a vision and a desire, but I cannot force you to love God, just like I cannot force my children to love me.

7th: We have DREAMS. I have had dreams of walking with God and seeing Rosalba standing with Jesus Christ. Could I paint these dreams? No. They were dreams to help me deal with the grief of losing Rosalba. They were to help me see there is much more to our lives than our minds and our bodies. To give me peace, knowing that indeed Rosalba and all those I have loved and cared for who have left this earth are in Heaven. It made me realize how little I know my own spirit and how little time I have spent to know it.

8th: We have been given PROPHECIES. This is a little-known topic that many people desire and fantasize about. Most prophecies have all been told already, and all that is left is the fulfillment of them. I'm excited with Jerusalem becoming the capital of Israel. This means the next prophecy will be the return of my Lord and Savior Jesus Christ. I'm always focusing on the prophecies now, it seems. It seems I am more anxious for Jesus to return now than I was before Rosalba died. I don't know what to think when the Bible says there won't be marriage in Heaven. I wonder if Rosalba will even recognize me or know me when I get there.

There are so many things for us to learn in the quietness of two who were once made into one and then were ripped apart by death. There are things we must learn about ourselves, and realize how much we didn't truly appreciate or thank God for the blessings we received with our spouse in our lives. It's a costly wisdom, and God knows we would not have asked for it. It's also true that coming through a great sorrow can make us stronger, and teach us what's really important. To survive the death of a loved one is no guarantee of greater wisdom. We can also become embittered, reclusive, and grasping. Yet if we can weather the storm, we'll have a better sense of who we are and what we want most in life. We'll learn to savor and cherish cool water, sunshine and wind, the smell of roses, and the love and friendships we have now.

I think of the death of Moses and the loneliness. He was absolutely alone in death and he had to be because it was between him and God. I was with Rosalba when she died, but in reality the cross was hers to carry alone, and in those final moments it was only between her and God. In death, men are and ever must be alone because of: 1: We lose all our senses. I remember Rosalba losing many of her senses as the cancer destroyed her body. 2. I also noticed there was no fear as she approached her last breath. No crying, no fear, no sorrow, and no "Forgive me for this or that." The spirit of Rosalba was taking over her body and mind, as promised in the Bible.

When we don't know what or how to pray, our spirits will pray to God in ways we will not understand. So, as our minds and bodies separate from our spirit, there is an elevation in the death of many a Christ-like one that much separates them from the living.

In life we also learn by occasional solitude to be independent of men. When in dying human help is gone, there will be no sudden, terrible surprise. After we learn this, we learn we need to seek in life companionship with God in solitude or loneliness. Then, having often been alone with God before, loneliness with Him in death will be no terrifying experience, but the repetition and consummation of some of the best experiences of life.

What is my final conclusion as of today, dealing with the death of Rosalba my spouse of twenty-five years? She is gone. Her time on this earth was achieved as far as God had predetermined before her birth. God raised her up in a challenging environment suited to make her the best child of God, wife, and mother to our children. God blessed me for twenty-five years with a wonderful wife, lover, friend, sister-in-Christ, and mother to two healthy, wonderful children. God chose the twenty-two years of her life before me and the twenty-five years with me, and now He will choose the eternity she will spend with Him. I have discovered just how much my focus on God changed with a wife and children in the middle of my relationship with Him. I found it difficult to manage the relationship with God and the cares of the world. I found I couldn't really appreciate the blessings God had provided me because I was not aware of my own spirit and how I was ignoring it, trying to keep up with the cares of life. I found my peace was limited to what I could see, taste, touch, hear, and smell. I realized most of my life in Christ had been lived in this way. Now that Rosalba is in Heaven and our children are gone, I once again have been able to fall in love with God. I have always missed knowing that nothing was going to be between me and God. I really enjoyed feeling that I could love something so much that it would hurt when the separation happened. After experiencing that pain with Rosalba's cancer and death, I now recognize the pain I have been feeling for a long time spiritually. It was the loss of my relationship with God and not putting Him first in my life. I would be the first to admit that I did sacrifice my relationship with God once I got married and had children. It seemed the voices of my wife and children were always louder than the voice of God.

I have learned we are never alone and we were never created to be alone. Even God saw that man needed a helper and created Eve, but Eve never replaced God in Adam's life or creation. Rosalba never replaced God in John Wilson's life, either. God is my Creator and will be for an eternity. Rosalba was a real blessing and helper in my life and helped me learn so many things. She provided two healthy and blessed children in Sarahi and John. This also wouldn't have happened without God's creative power. God has given me peace and joy after watching death, hell, and the grave grasp at Rosalba's soul, only to admit defeat at the actions of my Lord and Savior Jesus Christ. God won, proving His awesome power, Rosalba won, proving the promise of God, "For it is by grace you have been saved, through faith-and this is not from yourselves, it is the gift of God-not by works, so that no one can boast. Ephesians 2: 8-9." I won because I got the chance to see the Fruit of the Spirit of God in Rosalba's life on this earth. I was blessed to see love, joy, peace, some patience, kindness, faithfulness, gentleness, and definitely self-control. She never smoked or drank and ate more salad than most rabbits combined.

I will never forget Rosalba on this earth and I will never cease to miss her. I will, however, never cease to praise my God for the time He blessed me with her as the help I needed to be me. Now I guess Rosalba can tell God, "It's Your turn, I give up! John's all Yours now."

I love you, Rosalba. Te amo Siempre!

CPSIA information can be obtained
at www.ICGtesting.com
Printed in the USA
LVHW092202180219
607973LV00001B/239/P